The Irregular School

Should disabled students be in regular classrooms all of the time or some of the time? Is the regular school or the special school or both the solution for educating students with a wide range of differences?

Inclusive education has been incorporated in government education policy around the world. Key international organizations such as UNESCO and OECD declare their commitment to *Education for All* and the principles and practice of inclusive education. There is no doubt that despite this respectability inclusive education is hotly contested and generates intense debate amongst teachers, parents, researchers and policy-makers. People continue to argue over the nature and extent of inclusion.

The Irregular School explores the foundations of the current controversies and argues that continuing to think in terms of the regular school or the special school obstructs progress towards inclusive education. This book contends that we need to build a better understanding of exclusion, of the foundations of the division between special and regular education and of school reform as a precondition for more inclusive schooling in the future. Schooling ought to be an apprenticeship in democracy and inclusion is a prerequisite of a democratic education.

Written by a leading scholar in the field, *The Irregular School* builds on existing research and literature to argue for a comprehensive understanding of exclusion, a more innovative and aggressive conception of inclusive education and a genuine commitment to school reform that steps aside from the troubled and troubling notions of regular schools and special schools. It will be of interest to all those working and researching in the field of inclusive education.

Roger Slee is Professor of Inclusive Education at the Institute of Education, University of London.

The Irregular School

Exclusion, schooling and inclusive education

Roger Slee

Routledge
Taylor & Francis Group

LONDON AND NEW YORK

This first edition published 2011
by Routledge
2 Park Square, Milton Park, Abingdon, Oxon OX14 4RN

Simultaneously published in the USA and Canada
by Routledge
270 Madison Avenue, New York, NY 10016

Routledge is an imprint of the Taylor & Francis Group, an informa business

© 2011 Roger Slee

Typeset in Sabon by Wearset Ltd, Boldon, Tyne and Wear
Printed and bound in Great Britain by CPI Anthony Rowe,
Chippenham, Wiltshire

We are grateful to all those who have granted us permission to
reproduce the photographs listed. While every effort has been made
to trace and acknowledge ownership of copyright material used in
this volume, the Publishers will be glad to make suitable
arrangements with any copyright holders whom it has not been
possible to contact.

British Library Cataloguing in Publication Data
A catalogue record for this book is available from the British Library

Library of Congress Cataloging-in-Publication Data
Slee, Roger.
The irregular school : exclusion, schooling, and inclusive education / by Roger Slee.
p. cm. – (Foundations and futures of education series)
Includes bibliographical references and index.
1. Inclusive education. I. Title.
LC1200.S54 2011
371.9'046–dc22   2010032146

ISBN13: 978-0-415-47989-9 (hbk)
ISBN13: 978-0-415-47990-5 (pbk)
ISBN13: 978-0-203-83156-4 (ebk)

For Jeanette, Carly & Rowan

Contents

Foreword

Tony Knight

This book is a passionate account of education and exclusion. It provides a persuasive depiction of persons with disability, who try to adjust and survive in an educational system that fails to provide what is desperately needed.

The concept 'inclusive education' became public usage when it emerged within publications such as the *International Journal of Inclusive Education*. In a short time inclusive education was popularized in policy-making groups and mainstream educational research. We see this in politicians' adoption of the notion of inclusiveness within discussions of general policy. Another effect is how the language of special education has been reworked within lectures and public comment to reflect the respectability of inclusive education. A full ranging list of advocates has emerged, these include: teachers, school administrators, carers, politicians, parents, civil servants, teacher educators and researchers. Emerging from this multitude of responses was the difficulty in finding a common language capable of agreement, across a considerable divergence of data able to communicate complex ideas. This complex of writing concerning special and/or inclusive education, is too often enmeshed itself in obfuscation and jargon. Roger Slee observes the tendency within the writing 'to conceal ideas within a thicket of words'. He reminds us that there is nothing more undemocratic than a language that excludes, especially when an inaccessible language masks a paucity of thought.

This is the point where the book starts its journey. The writing combines a mix of humour, research and criticism. This is important given the depth of global poverty described, providing a social context for the analysis and central argument. The early chapters unlock the general intention of the writer to find a purpose for 'inclusion' within a substantive educational theory. The illusion of 'substantive freedoms' is carefully detailed and examined. Here the reader has to negotiate later parts of Chapter 3, describing the five 'scapes' of cultural flows in a globalized world. This is no easy task for writer and reader, as this is not the only set of allegories to negotiate. The political economy of 'exclusion' requires focused reading, in order to capture the context of broad social change, affecting an increasingly fragmented social and economic landscape. This is a lengthy and important chapter in 'contextualizing' the concept of inclusion within the twenty-first century where the neo-liberal social imagination promotes competitive individualism and strangles community.

Each early chapter describes and analyses the context of various modes of student disabilities, coinciding with the growth of professional groups and carers involved in each sub-division. It would appear that little professional discussion is held between each bureaucratic grouping. Slee lays bare a deep political struggle between the opposing views of disability studies and segregated education. The lists of academic researchers present a variety of interpretations that underline the 'depth, continuity, and heat of the political struggle'.

Chapters 5, 6 and 7 construct a bridge into a more speculative consideration of futures for inclusive education, and a more searching discussion of the irregular school. Slee makes the case that it is possible to make a principled choice for inclusion, only if there are informed principles guiding a general educational theory – and here is the rub – and the central point to this book. It is a 'call to action' – not what has been described as the 'hyperactivism' – between a multitude of competing texts. The general failure, in policy, to embrace new ways of thinking about children comes as no surprise. The general failure of policy in dealing with 'disability' is well acknowledged in this book. A serious omission has been the loss of demonstrating youth competence in schools as a policy direction. Slee outlines clearly the contradiction between exclusion as part of system rationality, and inclusion to general schooling. Inclusive education is a project of political struggle and cultural change. Here the contrast between the two approaches is clearly outlined. Both inclusion and exclusion require two very different systemic approaches to general schooling. Slee makes the point that inclusive education is a theory and tactic for educational reform. He makes the case that inclusive education is not special education – it is a general struggle against failure and exclusion. He describes the future for inclusive education as a 'grand reform movement'. Here he speaks of futures for inclusive education. He offers a set of starting points and methodological possibilities. This will require a change in function and the profession of educational work, hence changes in schooling requirements.

These final and important chapters are required reading for practitioners. Unless there is a change in schooling requirements, the world that the disabled will inherit will continue to be an unjust one. The present logic of special education institutions maintains an unjust aura with well-established systemic injustices, expectations and too few resources. Discussions with special education teachers reveal a firm adherence to institutional rules, and a commitment to learned beliefs and injustices. Slee makes the case that as practitioners 'we seek explanation for children's failure, distraction, anger, and defiance in their genetic and medical profiles'. These labels of 'defectiveness' are conferred over time upon these children. The journey for these children at school is too often painful, predictive and oppressive.

Readers of this book are requested to engage in a number of tasks, pursuant to a more inclusive education. Descriptions of 'irregular' schooling are cited as 'beacons of hope'. These include four broad propositions – well worth the read in-and-of itself. These propositions are an attempt to show (drawn from a range of successful studies) how inclusive education has been decoupled from special education. Demonstrated are a wide range of tables and suggested practices and policy guidelines.

The 'restorative' practice nominated by Slee comes with cautions and warnings for school practice. These are welcome and need to be read carefully. There are a number of references to democratic theory throughout the book – these may well be the foundations for future steps. Inclusive education, according to *The Irregular School*, is everybody's business in a school.

Tony Knight
Melbourne, 2010

Acknowledgements

It would be impossible to acknowledge everyone who has assisted me with the development of the ideas drawn together in this book. The more people I mention, it seems the more I leave out. Therefore I will keep this list short and say a general thank you to those I don't name directly.

Special thanks are due to Anna Clarkson at Routledge for her patience and kind encouragement.

Peter Aggleton and Michael Reiss read drafts of the chapters, pressed me for clarity and helped to build ideas so that they had meaning outside of my head. They were very supportive and gently pressed when they needed to.

My colleagues and students at the Institute of Education have been very generous in listening to my ideas as I have rehearsed them in classes and at the coffee table. It is a privilege to work with Felicity Armstrong, Barbara Cole, Michele Moore and Len Barton.

I must also mention those people who set me out on this line of thought. Tony Knight, Bob Semmens, Sandy Cook, John Lewis and Ken Polk changed the way I understood the world as I wandered into the world of juvenile justice and criminology in my graduate studies in Melbourne. Len Barton and Sally Tomlinson have been wonderful mentors and friends. I have also been fortunate to have Stephen Ball down the corridor as a friend to discuss ideas with and to talk to about the craft of writing. I have read through and drawn from interviews that I conducted with Julie Allan for another project. I am indebted to her for that work.

I acknowledge many others directly in the pages and I thank you for your work that has helped me to think through the problems raised in and by this book. Linda Graham sent me a paper that she wrote with colleagues in Sydney that returns to the interests of Tony, Bob, Ken, Sandy and I in raising questions about the deleterious impacts of categorizing students and sorting them out. It is good to see that our concerns from the 1980s are back on the table.

Finally, there are three people who have had to live with this project and me, and have shown great interest and forbearance throughout.

Jeanette, Carly and Rowan, this book is dedicated to you though it is hardly sufficient recompense for what you bring to my life.

Roger Slee
London
July 2010

1　Approaching accents

Ever wondered why your Welsh accent starts drifting off towards India the moment you open your mouth?

Is your brilliant Belfast brogue being tripped up by loose vowels?

Are you aiming at Albuquerque, NM, but somehow winding up in Poughkeepsie, NY?

Whether your accents are wonderful, wobbly or woefully embarrassing, *How to do accents* will give you the structure of your new accent, providing you with plenty of practical guidance and top tips to keep it firmly in the right place.[1]

> From the back cover of: Sharpe, E. and Rowles, J. H. (2007) *How to do accents*. London, Oberon Books

Timbre and pitch

Had I not had the good fortune to be raised in the small rural township of Hamilton in the western district of the state of Victoria in Australia, I would not have been blessed with an Australian accent. A thing of elegance and beauty in and of itself, the tonal lilt of my way of talking (pronounced: Oz-tray-yan) has not made it necessary for me to covet the tones of other English dialects. I dare say though if happenstance had not been so generous, if it had been Hamilton in New Zealand or Hamilton in Ontario for instance, I would be reaching inside of a copy of Sharpe and Rowles to affect those soft urbane southern Australian tones.

Browsing in Blackwell's Bookshop on the Charing Cross Road I was captivated by the plain-covered authority of Sharpe and Rowles's promise. (More precisely the promise attributed to their work by the publisher's contracted blurb writer.) Notwithstanding the inclusion of a CD to train the ear and my covert wish to sound like Michael Gambon or even Ken Stott, practically speaking, I think my sixteen pounds was better spent on a couple of George Pelecanos novels.[2] I am not at all convinced that the combined exercise of mimicking the CD while reading the text would unlock the mysteries or explain the nuances that are acquired and crafted through years of local habitation. An accent is not just sound – it's the fusion of sound, idiom and local knowledge, custom and disposition. Just as years ago when I came to realize that deaf education was not just the challenge of volume.

I can't blame you for wondering why a book in a series on 'educational foundations and futures' commences this way. Let me explain. First is a desire to write this book as if it is meant to be read by those affected by the topic; parents and carers of schoolchildren, *our* civil servants and political leaders, teachers, school administrators, advocates in community organiza-tions, support personnel, students, researchers and teacher educators. In other words I aim to bring the public back for a reconsideration of public education – its foundations and futures.[3] For this task we need to find and use a common language capable of communicating complex ideas and changing social relations.

Recently I was teaching with a colleague, Len Barton, at the University of Athens in Greece. Our discussions and the set readings for the course were in English. Len discussed a chapter I had written with the students who had read it the night before. They took to the issues I had raised in the set reading with surprising enthusiasm. A number of them had said that they had read many things that I have written, but that it was *'hard work'*. This remark, though not entirely unexpected, was deeply troubling. I have been painfully aware of my tendency to conceal an idea within a thicket of words.

As in other fields of education research, academic verbiage in inclusive education writing does neither the cause nor academics any favours. Scholars such as Edward Said, Raewyn Connell, Richard Sennett, John Kenneth Galbraith and a host of others set out the responsibility of the public intellectual to speak intelligently and understandably to the com-munity. Not to do so – finding refuge in obfuscation and jargon – dimin-ishes the potential for and the character of public debate. It raises the spectre of *death sentences* wherein language is reduced to a 'shapeless, enervative sludge'.[4]

This is not exclusively a matter of the aesthetics and craft of writing. Nor is it simply a matter of effective communication across different audi-ences. The issue of language is profoundly political. For as Art Pearl and Tony Knight declare: 'Nothing is more undemocratic than a language that excludes.'[5] For those claiming an interest in inclusive education, this is far more than an editorial matter; it is recognition that exclusion and inclusion are about real people who ought not to be abstracted. Addressing their plight should remain urgent. Playful post-modern deconstruction needs to exercise caution and reflect upon the danger of drifting towards conserva-tism in the social relations of research.[6]

Listening to the Greek women in the class it occurred to me that unlike many of us whose first language is English, they thought about their words whereas we tend to think with our words. In his recent novel, *Something to tell you*, Hanif Kureishi's main character, a psychiatrist whose life is played out 'on one page of the London A to Z', describes his sister as the kind of person who talks and talks until she finds something to say.[7] So my undertaking is to present complex ideas as precisely, clearly and economically as possible. I hope to achieve this without superficiality or serious omissions.

Second, I have a growing aversion to the recent deluge of education Do-It-Yourself manuals. These almanacs of tips for teachers are overcrowding the education shelves in British bookshops. My hunch is that this is a global phenomenon. Notwithstanding their profitability for the authors and their publishing houses, I don't consider the cumulative effect of these books to be at all educational. Too often they simply provide advice for deck chair rearrangement. Seldom is there a consideration of the dangers of cruising through icebergs. Together with the proliferation of reductive targets for schools and teachers, these manuals are one in an array of symptoms of atrophy in the leadership and management of schooling, and education. Titles such as *Getting the buggers to behave*, *Getting the buggers to write*, *Getting the buggers to think*, *Getting the buggers into science*, *Getting the buggers to add up* and *Getting the buggers in tune* may well produce a collective school staff-room smile.[8] They may guarantee large door earnings for authors doing the professional development circuit. Some teachers under the inspectors' gaze clamour for relief from tough struggles in the classroom. However, these and the innumerable other tip-texts forfeit educational potential to the allure of quick fixes for the symptoms of a crisis in education in a complex world. Moreover, the series to which I allude is deeply offensive in its language, is unaware of the complex politics of the term 'bugger', and presupposes an agonistic relationship between teachers and their students. Cowley's *The guerrilla guide to teaching* would seem to confirm this.[9]

The crisis to which I refer is not an attack on teachers and schools. We live in an age where the most frequently blogging teacher in Japan writes under the *nom de plum* – 'hopeless teacher'. The crisis has been assembled over time through the relentless tide of neo-conservative and New Labour policies.[10] Teachers work in a climate of distrust and blame. They are distracted from educating by compliance rituals and inspection schedules and sanctions that reach into the public purse with contestable assessments of their efficacy or value for teachers and students.[11] This book aims to offer hope for teachers, students and communities through different educational settlements in new times. Borrowing from the introduction to Mike Rose's inspiring research in *Possible Lives*: schooling is *'our most important democratic experiment'*.[12] As such, great care and consideration needs to attend our shaping of the laboratory under changing conditions.

I am trying not to be elitist in targeting this highly seductive and reductive pulp non-fiction. In 2004 Don Watson published *Watson's dictionary of weasel words, contemporary cliches, cant and management jargon*.[13] In this book, he takes a machete to the evasive language and poor ideas that litter management texts and periodicals. A Watsonian approach to 'eduspeak'[14] is overdue.[15] Teachers and other education decision-makers speak of inclusion and building social capital while reinstating segregation.[16] They speak of teaching and learning and simultaneously distract students from their education with rote training for a battery of standardized tests.[17]

> How much has changed since the Victorian love affair with examinations? We have become ever more attached in terms of the scale and regularity of assessment, with estimates that a typical student who stays in schooling in England until age 18 will have taken over a hundred external assessments.[18]

Even Ken Boston, a former Director of the Qualifications and Assessment Authority reveals ambiguity about testing when quizzed in a *Guardian* newspaper interview:

> We need tests for monitoring individual, school and national performance. The amount of time actually spent on them is minuscule. But if you look at the time spent on preparation for tests, there's a risk in some schools that it will distort the curriculum. You don't increase the weight of a pig by weighing it repeatedly. You do it by long-term nutrition and diet.[19]

Later in the same interview he speaks of rolling on-line tests that enable a constancy of examination and surveillance.

Education jurisdictions around the world converge when they speak of educational accountability and each generate compliance regimes through simplified targets.[20] Neo-liberal governments speak of educating flexible and adaptable students to become global citizens and restrict educational choices through narrow national traditional curriculum.[21] They emphasize the need for autonomous learners and disqualify the role of mistakes (or failure) in learning. They urge creativity and reify uniformity and standardization. Penketh has captured the irony of the attempt to impose standards of creativity in her acute analysis of the role of observational drawing in the examination of students in the English art curriculum.[22] The rhetoric is of educational excellence when in actuality it translates in practical terms as ranking on a table of international comparison that is often disrespectful of cultural specificity and geopolitical context.[23] The discourse of building professional learning communities is a vehicle for the confiscation of professional autonomy.[24]

Of course, this is an area where professional care has to be exercised as we negotiate the dilemmas of assuring ourselves of greater quality in teaching and learning on the one hand, and not falling to the depths of costly compliance regimes on the other. Jonathan Kozol puts it this way:

> So the question, again, is not if we 'need' standards in our schools but with what sensibilities we navigate between the two extremes of regimented learning with destructive overtones, on one side, and pedagogic aimlessness and fatuous romanticism on the other. Somewhere between the world of Dickens' Gradgrind and John Silber and the world of pedagogic anarchy, there is a place of sanity where education is intense and substantive, and realistically competitive in a competitive society, but still respectful of the infinite variety of valued learnings and the limitless varieties of wisdom in the hearts of those who come to us as students.[25]

Dulling England's civic imagination[26]

Returning to England to work in 2007 provided a lesson in the ascendancy of superficiality (populist reduction), and a lesson in the demise of consideration and analysis in public policy decision-making. These processes operate across political and cultural life as well as in education. Indeed a maxim for education policy could read – *the triumph of the slogan.*

To be precise, my return has been to London, which those folk living outside of the great conurbation tell me is not all that there is to England. This is a city that offers both the best and the worst of journalism on newsstands everyday. Still most of the large battalions of commuters who file underground with me – there are 3 million tube (underground train) journeys everyday in London – opt for the free newspapers (on offer in the morning – *Metro* – and in the evening – *The Evening Standard*). These flimsy tabloids dull the discomfort of travel time, or perhaps they add to it. The gossip sheets put temporal distance between the reader and the person they are pressed against. Imprecisely called 'news' papers, they carry large tracts of advertising and heavily précised versions of syndicated stories. A commuter catch-up on the latest in celebrity gossip or, as Helen Garner writes of tabloids and television in Australia, '...they allow us *to refresh our expertise in the scandalous lives of celebrities*'.[27] They broadcast salacious and unsavoury details of violent crime, track the data on gang stabbings in the capital, ensnare politicians and other public figures in the modern-day stocks for their human frailties, and monitor the dalliances, trading and transfers across the premier-league football market.

My point here is that both our sensibilities and demand for detail have been dulled by the supremacy of the headline and the evacuation of the essay. Wars and disasters are reduced to print headlines and sixty-second news-film narratives. The monotony of the ensuing human suffering becomes no more than dull sounds from another room. Disasters are reported and forgotten. Famine and poverty, unless championed by celebrities, do not rate. Complex social and economic problems are communicated in *pre-shrunk* mono-dimensional digestible form. Unable to invest time in writing or reading the extended essay, we are reduced to a cooking show approach to civic affairs: 'Here's an analysis we made earlier.' The language of power is persuasive, sanitized, and clichéd – staccato grabs shun debate or thinking otherwise.

Dulling our education imagination

In schooling in England similar trends emerge. Students and teachers, as we have said, must live and work within the confines of a narrowly defined National Curriculum. Stephen Ball incisively described this conservative artefact of middle-class culture as a 'curriculum of the dead'; it sustains the 'curriculum as museum'.[28] Narrow and traditional curriculum subjects endure and are *offered* to the children of the 'information age'. This national curriculum is jealously policed through standardized high stakes tests, the demands of the international PISA and TIMSS[29] competitions and the controversial Student Achievement Tests (SATs).[30] Add to this the spectre of tabloid vilification and the imposition of special measures that haunts those schools on the lower rungs of the published national league table of school performance. Therein exists not only a powerful cocktail for the control of activity in schools and classrooms,[31] but also for a series of perverse side-effects. One of the most obvious distortions is the determination of schools to keep out of the headlines by compliance with the requirements of the test. Thenceforth curriculum decisions are driven by second guessing what will be in the tests.

Curriculum narrows to test training, subjects lose potency and tests fall victim to their half-life.[32] Given that assessment shapes learning,[33] the character and quality of assessment schedules demands forethought and care. Ironically the Education Testing Services fiasco that resulted in the late and non-delivery of test results in England proved to be more persuasive for government than the evidence and advice it receives in submissions from researchers, head-teachers and teachers' organizations. Though the use of high-stakes accountability tests may produce 'short term benefits, it rapidly degrades'.[34] Gillborn and Youdell[35] invoke a medical metaphor from the stressful conditions of the casualty centre in hospitals to describe a rationing of resources to assist those students who appear likely to pull through school tests with limited support. The most needy perish. This they call 'educational triage'. Perhaps this is what the Cameron/Clegg Coalition government policy agenda means when it speaks of 'aggressive setting by ability'?[36]

Dylan Wiliam's recent analysis of test reliability and validity demonstrates that in the national testing of 11 year olds in England some 30 per cent of pupils may be awarded a higher or lower level than their actual attainment merits.[37] Stobart warns of the inflated claims and distorting effect of the high stakes assessment instruments used in England and the USA, and argues for a more intelligent accountability – assessment for learning.[38] In the USA, Johnson and Johnson highlight the damaging links between poverty, high stakes testing and failure through an extended and poignant case study of one of the poorest schools in Louisiana.[39] Despite the enormous investment of government and education bureaucracies in testing as an instrument for improving learning, argues Allan Luke, on the basis of the scores from current testing regimes, little can be said about the quality of learning or the capacity of pupils to apply lessons across divergent contexts and problems.[40] Yet this is the preparation of children for the so-called knowledge economy.

Elsewhere in jurisdictions as disparate as Queensland in Australia and Quebec in Canada there has been significant progress in curriculum reform. Though Queensland has shied away from the challenge of reform in deference to the conservative and politically popular option of a National Curriculum built upon traditional subject or discipline groupings, it had a chance to exercise educational leadership. Supported by the State's Premier as a smart state initiative, the New Basics[41] school reform research pilot was developed to counter the call for a return to rote, *back to basics*.

A rich portfolio of assessment tasks was carefully developed, drawing on criticism and advice from assessment and evaluation experts from around the world, to enable students to show mastery and teachers to evaluate the impact of elements of pedagogy and curriculum. John Ainley, a respected researcher and statistician from the Australian Council for Educational Research, independently undertook an evaluation of the testing and assessment schedules and items against the research protocols. His report submitted to the Ministry's Director General concluded that the research was sound and that the methods employed were capable of yielding substantive evidence on which to adjudicate the merits and shortcomings of the New Basics trial.

Upon conclusion of the research it was found that not only did the reforms in curriculum organisation, approaches to teaching (pedagogy) and rich assessment improve the attainments of students in the pilot schools, the drop in levels of student engagement and academic attainment during the middle years of schooling (especially Years 8 and 9) identified in the Queensland School Reform Longitudinal Study (QSRLS) had been arrested. In other words, the so-called Year 9 dip had been erased by achieving relevance of subject matter and teaching styles, by ensuring a coherence of challenge in both teaching approaches and assessment methods, by inscribing diversity and difference in the teaching approaches and subject matter, and by building relationships between students and teachers and students with each other that translated into caring classrooms.[42] A vindication of Dewey and Vygotsky, the results didn't end there. Teachers became more animated by and about their job. They talked with each other more about how and what they taught, how the students responded, and whether the students knew what the teachers thought they were teaching. Simply put, we had a basis in evidence to suggest that the project was building professional learning communities and a culture of learning on both sides of the teacher's desk.

What might we have learnt from the New Basics school reform trial?

- Quick fixes such as training pupils to perform well on simple tests of literacy and mathematics do not produce excellence in teaching and learning.
- Sustainable improvement of teaching and learning is built on meticulous research, design and evaluation that accounts for and learns from the complexity of teaching and learning.
- Greater value is attached to formative rather than summative assessment to improve both the quality of teaching and the levels of learning.
- Engaging teachers in the development, implementation, evaluation and leadership of change is essential.
- This element presupposes a condition of trust.
- Re-engaging and improving the professional knowledge of the skills of the education workforce is itself an educational process and goal.
- Authentic reforms require significant investment, financial and political.

What happened to New Basics? There is a postscript. It was quietly shelved. Despite its having been championed by a State Premier, Education Ministers (Secretaries of State for Education) and Directors General (equivalent to Permanent Secretaries) and having achieved its principal goals, the project was dropped. Perhaps there are two major reasons. First, there was the demonstration that education improvement is costly. Educational improvement demands a level of teacher professional development that was not previously embraced. I hasten to add that throwing money at schools is not in itself a recipe for achieving and sustaining improved student outcomes. Second, within the bureaucracy there was an influential and powerfully connected residue of opposition to challenges to the traditional approaches to the eight Key Learning Areas. Riding on a wave of political support for a national curriculum framed around conservative approaches to curriculum organization, bolder attempts to achieve coherence between knowledge organization, teaching, students and a changing world were not an option. Sloganeering that fuses nationalism and *back to the basics* has considerable traction (in a nation easily beguiled by the racist anti-immigration platform of Pauline Hanson and her One Nation political party).

Meanwhile in England, the aforementioned former Head of the Qualifications and Assessment Authority and former Director General of the New South Wales Department of Education, Ken Boston, had to muster all his political courage to suggest a themed approach to organizing knowledge in a school curriculum, an approach recommended by the Rose Report (2008) on primary school education.[43] The Cambridge University response to the Rose Review of primary school education led by Robin Alexander,[44] supported thematic organization for the curriculum and the final report of the Rose Committee recommended the organization of the curriculum into six broader areas rather than its traditional splitting up into fourteen individual subjects.

Offering superficial responses to complex problems is not just found in the pages of the '100 tips for teachers' texts. Sadly it is a function of the political process wherein educational research is considered an 'unhelpful irritant'.[45] Norman Fairclough's dissection of political rhetoric in *New Labour, new language* is instructive.[46] Crisp and self-evident messages seem to provide no option for interrogation or disagreement.

> Slogans, recipes, incantations and self-evidences ... are part of the process of building support for state projects and establishing hegemonic vision ... the statements and fragments do make a coherent joined up whole. They do not have their effects by virtue of their inherent logic. Discourses often maintain their credibility through their repetition, substantive simplicity ... and rhetorical sophistication.[47]

Who could resist a call to 'raise achievement'?[48] 'Personalizing learning' to ensure that 'the job of government is to seek for every pupil what any parent would seek for their child' is self-evident. Insisting on 'standards not structures'[49] is refreshing though ironic in a country where the expenditure on school inspection and the over-zealous testing programme would bank roll the education systems of developing countries or significantly improve schooling in the pain zones of disadvantage across Britain as identified by Wilkinson and Pickett and the Institute for Fiscal Studies.[50] Like the language of 'school effectiveness' and 'school improvement' before them, the current crop of policy epithets determine what can be said, what must remain unsaid, what is acceptable and what is off the policy-table.[51]

The recourse to 'spin' has become a hallmark of the education policy process, a leveller of public discourse. It is the language of power, 'And while it begins with the powerful, the weak are often obliged to speak it, imitate it.'[52] And, as Watson laments, the reductive effect on public language is laid bare. In my experience in the civil service I remember meetings that resembled choir practice; same sheets, same lyrics. Dominant words, couplets and phrases included a pastiche of neologisms and impossible alternatives:[53] 'co-opetition', 'capacity building', 'public–private partnerships', 'smart state', 'earning or learning' – everyone wanted 'policy with grunt'. Former head of Tony Blair's Delivery Unit, Michael Barber tells us:

Loaded with negative associations though the word has become, 'spin' really does matter; the danger comes when it is divorced from substance.[54]

In his book entitled *Instruction to deliver*, Barber sets out the delivery priorities for the Delivery Unit across key government portfolios (Table 1.1).

The education delivery priorities rest on the firm assumption that improvement in student attainment in tests is a measure of the quality of learning. Targets do not speak of the quality of the measures and thereby reveals a separation from substance that the engagement in a consideration of assessment for learning versus teaching to tests. Literacy becomes a case in point where turf wars and substantive conflicts over efficacy and evidence between phonics,[55] reading recovery[56] and the four resources model developed by Freebody and Luke[57] are ignored as governments and oppositions cast their policy nets. The paradox is that as teachers and students improve at the examination and qualifications challenge, faith in the rigour of the test or the worth of the qualification diminishes. Such has been the recent fate of the A level in England.

Panics around youth[58] attach priority to reducing truancy. Forcing children back into schools is no guarantee for engagement or learning. Strategies for forcing reluctant (truanting) pupils into schoolrooms have a long history internationally[59] and notwithstanding attempts to blame and criminalize parents of truanting students[60] and the expenditure of £885 million on schemes to reduce truancy since 1997, the government concedes no appreciable reduction in the level of truancy.[61] Patterns of pupil permanent exclusions, suspensions, managed moves and referral to Pupil Referral Units[62] suggest that truancy is a symptom of more intractable issues

Table 1.1 Delivery Unit priorities

Department	Delivery Unit priorities
Health	Heart disease mortality
	Cancer mortality
	Waiting lists
	Waiting times
	Accident and Emergency
Education	Literacy and numeracy at 11
	Maths and English at 14
	5+ A*–C GCSE
	Truancy
Home Office	Overall crime and breakdowns by type
	Likelihood of being a victim
	Offenders brought to justice
Transport	Road congestion
	Rail punctuality

Source: Adapted from Barber, M. (2007) *Instruction to deliver*. London, Politico's, p. 50.

that beset attempts to school our children.[63] A reversal of popular belief may suggest that the issue of disengagement from schooling is not the fault of the incompetent parent or of the child's chaotic pathology. Later in this book I will explore data showing the grip of the ADHD global pandemic[64] and the exponential growth of special educational needs.[65] My aim is not to deny the existence of childhood impairments and difficulties. There is a responsibility to sound an unpopular warning in some quarters[66] that the allure of the diagnosis and treatment may cast a net over a growing cohort to maintain order in schools.[67] Steven Rose illustrates the point:

> Children who are calmer at home and school are easier to parent and teach. However, Ritalin no more cures ADHD than aspirin cures toothache. Masking the psychic pain that disruptive behaviour indicates can provide a breathing space for parents, teachers, and the child to negotiate a new and better relationship, but if the opportunity to do this is not seized, we will once again find ourselves trying to adjust the mind rather than the society.

Reversing the tide of labelling and exclusion to bring society, education policy and the configuration of schooling into the diagnostic gaze could well invite pessimism and Canute-like resignation.[68]

Targets require substance too if they are to change the pitch and timbre of education to suit new times. Andy Hargreaves and Dennis Shirley write about the way in which football (soccer) clubs have enlisted data analysts in the attempt to leverage improvement for their players' and teams' performances.[69] In the course of their research they interviewed the Performance Analyst at a First Division League team in England. The club, like many others, was using a software package named ProZone, which analyses film recordings of the games. The Performance Analyst then catalogues the data for each player.

> Every touch of the ball – where they are, when they touched it, what they did afterwards ... There's nothing that's missed.... Some managers we were told, treat the data literally, as an unambiguous indicator of effort and effectiveness.[70]

The effect, according to Hargreaves and Shirley, was that some managers set targets for players for the number of steps they took in a game and allegedly placed microchips in players' shoes to record their performance. Complying with this new requirement to lift their step quotient, players were never still 'off ball' away from camera scrutiny. You could be forgiven for thinking that footballers too had been swept up in the postmodern fidgeting and restlessness pandemic: ADHD. Was the quality of play better? Did team performance improve? No. What appear to be and are offered as sensible targets may have regressive impacts if not applied judiciously.

The irregular school

The title of this book is offered provocatively – my tongue pressing firmly into my cheek. What is *irregular schooling* you may well ask? Irregular schooling is my retaliation to the ill-considered and over-used couplet, *regular schools*. The term, *the regular school*, is frequently offered as the counterpoint to the term: *special school*. It is also code for the implied *normal school*. It follows that there must be *normal or regular students* for whom these schools exist. And, as the logic proceeds, there are *other* children who are not normal, regular or valid – they are our in-valid population. Whether we call it regular or normal, neither the meaning nor the social impact change. Anne Deveson reflects this deflective deployment of language in her moving chronicle of her son's struggle with schizophrenia, the reactions of the outside world to him as someone with mental illness and his tragic ending of his life.

> We do not use the word 'mad' anymore. We have banished it, together with words like 'lunatic', 'asylum'; even the word 'insane' is rarely heard. These words evoke oppressions of the past; today the terminology has changed, become more technical and distancing, yet our oppressions remain.[71]

Special schools, it is traditionally contended, are places where expert knowledge about and skills for teaching impaired children reside; they are also a safe haven from the cruelty of the regular neighbourhood school. Some have argued that inclusive education results in the sacrifice of disabled children for the sake of misplaced ideology.[72] Indeed, inclusive education, like special education, is ideological.[73] Both are based upon alternative views of the world and the nature and form of schooling that will build that world. It is also true that regular schooling, as it stands, may be a dreadful experience for many disabled children, just as it is for many children of colour, poor white children, traveller and refugee children, and Aboriginal children. Indeed, perhaps one of the most memorable statements in my special education training came from the American criminologist Professor Ken Polk when he stated that, 'for many children the experience of school is the daily experience of humiliation and pain'. Segregated schooling grew out of an uneasy alliance between the radical compromise of parents of disabled children demanding some form of education for their rejected children, eugenics imperatives and dominant expert psychological and medical knowledge about disabled children. We will explore this history in our discussion of foundations. To maintain centuries later that segregation is acceptable because it provides 'choice' or because of the state of regular schools will not suffice. As Pierre Bourdieu affirms: 'Given the choice of two evils, I refuse to accept the lesser.'[74] The challenge is to make the physical, social, cultural and educational arrangement of schooling better for all. In the following chapters I will examine the institutional arrangements that they special and regular, describe and propose that neither is an accurate description or model for an education for the future. They are shibboleths to unsatisfactory knowledge and practices of the past.

Ferdinand Mount is disarmingly honest in describing the motivation behind his book, *Mind the gap*.[75] The book provides a chilling account of the 'baffled despair of the new underclass', and of the 'new class divide in Britain'.[76] Himself an operative in the Thatcher administration and a product of 'expensive independent schools', he is in possession of 'a very nice house in a conservation area ... a languid upper-class voice and a semi-dormant baronetcy'.[77] It was when proofreading a speech given abroad that he came to the sentence: '*Class divisions are fading in Britain*', that he felt 'an instructive twitch and came to a stop'. The repetition of the sentiment and words over time across different political parties rendered the demise of class in Britain an unexamined given in polite company. However, the lived experience for Britain's worst-off people suggests otherwise as is demonstrated in Wilkinson and Pickett's analysis of inequality in affluent societies.[78] The book, for Mount, became an exercise in what Antonio Gramsci might record in his notebooks as correcting the prevailing or hegemonic *common sense* or the dominant versions of truth.[79]

Mount provides a lesson in the value of hesitation and closer interrogation of utterances of conventional wisdom. For those who work in education and those who use it, this is an essential lesson. Schools are governed by conventional wisdom, by the sequential assemblage of habits, traditions, beliefs, practices and organizational preferences. The educational common sense is not unsettled by testing and league tables that forces the exclusion of students and the establishment of a residual or lower-tiered category of schooling for difficult and failing pupils. The pages of education policy pamphlets and speeches are replete with pronouncements about inclusiveness, social capital, equity, excellence and citizenship. Children, we are told, matter. Indeed, it seems now that *Every child matters*.[80] This was, and is, not always the case. This book will tell another story, invite us to critically re-examine our educational foundations and establish propositions for educational futures.

Not long after taking up a senior position in Education Queensland (the Queensland Ministry of Education) I was summoned to meet with executive officers from the Queensland Association of Special School Administrators (i.e. Principals of segregated special schools). The purpose of the meeting I sensed was to test the level of threat I would pose to Queensland special schools. Flattering though the thought of ending the segregation of disabled children is, the answer I had to give is derived from the real politic. A government that is particularly sensitive to poor press is not going to entertain the risk of this so-called minimization of choice. Remembering Bertolt Brecht's advice that, 'Taking obstacles into account the shortest line between two points might not be a straight line', I suggested that they had asked me the wrong question.[81] The inquisitors would be better off by asking: What knowledge, skills and dispositions do kids need to negotiate the world of the future? Then would follow the questions that address the arrangement of educational resources and the workforce to deliver our new educational settlements. My response was dismissed as tactical and not at all reassuring. Today, I stand by these questions. Other questions ought to have been asked as well. Can we be confident about the criteria for categorizing and sorting children? What do ethnic disparities in the diagnosis and referral rates of children tell us? What might the growing demand for alternatives tell us about the form of the regular school? Does our expanding knowledge of the pathology of children through the discovery of syndromes and now it seems, shadow syndromes,[82] advance their welfare and education or does it increase their vulnerability and threaten their education?

Challenging widely accepted beliefs and practices in education is a difficult and unpopular task. Compromise[83] is an essential element of democratic conventions.[84] However, where is the point where compromise evacuates principle? Reforms that embrace the practice **and** the rhetoric of social inclusion, capacity building, democratic citizenship, equality and excellence making every child matter, assessment for learning and excellence in teaching and learning necessitates critique and analysis before constructing answers. It requires a social intelligence that embraces changing contexts and fashions new building blocks.

This book will argue that in New Times[85] a new analysis is required that invites us to move beyond contests between special and regular given that neither is fairing so very well. Thomas and Loxley and Rizvi and Lingard are instructive in their recognition of the wisdom of eclectic adoptions of theory as 'thinking tools', to borrow from Bourdieu.[86] I hope that this book does not lead anyone to think that my position on exclusion has softened. My hope is that it contributes to understanding changing forms of exclusion and that it reaffirms inclusion as a rights issue. Inclusive education is first and foremost a political position; it offers an audacious challenge to the attachment of ascending and descending values to different people. In this respect it is, as Julie Allan asserts, an ethical project. Following Foucault, Allan argues that inclusive education is not a project to be done on a 'discrete population of children, but rather (as) something we must do to ourselves'.[87] In this respect inclusive education invites us to think about the nature of the world we live in, a world that we prefer and our role in shaping both of those worlds. Thereafter follow technical questions about research, resources, curriculum, pedagogy, assessment and the ecologies of schooling and human development.[88]

The structure and reading of the book

The major part of this book explores the foundations of inclusive education, establishing the case by mapping exclusion. It ought to be sufficient to announce the requirement for inclusive education, itself a restatement of the bold democratic experiment[89] as did Basil Bernstein:

> First of all there are the conditions for an effective democracy. I am not going to derive these from high-order principles, I am just going to announce them.[90]

The evidence gathered in the following pages shows that this is not the case. Assuming agreement on inclusive education, without stipulating its meanings and the implications of these different meanings, has in fact been its undoing.

The last chapter of the book embraces the series' claim to explore educational futures. Doing this depends upon a careful reading of the present. Hence the first part of planning a future is an analysis of the state of play across the dimensions of inclusive education.

Trading in futures, as bankers may now tell us, requires some caution. I always wonder if the people who don sandwich boards announcing the end of the world on the 28 March have another board at the ready for when they tread the streets on the 29th. Conclusions and futurology are, as Stephen Ball counsels, fraught.[91] History often assigns them to the intellectual scrapheap. For that reason I am simply going to describe reform initiatives internationally across very divergent contexts, explore their conceptual foundations and offer propositions for recognizing and dismantling exclusion as progress towards more inclusive forms of education. Within this discussion I will draw from Tony Knight and Art Pearl's proposition that schooling ought to be an apprenticeship in democracy and that this has implications for the form and for the conduct of an education. I will also consider the role of compromise in reform and diverging from where Norwich[92] concludes, put fundamental principles that don't bear compromise back on the table.

In Chapter 2 we will commence our consideration of the foundations of inclusive education by attempting to come to terms with exclusion. UNESCO assumed a global agenda to affirm *Education for all* as a concern for all children, particularly the most vulnerable.[93] I too intend to commence with a large canvas to establish exclusion as a general, though not always acknowledged, social condition.

2   The worlds we live in

He knows what could be done. He knows that each of these patients could rise from the deathbed but for the want of a dollar a day. He knows that the problem is simply that the world has seen fit to look away as hundreds of impoverished Malawians die this day as a result of their poverty.

Jeffrey Sachs (2005) *The end of poverty*. p. 9

But the truth is that both the broken society and the broken economy resulted from the growth of inequality.

Richard Wilkinson and Kate Pickett (2009) *The spirit level.*
Why more equal societies almost always do better. p. 5

The seeds of collective indifference

In his manifesto for ending global poverty Jeffrey Sachs, Director of The Earth Institute at Columbia University and a Special Advisor to the United Nations on the Millennium Development Goals, delivers a chilling message of human suffering set against a condition of human indifference. 'Eight million people', he writes, 'around the world die each year because they are too poor to stay alive.'[1] Detail depicts the depth of immizeration.

Every morning our newspapers could report, 'More than 20,000 people perished yesterday of extreme poverty.' The stories would put the stark numbers in context – up to 8,000 children dead of malaria, 5,000 mothers and fathers dead of tuberculosis, 7,500 young adults dead of AIDS, and thousands more dead of diarrhoea, respiratory infection, and other killer diseases that prey on bodies weakened by chronic hunger. The poor die in hospital wards that lack drugs, in villages that lack anti-malarial bed nets, in houses that lack safe drinking water. They die namelessly, without public comment. Sadly, such stories rarely get written.[2]

The year 2008 World Bank *Development Research Report* on global poverty concedes that extreme poverty is more 'pervasive' than it had previously reported: 'Alas the revised estimates reported in the present paper suggest that our celebrations in finally getting under the one billion mark for the "$1 a day" poverty count were premature.'[3] Moreover, 'Because of lags in survey data availability, these estimates do not yet reflect the sharp rise in food prices since 2005.'[4] There is more than a tinge of irony lurking in the pages of World Bank reports on world poverty. Given the Bank's adherence to 'interlocking conditions on aid and debt relief'[5] that favour the assemblage of international private interests in the developing world, the Bank appears disingenuous in its revelation of prematurely celebrating poverty diminution. A principal apparatus for raising the level of private sector involvement is through the provision of 'technical assistance' or TA, which may include: training, scholarships, studies and the provision of technical or expert advisers. Emmett and Green provide insight into the dimensions of the re-routing of aid money in this way from the developing world to the developed world:

> But rich countries that spend most of their aid on TA are spending too much money on international consultants … As much as 70% of aid for education is salaries. In some countries, 100 days of consultancy bills cost the same as paying teachers' salaries for a year or keeping 5,000 children in school. A study of TA in Mozambique found that rich countries were spending a total of $350 million per year on 3,500 technical experts, while 100,000 Mozambican public sector workers were paid a total of just $74 million.[6]

The World Bank and its 'sibling' the International Monetary Fund, as Philip Jones[7] characterizes it, hold considerable global sway over national government policy frameworks. The World Bank's rating of countries influences their ability to borrow from private banks and fund holders, including loans for military requirements. The Bank's commitment to education as a development tool rests on a belief that moulding human capital for the global knowledge economy together with building the private sector will lift people and nations out of impoverishment. As an aside, Jones observes the deluge of watery metaphors such as 'rising tides lift all boats' and the 'trickle down effect of the market' to justify the dismantling of the formerly dominant Keynesian approaches to development work.[8] Moreover, human capital theory has '…appeal to policymakers because of its simple solution to complex problems'.[9] Through structural adjustment programmes, the Bank expresses its consistent adherence to a neo-classical belief in market-driven economic development as a panacea for poverty and debt. Its sympathy towards an unfettered market and to scaling down the size of government in education could be seen in its appointment of Maris O'Rourke who had been the Director-General of Education in New Zealand during its most ardent phase of '*Rogernomics*'[10] and the dismantling of the public sector to the position of Director of Education from 1995 to 2001.

Dambisa Moyo believes that while the donors' conditions 'made sense on paper', its workings tied aid in three ways:

- tied to procurement – spending on specified goods and services frequently originating from the donor country;
- specifying the sector or project for aid expenditure;
- anchoring aid to specific economic and political policies.

In practice she argues, 'conditionalities failed miserably'. Not only did aid money find its way back to the shopping malls in the countries of origin through the payment of consultants through technical assistance, the conditions failed to address 'corruption and bad government'.[11]

The year 2005 University of Toronto Massey Lectures were delivered by Stephen Lewis the then United Nation's Secretary General's special envoy for HIV and AIDS in Africa and commissioner to the World Health Organisation's Commission on Social Determinants of Health. The five addresses collectively published as *Race against time*[12] commenced with a lecture uncompromisingly entitled *It shames and diminishes us all*. In this oration, Lewis is an impressive speaker and public intellectual he considers the complicity of the developed world in the degradation of Africa.

> I have to say that the ongoing plight of Africa forces me to perpetual rage. It's all so unnecessary, so crazy that hundreds of millions of people should be thus abandoned.

His rage has its targets.

> It is important to remember that Africa was left in dreadful shape by the departing colonial powers, and was subsequently whip-sawed between ideological factions in the Cold War. But rather more decisive, it was also delivered to the depredations of the so-called IFIS – the collection of International Financial Institutions dominated by the World Bank and the International Monetary Fund ... and including the African Development Bank and other regional development banks. The result of the IFIS' destructive power over Africa was to compromise the social sectors, particularly the health and education sectors of the continent to this day.[13]

The World Bank and the IMF, as we have observed, applied Structural Adjustment Programmes driven by 'conditionality'.[14] Simply put, conditionality refers to the stringent conditions attached to loans from the World Bank or the IMF. Drawing on data from Action Aid International-Emmett, Green, Lawson, Calaguas, Aikman, Kamal-Yanni and Smyth further illustrate the damaging impact of conditions that are tied to aid:

The IMF lends money to poor countries under strict condition that they pursue 'sound' economic policies. If the IMF pulls out, the rich countries will follow. While the IMF is right that countries should manage their economies carefully, its overly rigid stance on public spending is incompatible with achieving the Millennium Development Goals on health, education, and water and sanitation. In Kenya 60,000 teachers are needed to cope with thousands of extra pupils who started coming to school after tuition fees were abolished. But the IMF target to reduce Kenya's public sector wage bill from 8.5 per cent to 7.2 per cent of GDP by 2007 means that teacher numbers have been frozen at their 1998 level.[15]

These conditions reflect the Bank and the Fund's steadfast adherence to Hayekian economic targets wherein the interests of quasi-markets govern policy.[16]

The conditions ranged from the sale of public sector corporations, to the imposition of 'cost-sharing' (the euphemism for user fees imposed on health and education), to savage cutbacks in employment levels in the public service, mostly in the social sectors. To this day, the cutbacks haunt Africa: the IFIS continue to impose 'macroeconomic' limits on the numbers of people (think nurses and teachers) who can be hired, and if that doesn't do the trick, there are financial limits placed on the amount of money that can be spent on the social sectors as a percentage of a country's gross national product (GNP). The damage is dreadful. One of the critical reasons for Africa's inability to respond adequately to the pandemic can be explained by user fees in health care ... at the heart of structural adjustment policies there lay two absolutes: Curtail and decimate the public sector; enhance, at any cost, the private sector.[17]

It is crucial that we understand the contexts in which aid becomes another target for fiscal deregulation. The following extract from Beyers and Hay outlines the dimensions of the extreme suffering in the furnace of poverty and the HIV and AIDS pandemic in Southern Africa alone:

South Africa has one of the highest rates of infection of HIV and AIDS in the world. A total of 21.5% of adults aged between 15 and 49 years are infected (UNAIDS, 2004), although the South African HIV Survey estimate it conservatively at 16.2%. The country has the highest death rate in the world, namely 21.32 per 1000 people (Central Intelligence Agency, 2005). The number of HIV-positive people is estimated at approximately 4.7 million of the total population of 44 million, and 60% of those infected are younger than 25 years. Its neighbours Swaziland (38.8%) and Botswana (37.3%) have the doubtful honour to have the world's highest HIV and AIDS infection rates.

Well over one-third of the people living with HIV and AIDS in the world at the end of 2003 were living in Southern Africa. This amounts to an estimated figure of 14.4 million people of the world total of 37.8 million. Southern Africa further was home to an estimated 5.91 million orphans due to AIDS at the end of 2003.[18]

The World Bank and IMF responded to the pandemic by offering the afflicted African nations loans, with suitably small interest rates, to fight the pandemic and poverty! The impact of the proposed loans and the enforced SAPS was the 'rending of the fabric of African society'.[19] This stands in stark contrast with 'other worlds'. Reflecting on the level of subsidy to European and US farmers in 2005 of $350 billion (five times the amount spent on foreign aid), Lewis reckoned that while every cow in the European Union is subsidized to the tune of $2 a day, 400 to 500 million people in Africa are condemned to live on less than a dollar a day.[20] While collective outrage finally shamed the Bank and the G-8 leaders to write off $40 billion in debts owed by 18 African countries on 11 June 2005 the impact has not eased the grip of the debt manacles. The debt remains at around $200 billion.[21] Again I defer to Lewis's passionate summation:

> ...between 1970 and 2002, Africa acquired $294 billion of debt.... Over the same period, it paid back $260 billion mostly in interest. At the end of it all, Africa continued to owe upwards of $230 billion in debt. Surely that is the definition of international economic obscenity. Here you have the poorest continent in the world paying off its debt, again and again, and forever being grotesquely in hock.[22]

Poverty and development work is a problematic *business.* My point here is not to diminish the work of individuals, and organizations, who sometimes make extreme sacrifices as they work in dangerous circumstances to alleviate disease, poverty and suffering. Rather it is necessary to consider the overall impact of international development processes and the ways they intensify suffering and distress. Moreover, as Moyo asserts, it is time to stop pretending that the aid-based development model will work for the world's poorest countries.[23] Like Moyo, Riddell argues that new relationships have to be forged and political will exercised.[24] Such a relationship cannot coexist with a world that decides to look away.

Other worlds

To compile this portrait of global poverty and the attendant human suffering I selected a small brush and canvas. The picture offers only a series of broken outline strokes. This is but a part of one of the four to seven continents, depending on how we count them. There is no shortage of choice to enter into a portfolio of world of poverty.

The urban streets and rural villages of India offer extremes of deprivation despite claims of the economic upturn ushered in by global flows of
capital, technology and ideas. There are rubbish-heaps in the Philippines
where people live, families scavenging for their sustenance amongst the
refuse. The unremitting suffering experienced by people displaced by war,
who are congregated and contained in camps and ghettos in strange lands
silently bearing their grief, hunger and fear while those who take freedom,
food, shelter, respect and dignity for granted lock in a diplomatic arm-
wrestle with each other to shed responsibility. What a response-sapping
representation it would be (is).

Of course, poverty and the politics of international aid are far more
complex than I have here rendered them.[25] What particularly interests me
is the reaction of those of us who are not directly affected. There are
choices to be made.

- Some engage directly in the struggle against poverty and pandemic,
  they are in the field as it were. Here we may read 'field' as having
  broad applications.
- Many give to established charities, perhaps they subscribe to a programme where they develop a relationship with a named child, and in
  that way they make their important contribution.
- Some enlist in groups of activists aimed at influencing the politics and
  trade practices of the developed world.
- We may find the direct action that causes disruption to our lifestyle
  and routines tiresome and be deflected from thinking about the issues
  by our disdain for these 'radical elements'.
- We may be spurred by the large-scale benefits – cultural events, popu-
  lated by the A-list folk. The direct pleas and subliminal flow of phone
  numbers across the bottom of the screen impress on us a notion that
  we have the capacity to act.
- We may be appalled by the brief glimpses of suffering on the media
  and turn away.

Globally there has been a sustained level of help that jars with the global
flows of power and markets that worsen the plight of millions. But funda-
mentally there has grown a *collective indifference* to suffering amongst
those who are not suffering. How else in 2002 could millions of Australians countenance the silent painful protests of desperate Afghan asylum
seekers as they sewed their lips together as part of a hunger strike in a
detention camp 320 miles north-west of Adelaide in the desert outside the
township of Woomera?[26] While *The Age* newspaper in Melbourne reported
that there were fifty adults (men and women) and four children who had
sewn their lips together and *The Independent* in England reported seventy
adults and three children, the Department for Immigration contended that
it involved four men. The credibility of the then Howard government and

the Minister for Immigration Philip Ruddock is further diminished when we also consider the fabrication of evidence by the government prior to an election that boatpeople were throwing babies overboard to heighten panics over immigration.

They walk amongst us

That's but one snapshot of the worlds we live in that illustrates notions of the developed and developing worlds. We totter as we gaze across the giddying gulfs between these worlds. We have learned to live in a condition of separation, neglect and antagonism. We deflect, albeit unconsciously, in a condition of collective indifference. The dominant news-talk, social anaesthesia as Baudrillard might put it,[27] is about security and terror, about the forces of good and evil. Vast fortunes and the lives of young poor people, argues Sachs,[28] are sacrificed at the altar of the war on terror. Animosity deepens and enshrouds all in the name of religion and patriotism. Attack and reprisal is the new international dialogue. Like Sen[29] before him, Sachs suggests that the real risk for security is poverty. Debates about the nature, targets and perpetrators of terror build indifference to the base problems that divide and exclude people.

Poverty is of course relative. We cross boundaries between affluence and poverty on our journeys into work each day. Even if we do not physically cross the boundaries, there are the daily reminders of their existence: the homeless, street beggars, people with mental health problems who are condemned to live on the street in the name of 'care in the community', the inter-generational unemployed who often live vicariously through television and radio, disabled people obstructed from participating in the workforce, children who are on free school meals and who can't participate in school excursions and so the list extends.

There are worlds within worlds and here too, poverty, social exclusion and profound suffering walk amongst us. The Innocenti Report Card 7, *Child poverty in perspective: An over-view of child wellbeing in rich countries*[30] assesses the lives and well-being of children and young people in twenty-one nations of the industrialized world. Drawing on data from forty

Table 2.1 US child poverty rate, by ethnicity, 1997

	% in poverty	*% of total population*
White	12.4	65.3
Black	37.7	15.6
Hispanic	36.8	14.6
Native American – Inuit	32.5	0.9
Asian – Pacific Islander	20.8	3.6
Total	20.3	100.0

separate indicators across six dimensions: material well-being, health and safety, education, peer and family relationships, behaviours and risks, and young people's own subjective sense of well-being, the report concluded that the United Kingdom (UK) and the United States (US) find themselves in the bottom third of the rankings for five of the six dimensions reviewed.[31]

Calculations by Rainwater and Smeeding[32] depict child poverty in its ethnic hue. While 'white' Americans represent 12.4 per cent of the percentage in poverty, the numbers for other ethnic groups suggest that poverty is not benignly dispensed.

The Fabian Commission on Life Chances and Child Poverty reported in its *Narrowing the gap* report that one in every five children in the UK grows up in poverty, some 3.5 million children.[33] Disaggregating its data, it is possible to see the disproportionate concentration of poverty on particular groupings within the population. A child living in a household where there is a disabled parent increases the risk of poverty from 19 per cent to 30 per cent.[34]

> 73.3% of families with disabled children have an income below the UK mean income, and 30.7% suffered 'absolute low income' as defined by the government.[35]

This is hardly surprising when we know that 49 per cent of disabled people of working age in the UK are employed, compared with 81 per cent of non-disabled people.[36] The risk of unemployment and poverty among Pakistani and Bangladeshi families is 61 per cent, nearly three times the average.[37] At school this means that:

> Over 30% of Pakistani and Black children are eligible for free school meals, as are over 50% of Bangladeshi, Gypsy/Roma and pupils of Travellers of Irish heritage, as compared to just 14% of White pupils.[38]

Toynbee and Walker[39] draw on other data sets to make sharp comparison with the simultaneous rise and concentration of wealth in the UK.

> Pay for top executives has been rising by many multiples more than average pay ... in 2006–7 chief executives' pay in the FTSE 100 companies soared by 37% over the previous year. In that year national average pay increased by 4% while the chancellor, Gordon Brown, insisted that public-sector pay increases be held at 2%. This vast percentage increase in top pay was no freak occurrence. In 2005–6 chief executive pay advanced 28%; the previous year it rose 16% and the year before that 13%. Between 2000 and 2007 FTSE top 100 chief executive pay grew 150% while median earnings across the whole population grew by just 30%.

Of course this picture is also incomplete. Consider the capacity of the most affluent income bracket to reduce or excise tax responsibility. While the 2007–8 minimum wage for a 39-hour week would bring £215.28 to the family table this is 64 per cent of the poverty line, which has been set at £332 a week.[40] Child tax credits would add to this, but it remains the case that many of the UK's children living in poverty come from households where one adult is in work. The grim reality is that '...more than half of all child poverty (54 per cent) occurs in households where at least one parent is doing some paid work'.[41] Again the comparisons across the class divide are staggering: 'To the top pay average of £737,000 in 2007, add bonuses, pensions and share options ... (taking) total average earnings to £3.2 million.'[42] Add to this the imposition on taxpayers in the UK on minimum wages to share the collective burden of subsidizing individual avarice in the banking industry and the swelling ranks of the unemployed following the near collapse of the financial sector. The need to acknowledge and confront the growing inequality, and the social dysfunction that accompanies it, in affluent societies such as the UK is all the more urgent.[43]

Sadly the UK is a variation on the theme of social division throughout what we loosely call the developed world. Activist and educator Jonathan Kozol has written at length about the intransigence of the separation between rich and poor in the US.[44] Taking us to East St. Louis, Illinois he reports on a city which is '98% black, has no obstetric services, no regular trash collection, and few jobs'.[45] Nearly one-third of the families live on less than $7,500 per year. He speaks of the city's inability to afford to repair its dilapidated sewage system and of the women cleaning faecal matter from their sinks; of the children with high traces of lead in their blood courtesy of the preponderance of tax-exempt chemical companies that are located near the housing projects. Opposite on the other side of the Mississippi River are the Illinois Bluffs; places of affluence where the white folk live shielded from the suffering of their neighbours. Subsequent portraits of the conditions of the poor in the US such as those in Kozol's *The shame of the nation* confirm Jones's conviction that 'Poverty is a stubborn enemy'.[46] What Kozol demonstrates is that in some regards the legislative achievements of civil rights movement are in fact a pyrrhic victory.

> What seems unmistakable, but, oddly enough, is rarely said in public settings nowadays, is that the nation, for all practice and intent, has turned its back upon the moral implications, if not yet the legal ramifications, of the Brown decision. The struggle being waged today, where there is any struggle being waged at all, is closer to the one that was addressed in 1896 in Plessy v. Ferguson, in which the court accepted segregated institutions for black people, stipulating only that they must be equal to those open to white people. The dual

society, at least in public education, seems in general to be unquestioned.[47]

Some fourteen years later Kozol cites the work of Gary Orfield and his colleagues at the Civil Rights project at Harvard University to note the 'evisceration' of integration and the systematic reassertion of segregation.[48] He identifies a school in Kansas City, Missouri where there is a 99.6 per cent African American cohort of students that describes itself as a school for students from diverse backgrounds.[49]

> Racial isolation and the concentrated poverty of children in public school go hand in hand, moreover, as the Harvard project notes. Only 15 percent of the intensely segregated white schools in the nation have student populations in which more than half are poor enough to be receiving free meals or reduced price meals. By contrast, a staggering 86 percent of intensely segregated black and Latino schools have student enrolments in which more than half are poor by the same standard. A segregated inner-city school is almost six times as likely to be a school of concentrated poverty as is a school that has an overwhelming white population.[50]

Elsewhere calls to the City of Sydney (Australia) Council from people seeking assistance for homelessness during the year 2005/2006 numbered 51,700, up from 46,864 during 2004/2005.[51] Of course such data only reports those who call and they represent the urban centre of a large sprawling metropolis. Those homeless people living outside the centre of this large conurbation do not figure in the data.

Jack Layton[52] found that confronting the challenges of homelessness in Canada were intensified by a chronic lack of data. Where data are available they are seriously short of the mark. Seldom do they account for people on park benches, in diverse nooks and crannies, in bus shelters, on sidewalk grates, under bridges and in tunnels, in squats, parking garages, cars, tents, emergency shelters or in cheap hotels or motels. Reading the 'executive summary' of the Report of the Mayor's Homelessness Action Task Force (Anne Golden, Chair) entitled *Taking responsibility for homelessness: an action plan for Toronto* is revealing if only an incomplete account of a problem that has become much worse since its publication.[53]

To summarize, the two studies commissioned by the Task Force found that:

- Almost 26,000 different individuals used hostels in Toronto in 1996, about 3,200 on any given night (the number is much higher in the winter). 170,000 different individuals used shelters over the nine years between 1988 and 1996.

- The fastest-growing groups of hostel users are youth under 18 and families with children. Families accounted for 46 percent of the people using hostels in Toronto in 1996.
- 5,300 children were homeless in 1996.
- Between 30 and 35 percent of homeless people suffer from mental illness. The estimates are higher for some population groups; for example, 75 percent of homeless single women suffer from mental illness.
- 4,400 people in 1996 (17 percent of hostel users) stayed in the hostel system for a year or more. This group of 'chronic hostel users' takes up about 46 percent of the beds and services.
- At least 47 percent of hostel users come from outside Toronto.
- More than 100,000 people are on the waiting list for social housing in Toronto.
- Poverty is getting worse among the applicants for social housing; more than one-third of the people on the waiting list have incomes of less than $800 a month.
- The number of families on the social housing waiting list has increased greatly: more than 31,000 children are on the waiting list. At the current rate of placement, families would have to wait 17 years to obtain housing.

(City of Toronto, 1999: 4)

The third annual homeless assessment report tells a grim if incomplete story of the marginalization and disadvantage of a large group of US 'citizenry'.[54] They report that on a single night in January 2007 'there were nearly 672,000 sheltered and unsheltered homeless persons'.[55] Nearly two-thirds of these people were in families, and 42 per cent were sleeping on the streets. Of course, these data are radically incomplete given the difficulty of identification.

I said earlier that representing poverty is a complicated and overwhelming task. I have referred to and used data that draws from the 'poverty line' measure of threshold income as a way of representing poverty. Where possible I have tried to find data where the poverty line is set after housing costs. The poverty line remains an arbitrary index that selects an *'austere income-based poverty line ... based on earlier government calculations about emergency food needs for families'*.[56] This single index measure is convenient but, as Connell reminds us, seriously understates levels of economic and social deprivation. It fails to account for availability of:

> ...types of resources beyond income and wealth that cannot be cashed out on an individual basis, but where inequality is materially significant: for example, access to public institutions such as libraries, colleges, and hospitals; to public utilities; and to safety and community health.[57]

Frequently and in a range of ways the problem of poverty is reduced or distilled by governments and researchers as pathological; something inherent to the make up of poor people themselves. There is also a tendency to homogenize the poor as a single group. Poverty is an issue that cuts across different identities, though some people are more vulnerable. Disabled people,[58] women as single supporting parents,[59] refugee and traveller people,[60] Indigenous people still dealing with the impact of invasion and colonization[61] are some of the people who are more likely to experience prolonged disadvantage. I have tried to show this through a selection of data from different locations around the world. A key point to be drawn from Connell and others before her is that poverty is not a characteristic of the categories of people themselves, it is socially constructed. Poverty is an outcome of particular political, economic and social relations. We will return to this point, the social construction of identity, throughout the book. Wilkinson and Pickett take up the politics of material success and social failure:

> The contrast between the material success and social failure of many rich countries is an important signpost. It suggests that, if we are to gain further improvements in the real quality of life, we need to shift attention from material standards and economic growth to ways of improving the psychological and social wellbeing of whole societies. However, as soon as anything psychological is mentioned, discussion tends to focus almost exclusively on individual remedies and treatments. Political thinking seems to run into the sand.[62]

Somehow many of us in advanced capitalist states fail to see and or respond to this. We find our comfort zone within 'opaque' geographies of exclusion 'that do not make the news' and remain concealed and largely ignored.[63] I place myself in the frame. This is the condition of collective indifference that touches us all in various ways. Let me present three stories, vignettes of where our civic responsibility or Third Way[64] conscience goes missing. The purpose of the vignettes is to demonstrate that the global problem I am describing has local faces. One of the stories comes from David Harvey,[65] the other two come from my time working in the Queensland civil service. In telling these stories I am going to add the spectre of schooling (remember this is a book on educational foundations and futures?). I do this because it was as an education worker that I constantly travelled from one world to another, only sometimes being forced to admit my complicity in the local separations of these worlds.

Vignette one: the value of labour

Death in the Broiler Belt

In *Justice, Nature & the Geography of Difference* David Harvey (1996) takes us to the township of Hamlet in North Carolina deep in what he calls the 'Broiler Belt'. The 'Broiler Belt' refers to the broiler chicken production industry that forms a '…*vast arc running from Maryland's eastern shore through the Carolinas and across the "Deep South" into the Texas Panhandle'* (Harvey, 1996: 335). Valued at more than $20 billion a year, the broiler industry holds considerable political sway. Linked to the chicken production industry is the chicken processing industry 'employing 150,000 workers in 250 or so plants, mostly located in very small towns or rural settings'. While the chicken production industry attracts critical scrutiny from animal rights and environmental groups, the processing industry has done little to improve the poor conditions of its workforce. At the Imperial Foods plant in the town of Hamlet on Tuesday 3 September 1991 a serious fire broke out in the factory claiming the lives of twenty-five of the 200 workers and seriously injuring another fifty-six workers. This was a very serious industrial accident by world standards.

Harvey contrasts the public response to this incident with the 1911 Triangle Shirtwaist Company fire in which 146 employees perished. Whereas the Hamlet fire failed to register significant media and community reaction, over 100,000 people marched in protest down Broadway in New York and won improvements in workplace conditions following the Shirtwaist Company disaster. Eighty years later and 'despite a dizzying matrix of laws, regulations and codes enacted to protect workers, most of the Imperial workers died as the women in New York had: pounding on locked or blocked fire doors' (Harvey, 1999: 336). To explain the failure of the Imperial Foods disaster to excite public and official condemnation Harvey unfashionably though persuasively enlists a Marxist analysis of the conditions of the labour market. The steady decline of agricultural employment across the US results, he argues, in a 'relatively isolated industrial reserve army … far more vulnerable to exploitation than its urban counterpart' (1999: 336–337).

> Those living in relatively geographically isolated rural towns of this sort are, consequently, easy prey for an industry seeking a cheap, unorganized, and easily disciplined labour force.
>
> (Harvey, 1999: 335)

The mobility of industry operations makes it possible to select geographically isolated workers whose lack of alternative employment presses them to accept sub-minimum wage and unsafe employment conditions. Moreover, the dispersal of the workforce as industry seeks out 'affordable' workers limits opportunities for the political agency of workers, for organization and resistance. Fragmentation, concludes Harvey, also characterizes progressive politics as it narrows to the new social movements that in their focus on gender, race, ethnicity, ecology, sexuality, multiculturalism, and so on provide 'a working alternative to class politics of the traditional sort and in some instances have exhibited downright hostility to such class politics' (1996: 341). In this new political configuration Harvey argues that the chickens will command more sympathy than the workers:

> The general tone in the media, therefore, was to sensationalise the horror of the 'accident', but not to probe at all into its origins and certainly not to indite capitalist-class interests, the Republican Party, the failures of the state of North Carolina or OSHA (Occupational Safety and Health Association) as accessory to a murderously negligent event.
>
> (Harvey, 1996: 341)

Vignette two: out of sight, never mind

Community School, Gulf Country, Queensland

As the Deputy Director General of *Education Queensland* (that state's Education Department) between 2000 and 2004 my portfolio included *Partners for Success*. *Partners for Success* was the banner under which we gathered resources, programs and policies connected with Indigenous or Aboriginal education. I therefore had the real privilege of visiting Aboriginal community schools across the state such as Cherbourg State School led by an Aboriginal principal, Chris Sara. The Cherbourg story is an inspiring testament to comprehensive school reform and educational and community leadership that transcends disconnected targets. To be sure the school hits the targets, but this wasn't achieved by target practice. The aim was to achieve cultural change through the reconstruction of the school's ethos, community relationships, programmes and pedagogy.

Under a rallying call of *strong and smart* Sara dispelled prevailing myths and negative stereotypes about Aborigines, established and elaborated over years of European Australian oppression. The school worked with community elders to rebuild their children's pride in their Aboriginal identity and traditional culture. Sara and the teachers worked with families to instil within the children a drive for academic success on the basis that doing well meant that they would have to be better not just as good as the town's (whitefella) children. This is a story of possibility and future that we will revisit.

I also visited places (same state, but different world) in the paralysis of another story. These are places light years away from *strong and smart*. Such a place is an Aboriginal community in the Gulf country of northwest Queensland. The community location is not the traditional land of its inhabitants. Aboriginal people had been removed from their traditional lands and resettled here in the 1930s following devastation from cyclones. I recollect stories that as Aboriginal people attempted to return to their tribal land, they had been forcibly moved back to their new location. The significance of this for a people whose religious, cultural and economic life is intrinsically situated in their land cannot be overstated. Their resettlement included little in the way of infrastructure – traditional cultural (tribal) or European. Dispossessed and on different people's land where spiritual connection to the land is at the centre of community life, the Aboriginal population was conscripted into European religious and social observances and expectations. Readers may not know that until relatively recently Aboriginal people in Queensland had to carry a licence that governed where they were permitted to live and travel. In this way they were tied to the missions and communities. This was considered by European society to be preferable to dwelling on town fringes. The permit regulations and surveillance proceeded from a colonial European science that cast Aboriginal people as pathologically inferior, indolent and criminal. The pioneers of South Africa's rule of Apartheid had travelled to Australia to learn how to contain and control indigenous people. Readers may not be aware that in spite of the abundance of evidence of systematic genocide against Aborigines at the hands of the invading Europeans (Reynolds, 2001), a Labor government in Queensland attempted to alter the Queensland school curriculum to remove the word invasion from the course of study.

My visit was extremely confronting and haunts me still. The local District Director for Mt Isa, Alan Baillie spoke with me about the visit beforehand to prepare for the encounter. He had taken city folk up there before. He was positive about the people and about the efforts that were being made to build community and improve the educational support for children at the local school. He spoke with genuine pride and concern about the mostly young teachers who took positions in the school until, ground down, they returned to more salubrious parts of the state. As we travelled the considerable distance from what had always been to me the remote Mount Isa base, a new (old) world emerged. Alan had been influential in teaching me how to look at the Australian landscape afresh, to apprehend the complexity and beauty that I wasn't equipped to understand or value. It is not uncommon for people who live along the eastern and southern coastline of Australia to talk about most of Australia as being empty. We see expanses of red dirt sparsely punctuated by trees and scrub, a Fred Williams canvas, and call it desert and deserted. Many see it differently and value the deeply spiritual qualities of land and place, taking their cues from the descendants of the original inhabitants and custodians of the land.

The small plane took some time to get to the community. Driving in from the landing strip airport, I stared out from the air-conditioned government-issued Toyota Land Cruiser at an unfolding scene of colonial desolation. These people await post-colonialism. Nothing could prepare me for this trip. I retain no sense of the chronology of what I saw. There was a general store, a shed from which goods and food were sold, outside of which sat a number of people in the blistering heat and dust. There were some children playing in the dirt. We saw a small hospital building. Maybe one or two wards, next to which were houses for the medical staff. High wire fencing surrounded the houses for these 'itinerant' workers. A black silhouette against the red and blue backdrop was the burnt-out remains of the original police station; a memento from a riot that could at any time reignite. Next to it was its replacement. The housing that I recall seeing was very basic, a result of the physical restrictions of moving building materials to this isolated part of the continent, wear and tear and grinding poverty the like of which I had not seen in Australia before.

Arriving at the school, we waited for the principal to unlock the heavily secured gate. We exchanged greetings and had a 'cuppa' in his office. He was warm and friendly, it seemed he really valued the contact with Alan who was one of his important links to the world from which he had come. Then followed the walk around the school. I had done many of these walks and always enjoyed them as I got to talk with kids and teachers about their schools and lives. Such visits grounded and re-educated the erstwhile professor. Many visits have made an indelible impression on me:

- Miss Smith signing to her children, those who could easily hear her and those who couldn't, because of the prevalence of Otitis Media amongst Mt Isa's Aboriginal children.
- A New Basics pilot-school teachers' meeting where they presented their children's work to each other in their own time and spoke with exhilaration of how they had developed new teaching approaches and utilized a range of assessment practices to see if the kids got it.
- The colour drained from a Deputy Principal's face as we walked around the school and she noticed one of the Year 7 kids running across the school building roof.
- A discussion with a group of young people in a high school who used wheelchairs who were constantly embarrassed by the inadequacy of toilet facilities; the 'disabled toilet' (a curious term) was in a remote location so that users were often late to class, or other toilets lacked space and facilities.

This school walk around was of another order, another world. First, the school was barricaded behind a perimeter high wire fence with barbed wire at the top. The windows and doors had intruder-proof bars and mesh that were locked when the children took their lessons inside. I had done a short stint of teaching at the now closed Victorian Pentridge Prison where it was customary for prison officers to unlock doors to let us into the classroom, but it was alien to school visits outside of a prison. He (the Principal) explained that this was necessary for the safety of the children and the teachers. Inside, the classrooms were like others. Children, and there weren't many, worked at computer terminals only momentarily interested in the visitors. It is difficult to describe the impact of reading the blackboard (or was it a whiteboard?) in the classroom. Like other schools there was a section where the rules were written as a reminder. Unlike other school rule charters, this one was divided into three sections: Rules for School/Rules for Home/Rules for Community. My eyes fixed in terror on one of the rules in a child's handwriting in the community section. *'DON'T HURT OR KILL ANYONE.'* We spoke of the unspeakable horrors that many of the children faced daily living with dispossessed and impoverished people, living with alcohol and substance abuse (despite the prohibitions) and living in the shadow of violence.

Then it was morning tea and a meeting with the elders. They were all women. One spoke quietly and unemotionally about her forgotten community, about the needs and hopes for the children. There was genuine affection for Mister Baillie and the teachers, but there was a clear message that they lack sufficient support from 'central office'. There followed questions about what I could do. The teachers looked on in respectful silence as I fumbled through an enormity of issues I could barely grasp. Alan engaged with the folk to talk of small progresses and his hopes for the future of Partners for Success. I quietly had another cuppa and lunch during which time we were introduced to a local policeman (who like the teachers seemed very young). He spoke of his perspective on building community and the importance of schooling.

We drove around again looking at the Spartan housing, shanties, a water hole where kids were swimming and then it was back to the plane. What safety there was bouncing around in a flimsy plane towards what used to be the remote township of Mt Isa. The Isa, as it is called, now felt like a secure metropolis. This was not an Australia that I had ever encountered or believed possible. My overwhelming thought all day was that I had somehow been transported into film footage from Soweto or somewhere similar. In the plane I looked through tears at Alan whose return look was sympathetic – he was well used to the shock felt by foreigners as they got to know the Australia few talk about. Returning to my everyday work I tried to relate these events and reconcile my shame. The edge dulled over time, diaries and in-trays displaced the sense of crisis. Although busy with policy and management of Partners for Success, I drifted into our collective indifference.

Vignette three: a purchase on paradise

'Blockies'

Let's stay in Queensland. The third of these vignettes is set on the outskirts of a town we'll call Larkin. It is a little less than 400 kilometres away from Brisbane, the capital city of this north eastern Australian state. The staple products of this shire are grain, beef and wool. When I visited Larkin it, like most of Australia, was in the deadening grip of a ferocious drought. In the 1960s there was the discovery of oil deposits in the Larkin shire. With a population of around 800 people Larkin services an expansive rural population that was recorded as approximately 3,600 in the 2006 census. When drilling down to the data returned from the shire sub-divisions the figures become rubbery. The non-return rate was great as families were on the move in search of potable water. The town's school comprises the Prep Year through to Year 12 with a total population that hovers around 450 children. Like many schools in rural Queensland the school is a community hub providing more than just the schooling of the local children. There has emerged a set of difficult, perhaps unique, issues that the District Director (DD) alerted me to.

Speaking to a group of education department personnel about disadvantage and education and the challenges for inclusive schooling, the DD asked a question about rural poverty in the seminar and I gave a typically urban-centric response. I had imagined that he was talking about the children of

farmers feeling the pinch of our frequently unforgiving climate. State governments, churches and welfare organizations had mounted relief programmes
and even banks were starting to listen to calls for rural debt tolerance. The
plight of farmers, their families and the people living in the townships that
service the rural industry affected by long-term drought are indeed serious.
Only when the impact expresses itself at the supermarket till do we start to
take notice. Increased rates of suicide, mounting mortgage foreclosures and
bankruptcy rates and the relocation of people from the bush to the city, drug
and alcohol abuse, mental illness and domestic violence are neglected hall-
marks of country life. These indicators of protracted hardship do not make
as immediate an impression as does an increase in the price of milk or bread.
The effects of drought are uneven across farming communities but remain
dire for those affected. A separation between city and the bush based on
more than geographic distance muffles sympathy.

Choosing to have a word with me later the DD politely suggested that a visit
to Larkin would be the most effective way of addressing my ignorance. He was
not simply talking about these pressures that had driven into the well-being of
rural towns right across the continent; he was speaking about a unique
problem. Some years prior to my visit, real estate developers, we'll rename them
Capital Developments, had advertised large 'blocks' of land at unrepeatable
bargain prices. Unsuspecting purchasers, mostly from the poorer outer suburbs
of Sydney and Melbourne, took to the buy line: 'Move to your 30 acre rural
retreat, close to a bustling rural town.' Folk with a rural dream looking for their
*'Sea Change'** were also told that it was a short trip to the tourist Mecca of the
Gold and Sunshine Coasts. The developers financed purchasers' loans. Accordingly purchasers would own their block on receipt of the final payment.

There were unstated pitfalls for the prospective purchasers. This was not
the soil on which to build an idyll of self-sufficiency. The sub-divided land in
question did yield rocks and thistles aplenty, but little else. The services to
the blocks were meagre so that many had insufficient water and electricity.
Though the 2006 census data fails to reflect the concentration of poverty, the
overall impact is clear.

> ...in (Larkin) Shire the median weekly individual income for persons
> aged 15 years and over who were usual residents was $327, compared
> with $446 in Australia. The median weekly household income was
> $623, compared with $1,027 in Australia. The median weekly family
> income was $744, compared with $1,171 in Australia.
> (from the report of the Community Economic Development Officer on
> ABS Census Data, File Reference 14/9/1; 6/4/5; 3/1/2)

The data is predictable for rural Australia in decline. The large number of
people living on rural sub-divisions outside of Larkin results in an increased
reliance on services, and 'community indicators show (the) impact on areas
of unemployment, crime, domestic violence and health' (p. 6).

On arrival people found that their blocks were kilometres from the centre
of the town. The blocks fronted graded gravel roads and had limited access
to services, power and water. A worker from a welfare organization reflects
on having visited cubby houses with tarpaulin roofs and dirt floors – making

them unbearable in the 42 degrees summer heat. Toilets were a hole in the ground.

We set off early in the morning from the District Office to visit Larkin State School, taking in a tour of the blocks en route. The landscape that passed seemed unremarkable.

Leaving the main road some distance before the town, we drove down recently graded but unsealed roads with signposts naming each street that struck off from the intersections. The blocks appeared pretty barren, yielding little more than rocks and thistles. Placed on many of the blocks that I saw were large freight containers that substituted for housing. On others was an assortment of haphazard shanty constructions. Still others had something more substantial. Our guide pointed out security systems that had been set up in some. There seemed to be nothing to take, maybe the parts from the thirsty old model cars resting by the shanties, I thought. But alarms had been installed because of the high incidence of crime; theft of building materials, household belongings and protection for drug production. As the dimensions of what I was seeing started to form in my mind, I looked back at the street signs with their names: 'Fortune Road', 'Sunnyside Road', 'Diamond Road', 'Hope Road'. What a savage infliction of irony.

These block dwellers were derisively called *blockies* by the established Larkin folk. The lines had been drawn between the *blockies* and the townspeople dividing the school population. Evidence of the differences included: children from the blocks having sporadic attendance contingent on receipt of welfare that enabled the parents to drive the kids into town or travel several kilometres to the bus stops; children coming to school dirty and hungry; children not having the books and materials to do lessons or homework. The school principal spoke to me of the increased call on counselling staff and welfare agencies to deal with the impact of poverty and these transitory children. The principal estimated that there were at least 150 school age children living on the sub-divisions who were not attending school. Student Disciplinary Absences (suspension and expulsions) at the school had grown by 430 per cent in five years. Animosity was growing between the town folk and the *blockies* because of the unruly behaviour of these itinerant children.

The school and its teachers worked assiduously in meeting the educational and social needs of this new and challenging population. The school, however, struggled daily in the face of significant and unfamiliar challenges and limited resources. This is a story of a world with which most Queenslanders remain unfamiliar.

---

* *Sea change* is the title of a very popular Australian Broadcasting Commission television drama that depicts the progress of a single-parent family that leaves Melbourne city-life for the unencumbered tranquillity of life in a coastal town.

Drawing together the strands...

This chapter has been a depressing expedition through worlds within, or at the fringes of, other universes. The unifying thread has been exclusion born of poverty and disadvantage. I have merely hinted at the extent, divergent forms and devastating impacts of poverty and disadvantage. Our excursion has herded us like tourists around the globe, pausing only momentarily to get off the bus to view a range of poverties to form a view of the whole. Of course we have noted the irony that we do not have to travel far to bump up against poverty or social exclusion, it is a constant if unacknowledged companion.[66] The portraits of poverty reveal what sociologists of education call 'intersections' of exclusion.[67] In other words, in different societies different individuals and groups become more vulnerable and susceptible to exclusion. Disabled people, for example, are more likely to experience poverty as they are more frequently excluded from the labour market.[68] And it must be said that within this broad descriptor, disabled people will experience more overt forms of discrimination and oppression. Mental illness presents challenges that estrange, to use Bauman's words, like no other.[69] It is also important to take stock of Wilson and Pickett's contention that it is not just a question of income level. They argue that in more unequal societies all people do worse across a range of social and individual well-being indicators.[70]

Kozol describes there being an unofficial apartheid between black and white in the USA where there are '*death zones*', places devoid of white faces.

> In Boston, the press referred to areas like these as 'death zones' – a specific reference to the rate of infant death in ghetto neighbourhoods – but the feeling of the death zone often seemed to permeate the schools themselves. Looking around some of these inner-city schools, where filth and disrepair were worse than anything I'd seen in 1964, I often wondered why would we agree to let our children go to school in places where no politician, school board president, or business CEO would dream of working.[71]

In a world fragmented by war and conflict, the rising tide of people forced from their countries, by conflict and or poverty, forges new exclusions.[72] This list could be extended. Exclusion is pervasive, reaching across all communities with dramatic and subtle manifestations. There are the very obvious forms of exclusion the recognition of which generates little controversy. There are also exclusions that are claimed to be 'natural' and necessary. It must be quickly said that such claims are usually made on behalf of those to be excluded.

I am puzzled and alarmed by our capacity to turn away from exclusion, the indifference or determination to *look away*, as Sachs reports from his portrayal of Malawi, in the face of the subjugation of 'others'. Poverty is sustained both by indifference to the plight of those who live in its grip and by the determination of others to strive so as not to fall into its clutches. This, as Rizvi and Lingard's analysis shows, is the neo-liberal mantra of competitive individualism that informs global education policy-making.[73] Bauman usefully employs Doel and Clarke's notion of *ambient fear* to describe this condition.[74]

When I worked in Australia, I was genuinely alarmed and distressed when confronted by the sufferings in the Aboriginal community and the rural back blocks. I did not recognize these places as part of the country I inhabited. Indeed, so many Australians are able to maintain physical and temporal distance and speak to the world about the 'lucky country'. What entitles us to ignore such depth of suffering in our own locale? Why do we not fess-up to our role in its reproduction and maintenance? Yet we do resist acknowledgement and engagement in reparation. This is a matter of collective indifference to apparently isolated circumstances. More troubling is that we apply this same conditioned response in our near and frequent social relations. This ought to be the heart and head of discussions about exclusion and inclusive education before launching into the technical or logistical questions of organizing our schools and education resources. In this respect inclusive education is, as Julie Allan reminds us, an ethical project.

> The ethical project of inclusion does three things. First, the project forces us to see inclusion not as something that we do to a discrete population of children, but rather as something we must do to ourselves. Second, the ethical project allows us to 'experience ourselves as animated' (Brenauer, 1999: xiii), as 'capable of finding new secrets, possible freedoms, and inventions that take us in unexpected directions and breathe life back into the human project' (Ransom, 1997: 178). Finally, the project allows us to be optimistic about what we can change...[75]

Allan's point is sustained by analysis of our collective role in the production of disability and disablement. Disabled people continue to reside at the margins of civic life because we not only allow it, but also because we create, enforce and sustain disability. This is what Oliver refers to as the politics of disablement.[76] Herein lies a difference between individual pathology and social pathology. C. Wright Mills famously refers to this as the misrepresentation of social issues as personal troubles.[77] We will return to this distinction, as it is central to liberating ourselves from redundant traditional special and regular education assumptions to imagine a new order of schooling.

Collective indifference is a useful concept, but it is also flawed: useful because we can name the phenomenon of permitting exclusion either by consent or by apathy, and flawed because it separates us from our agency in the reproduction of oppressions. Let us consider why and how some people are denied social sponsorship in institutions such as schools. Just as important as identifying cultures of exclusion is the formation of an understanding of how we settle for that.

This is complicated as accompanying questions of intention loom to confound us. People, believing that they are helping, may be propping up the edifice of exclusion. We will consider, for example, the mixed objectives in the origins of special schooling. Simultaneously we see advocates proposing segregated special education as a means for ensuring that excluded children receive basic education where none was provided. Others saw it as a link in the chain of eugenics. At play here is a complex amalgam of history, ontology (the nature of being) and epistemology (the investigation of knowledge). In the next chapter I will attempt to unravel collective indifference as a platform for a consideration of the emergence and 'progress' of inclusive education.

3 Unravelling collective indifference

> Lack of respect, though less aggressive than an outright insult, can take an equally wounding form. No insult is offered another person, but neither is recognition extended: he or she is not seen – as a full human being whose presence matters.
>
> Richard Sennett, 2003: 3

> All societies produce strangers; but each kind of society produces its own kind of strangers, and produces them in its own inimitable way.
>
> Zygmunt Bauman, 1997: 17

A world that looks away

We have encountered through Jeffrey Sachs, a doctor working in Malawi in Africa.[1] I return to that chilling phrase in his depiction of the plight of these forgotten people: 'the world has seen fit to look away'. Looking away is a human reflex when our sensibilities are confronted. It is habitual and, after time, simply no longer recognized. It is a form of indifference that we have come to share. This chapter will develop a notion of *collective indifference* to suggest why exclusion so often goes unchallenged and why inclusion is so difficult.

Collective indifference is not just a means of coping with the ongoing suffering of the developing world, it refers also to the ways in which we have come to routinely ignore suffering that stalks us in our own neighbourhoods. I will also argue that collective indifference is an acquired condition. Bestowed understandings, expert professional knowledge and interests, and political imperatives converge to allow us to avert our gaze. Of course this process is not always straightforward, systematic or coherent.

Rizvi and Lingard[2] adopt Charles Taylor's concept of the modern social imaginary[3] to argue that with the passage of time globalization has deepened, extended and hastened the neo-liberal social imaginary. In this way of imagining civil society human connection is dismantled in preference to competitive individualism. Competitive individualism saturates education policy discourse and it drives the desires and hopes of individuals and families as they are pitted against each other to claim places at better schools, secure private tuition to leverage test performances, and dissuade schools from enrolling those who are perceived to compromise this drive to achieve rapidly multiplying government targets.

This chapter also extends our discussion of exclusion as a necessary prelude for a consideration of the origins and 'progress' of inclusive education. Tony Knight[4] urges that inclusive education should be cast and understood as a relational concept, a means to an end. In this respect, Basil Bernstein, who 'announced' inclusion as a right and requirement for democracy, accompanies him.[5] It must be stressed that in establishing its critical properties Bernstein distinguishes inclusion from *absorption* or assimilation. The French sociologist Alain Touraine expounds upon the dangers of inclusion becoming a shield for absorption and continuing oppression:

> In a world of intense cultural exchanges, there can be no democracy unless we recognize the diversity of cultures and the relations of domination that exist between them. The two elements are equally important: we must recognize the diversity of cultures, but also the existence of cultural domination.... The struggle for the liberation of cultural minorities can lead to their communitarianization, or in other words their subordination to an authoritarian cultural power.[6]

Researchers like Knight are interested in the interrogation of the purposes of education. Inclusion will not in or of itself suffice. A parallel can be found in Nobel Prize-winning economist Amartya Sen's work *Development as freedom*, where he argues that the purpose of development is to 'expand the real freedoms that people enjoy'.

> Viewing development in terms of expanding substantive freedoms directs attention to the ends that make development important, rather than merely to some of the means that, inter alia, play a prominent part in the process.[7]

Too frequently theories of inclusive education commence with technical considerations of the means for achieving inclusion. Inclusive education is thus reduced to a list of policies, strategies and resources. These activities to pursue inclusive education represent a necessary and important discussion, but it must be the second order discussion. The first requirement is to establish our goals and aspirations. Inclusive education commences with the recognition of the unequal social relations that produce exclusion. From that point we can pursue a less capricious process of developing our strategic discussion.

Let me hasten to point out that I have no argument with many traditional special educators who mount their critiques of inclusion on the failed relocation of segregated students in new surroundings where they continue to occupy marginal status and identity.[8] As Bernstein and Touraine instruct respectively, this is a manifestation of *absorption* or *communitarianization* rather than inclusion. Not a new predicament for vulnerable minorities, indigenous education advocates exposed how establishing quotas for university enrolments of indigenous students, devoid of strategies to dismantle Eurocentric curriculum and pedagogy, inexorably re-confirms their identities of failure and drives them out of higher education. Lobbying for access must aim for more than adding to the numbers of minority students on the enrolment register. Unless we simultaneously change the bias of curriculum, pedagogy and assessment and address the minutiae of the school's cultural package, then schools will continue to shun the possibility of inclusion.[9] To abandon the principle of inclusion because the logistics appear too difficult, in the manner suggested by Michael Farrell in his celebration of the special school, reveals conceptual aridity and political timidity.[10]

Armed with provocations and challenges from Slavoj Zizek's book, '*In defense of lost causes*', let us prize open this deflective struggle between the alternatives of special and regular schooling for disabled children.[11] Considering the corrupting force of Marxist revolutions Zizek cautions that within each revolution '...there was a redemptive moment which gets lost in the liberal-democratic rejection – and it is crucial to isolate this moment'.[12] This, we could reasonably contend, has happened in the once radical project of inclusive education.

Farrell asserts that '...at the heart of calls for the ultimate closure of special schools, lies a diminution of the importance of providing the best education possible for children, including children with SEN [special educational needs]'. For Farrell, 'The danger is that inclusion will come to be seen as more central to the work of schools than education.'[13] To illustrate this proposition he invents the metaphor of a fire department committed more to multi-ethnic, sexuality and gender representation than to the requirement for fire-fighting knowledge and skills.

Much of Farrell's critique of inclusive education and its attachment to a human rights agenda rests on the problem of what economists might refer to as *bracket creep* or the inflation of the number of groups identified as excluded and oppressed. Linda Graham and Naomi Sweller refer to this as category creep.[14] Herein lies a paradox. A glance at the *Diagnostic and statistical manual of mental disorders IV*[15] compendium of mental disorders that governs the criteria for children's achievement of SEN *'status'* and/or their disqualification from neighbourhood schools reveals an ever-expanding raft of behavioural disorders and syndromes available to apply to children and adults. We await DSM V in 2012 for further calibration and categorization of an increasingly disordered, needy and treatable population.[16] The consultations are now well advanced to enlarge the catalogue of syndromes and disorders *available* for application to school pupils.[17] Hence there exists an element of unacknowledged irony in Farrell's derisive adjudication of the human rights lobby:

> Inflation strains credibility, leading people to ask how many oppressed groups can be found in a society before the bizarre situation is reached where everyone is oppressed or excluded and there is nobody left to oppress or exclude them ... Given this increasing lack of credibility, it can be argued that it is not being educated in a special school that might oppress pupils. The main oppression and exclusion that pupils in special school and their parents have to fear is that of political correctness seeking to force an over-zealous inclusion agenda even if it means denying the child a good education.[18]

Applying this logic, I ask myself: who will be left as the 'normal child' once the cartographers of human disorders hang up their tools, dust off their workbench and fold their aprons?

Like Baroness Warnock[19] and many others, including Kauffman and Hallahan,[20] Kauffman and Sasso,[21] Kavale and Mostert,[22] and Mostert, Kavale and Kauffman,[23] the correct observation that children who migrate from special schools to their neighbourhood schools too frequently experience marginalization within the mainstream is proffered to abandon the principle and practice of inclusion. Indeed, Farrell dismisses the life stories from the voices of former special school students in Derrick Armstrong's research in large measure because the deleterious experience of students in regular education is not considered within his report.[24] The argument can be unravelled further.

Let us recall Zizek to allow some level of confusion before ruling a line through what history has thrown up for us:

> ...the goal is to leave behind, with all the violence necessary, what Lacan mockingly referred to as the 'narcissism of the lost Cause,' and to courageously accept full actualization of a Cause, including the inevitable risk of a catastrophic disaster.... To paraphrase Beckett's memorable phrase ... after one fails, one can go on and fail better, while indifference drowns us deeper and deeper in the morass of imbecilic Being.[25]

A contingent concept, inclusive education is condemned to train its critical eye to the changing conditions of education. Indeed, the eye must be capable of complete oscillation, turning inward and outward. Barton[26] and Oliver[27] press us to honour our obligation to consider our own privileged position as educators and researchers in the processes of exclusion. It assumes, or it should, an alternative vision of the purposes, character and practices of schooling. At the heart of inclusive education lies, as argued by activists and scholars such as Ballard,[28] Barton[29] and Armstrong,[30] the '*overwhelming question*':[31] What kind of world do we desire? Is it a world where we can comfortably rationalize exclusion and segregation of different groups of people? What is the nature of justice and democracy? Does this not apply to people we describe as having special educational needs? Other *first-order* questions arise:

- What is exclusion?
- Who is in and who is out?
- How does this happen?
- How do we learn to recognize, expose and dismantle it?
- Inclusion into what?

This chapter provides a bridge where we will move from the generality of exclusion as a social condition to specificities of exclusion as an institutional feature or part of the grammar of schooling. I want to consider how people develop, impose, police and protect economic, social and cultural barriers that simultaneously anoint and discard people. I will argue that at least two mechanisms are in operation concurrently to construct orders of inclusion and exclusion. These overlapping mechanisms are:

- bestowed understandings; and
- professional knowledge and interests.

It is also important to place you and me in the frame to declare our complicity in or our rejection of, the 'order of things' (the way things are). Michele Moore, the Editor of *Disability & Society*, often reminds students in her classes that just as exclusion is based on sets of decisions and actions, so too is inclusion. Doing this establishes agency, our power to act. Put simply, there are choices to be made. The current organization of education has consequences. Some pupils are smiled upon, actually and metaphorically. They enrol without fuss; they find that the culture and organization of the classroom and what they are learning complements the culture and disposition of their family life.[32] They receive their lessons, their learning at school is often augmented by family resources, they turn in their assignments and they stride across the graduation stage as school and family enter into a mutual celebration of success. Privilege begets privilege. Silly hats are heaved heavenward.

Not so for all students. In Queensland, for example, students with disabilities were not enrolled, they were '*placed*' in schools. Until relatively recently, parents and caregivers of these children were referred to the provocatively named *Low Incidence Unit*; the agency that would manage their child's or their *low incident's* conditions of engagement. Oftentimes such referral heralds a rude awakening for parents that school will be a hostile terrain for them and their children to navigate.[33] Theirs will most likely be a struggle to assert their children's right to access the school, the classroom and the curriculum. The message will frequently be that their child is worth less than the regular children whose education is disturbed and threatened by the presence of their disabled child. To use Bauman's poignant couplet, their child is consigned to the ranks of the 'surplus population'.[34] In the competitive education marketplace schools compete to attract those students whose academic potential will improve and sustain the school's position on the academic league table. This is the perverse impact of so-called choice in many jurisdictions.[35] In this competitive environment schools are very anxious about risky students.[36] A series of conditions may be attached to the placement of the disabled child including:

- where their instruction will take place;
- who will conduct that teaching (if not a specialist teacher, more likely a teacher aide);
- the duration of schooling; and
- the resources required for their child.

In some jurisdictions parents of disabled children may be required to pay additional fees to the school to procure a teaching assistant for the child as a condition of their placement. Parents will sit through meetings to review and renew Individual Education Plans.[37] Couched in terms of collaboration, according to Kearney's research in New Zealand schools, this exercise is more often than not a compliance ritual.[38] Adopting technical and sometimes intimidating language, expert professionals assist in the limitation of expectations in keeping with the reductive force of the disabling labels they confer on children.[39] Moreover, the language of special educational needs serves to remind the ordinary or the regular teacher – the teacher of ordinary or regular children – that s/he can look away from the exceptional child. They are excused while aides and other support staff provide a symbolic partition around the disabled or challenging child. There is a growing literature lead by researchers including Balshaw in the UK, Giangrecco in the USA and Bourke in Australia that questions the educational efficacy and highlights the stigmatizing effects of this form of inclusion support.[40] Moreover, it may well be argued, as Douglas Biklen suggested many years ago, that in the regular school classroom, the providers of support and assistance are at risk of becoming as marginalized as the children they work with.[41]

I am reminded of when, years ago, a parent was making a submission to a regional review of a special education services panel in northern New South Wales, in Australia. Exhausting her prepared and polite remarks to the be-suited officials, she looked down and spoke to the floor in a lowered and exhausted voice. However it was spun, she observed, inclusive education in that region was merely 'scraps from the table for children who, when all is said and done, are sometimes tolerated but never welcome'. This remark has haunted me ever since. Setting aside politeness and deference may be exactly what is required for registering less powerful lay voices.

Making indifference collective – antecedents

Following Alain Touraine, Kevin McDonald has had a longstanding interest in social movements and 'struggles for freedom'.[42] His analysis of developing and competing understandings of globalization sheds light on shifts in social theory depicting a 'new uncertainty about fundamental categories to make sense of being and acting in the world'.[43] As Rizvi and Lingard remind us globalization is a highly contested notion:

> It refers not only to shifts in patterns of transnational economic activities, especially with respect to the movement of capital and finance, but also to the ways in which contemporary political and cultural configurations have been reshaped by major advances in information technologies. It is a concept that is used not only to describe a set of empirical changes, but also to prescribe desired interpretations of and responses to these changes ... globalisation affects the ways in which we both interpret and imagine our lives.[44]

Referred to as the Washington Consensus, early globalization theory was framed around analyses of global corporations and the finance industry, media and the emergent information technologies that facilitated a new-found real time or simultaneous global reach. In its early articulation, McDonald observes,[45] globalization theories expressed a notion of an outward movement by the West, the 'golden straitjacket',[46] and the modernizing forces of capital thereby creating what Giddens described as a borderless or 'runaway world'.[47] Subsequent postulations have enlivened and added new textures to the discussion of globalization. In a shift from 'structures to flows'[48] researchers such as Manuel Castells,[49] in his analysis of networks showing global transformations from the industrial paradigm to the information paradigm, argues that the shift to networks has accordingly weakened the authority and power of government, traditional social institutions and nation-state borders. Arjun Appadurai,[50] consistent with Charles Taylor's 'modern social imaginaries', augments economic and institutional analyses to consider the critical role of culture in new globalizations. As indicated previously by Rizvi and Lingard, people experience multiple worlds in multiple ways. New social geographies emerge where neighbourhood, community and network become more complex, expansive and fluid concepts and experiences. Appadurai traces five 'scapes' of cultural flows in a globalizing world:

- **Ethnoscapes** – population shifts: immigration, tourism, guest workers, exiles/refugees.

- **Technoscapes** – global technology networks: Internet/World Wide Web, transport systems.
- **Financescapes** – complex and changing flows of international finance.
- **Mediascapes** – global media incorporating television syndicates, the Internet, magazines and audio and film streaming.
- **Ideoscapes** – the movement of ideas that are developed in one locale, and gather international significance.

For Appadurai understanding global patterns is as much about disjuncture, fragmentation and dislocation as convergence. 'Glocalization', the reassertion of the local against pervasive globalization, becomes a key analytic focus. Hence explanations are not always tidy, nor are they sequentially ordered. Appadurai offers a 'salutary reminder' that:

> …globalization is itself a deeply historical, uneven and even localizing process. Globalization does not necessarily or even frequently imply homogenization or Americanization, and to the extent that different societies appropriate the materials of modernity differently, there is still ample room for the deep study of specific geographies, histories and languages.[51]

Law and Urry have described the world, or more precisely 'worlds' as a pluriverse,[52] a world that defies depiction or characterization through generality, but is better explained by the specificities of its disjuncture and convergences. Under these conditions the case for a non-linear reconsideration of the organization of 'schooling' seems overdue. More particularly our reconsideration needs to be mounted within the context of the changed worlds inhabited by shifting populations of young people with complex and hybrid identities[53] who no longer see school or family as the custodians of information.[54]

A political economy of exclusion

Richard Sennett delivered the 2004 Castle Lectures in Ethics, Politics and Economics at Yale University. They have been published as *The culture of new capitalism*.[55] Obliquely summoning the frequently offered adage: 'Don't wish too hard, you might just get it!' Sennett elegantly captures a broad vista of social change as represented by the changing relations of production, employment and labour market organization. He prefaces his lectures by remembering how in the 1960s 'serious young radicals' targeted large corporations and government organizations, including state socialism, as bureaucratic prisons. Their 'size, complexity and rigidity' 'fixed people in an iron grip'.[56] The young radicals have been granted their wish; the wall came tumbling down. Governments and corporations are evacuating predictable and protective institutional forms. Jessop describes this as a shift from the Keynesian National Welfare State to the Schumpterian Workfare or Competition State.[57] Sennett remarks:

> Yet history has granted the New Left its wish in a perverse form. The insurgents of my youth believed that by dismantling institutions they could produce communities: face-to-face relations of trust and solidarity, relations constantly negotiated and renewed, a communal realm in which people became sensitive to one another's needs. This has certainly not happened. The fragmenting of big institutions has left many people's lives in a fragmented state: the places they work more resembling train stations than villages, as family life is disoriented by the demands of work. Migration is the icon of the global age, moving on rather than settling in.[58]

As a footnote I direct your attention to the Canadian public intellectual and politician Michael Ignatieff's observation that notwithstanding the elevation of needs to rights in the welfare state, there was no guarantee of solidarity:

> Respect and dignity also depend on whether entitlements are understood to be a matter of right, a matter of deserving, or a matter of charity. In many Western welfare states, entitlements are still perceived by both the giver and the receiver, as gifts. To be in need, to be in receipt of welfare, is still understood as a source of shame. Needs may make rights in law, but they do not necessarily make rights in the minds of the strangers at my door.[59]

For Ignatieff, 'we remain a society of strangers'.[60] Neither proponents of *The Third Way* nor its critics have resolved the ambiguous relations of providing for entitlement while limiting the sense of uselessness, shame and hostility that accompanies dependency.[61]

Half a century of wealth creation, argues Sennett, has produced greater economic inequality and social instability. Ours remains a detached society, *'a crowded city of lightly engaged people'*.[62] In the new culture of global capitalism a new culture (values and practices) has emerged that tears apart notions of the supportive community. In the new capitalism Sennett suggests that the 'ideal man or woman' has to confront three challenges in a climate of 'unstable, fragmentary social conditions'.[63] To précis, the challenges are:

1 **Time:** how to manage short-term relationships, and oneself, while migrating from task to task, job to job, place to place.
2 **Talent:** how to develop new skills, knowledge and dispositions and mine potential abilities as technology reshapes labour.
3 **Surrender:** how to let go of the past. Experience, loyalty and human

attachment are no longer prized. A new personality trait is required akin to the new consumer who hungers after the new even if the old is perfectly serviceable.

This is a capricious world, a feckless new disorder built on what McDonald calls *fluidarity* rather than now redundant notions of solidarity.[64] New communities in virtual worlds are built on contingent, conditional and expendable values. In the new political economy people lose self-narrative as they try to traverse the fragmented social and economic landscape.

> The new institutions ... are neither smaller nor more democratic; centralized power has instead been reconfigured, power split off from authority. The institutions inspire only weak loyalty, they diminish participation and mediation of commands, they breed low levels of informal trust and high levels of anxiety about uselessness ... the cutting edge has capitalized on superficial human relations.[65]

At the heart of Sennett's analysis, and it is an analysis built from the heart, are notions of *usefulness, commitment, trust* and *value*.

Like Bauman, Sennett is concerned about human waste or perhaps more accurately, the wasting of humans. The 'spectre of uselessness', as he calls it, casts a long shadow formed by the search for global sweatshops, the impact of automation and a combination of ageism and skills exhaustion.[66] To his list we might add: disablement, conflict and war and forced migration. In Bauman's terms economic progress creates flawed consumers and hence a 'surplus population'.

> In a society of consumers, they are 'flawed consumers' – people lacking the money that would allow them to stretch the capacity of the consumer market, while they create another kind of demand to which the profit-oriented consumer industry cannot respond and which it cannot profitably 'colonize'. Consumers are the prize assets of consumer society; flawed consumers are its most irksome and costly liabilities.[67]

The migration of surplus people or collateral casualties to the social margins as a consequence of the redundancy of their labour builds and intensifies individual competition, estrangement or disengagement and fear and prejudice against an increasing array of threats for those who grimly hang on to social respectability. The stakes are high in a post-stakeholder society.

> Causes of exclusion may be different, but for those on the receiving end the results feel much the same ... stripped of the self-confidence and self-esteem needed to sustain their social survival, they have no reason to contemplate and savour the subtle distinctions between

suffering by design and misery by default. They may be excused for feeling rejected, being incensed and indignant, breathing vehemence and harbouring revenge – though having learned the futility of resistance and surrendered to the verdict of their own inferiority they could hardly find a way to recast all such sentiments into effective action. Whether by an explicit sentence or by an implied though never officially published verdict, they have become superfluous, unnecessary, unneeded and unwanted, and their reactions, off the mark or absent, render the censure of self-fulfilling prophecy.[68]

Absolution from responsibility for our production of the outcast is offered in the so-called impersonalized forces at work:

> ...the production of human waste has all the markings of an impersonal, purely technical issue. The principal actors in the drama are 'terms of trade', 'market demands', 'competitive pressures', 'productivity' or 'efficiency' requirements, all covering up or explicitly denying any connection with the intentions, will, decisions and actions of real humans with names and addresses.[69]

In a state of *ambient fear* we turn from, or we turn on, the *Other*, the stranger, the surplus population as we secure our survival and privileges.[70] In times of recession we witness the rapid metastasizing of racism and the loathing of immigrant, refugee and disabled people. *Mixaphobia* replaces liberal multiculturalism and diversity discourse.[71] This is the foundation for exclusion, the incubus for the cultural values and practices of institutional life. The social and cultural gravity is competitive individualism. Herein lies the dismantling of community. Let us examine the ways in which collective indifference to the excluded operates in and is sustained by schools.

1 Bestowed understandings: the making and unmaking of people

In *The world in six songs*, onetime member of the band Blue Oyster Cult, record producer and neuroscientist, Daniel Levitin reminds us of musicologist David Huron's observation that 'music is characterized by its ubiquity and its antiquity'.[72] So too for exclusion. Both of these facts dull our sensibilities. Exclusion is a part of the grammar of our past. It is the wallpaper of our daily lives. Exclusion is everywhere and it has been there for a long time. This helps to explain both its invisibility and resilience over time.

In the arts we celebrate the aesthetic of 'normality'.[73] Representation of disability in literature, children's rhymes and stories, art, film and television, and music is built on distortions, caricature, degradations and demonization.[74] The *freak show* is never far away; it remains a part of our cultural sediment.[75] These distortions leach into and infect everyday experience; they become the ubiquitous subconscious etchings of the common sense. Add to this the progressive legacy of science and medical knowledge about human impairment and disability together with the built and institutional environments that we inhabit and you have a powerful cocktail for the estrangement and exclusion of disabled people. The transmission of exclusionary attitudes towards other minority identities is a constant feature of cultural life.

Fixing attitudes and finding resources?

Repeated explanations for the failure of inclusive education have formed around 'attitudes' and 'resources'. The former examines the obstacle presented by the negative attitudes of head-teachers (principals), teachers and or parents of the children whose place in the school is not challenged (the so-called normal children). The attitudes of parents of disabled pupils are also gathered to explore the extent to which they have *accepted* the limitations of their children; a test of submission to social will. The latter, resources, is used as a defence for segregation or prohibiting the enrolment of the disabled child. Both areas of research are problematic.

Much of the 'attitudes towards inclusive education' research is itself problematic and plays a part in compounding exclusion. How so? Researchers arm themselves with survey instruments to map, scope and describe these obstructive attitudes and their holders. Following their counterparts in the US and elsewhere,[76] researchers based at Macquarie University in Sydney embarked on a series of funded projects to identify attitudes towards the integration of disabled students into mainstream schools in New South Wales amongst teachers and resource teachers,[77] school principals,[78] school psychologists[79] and pre-school directors in Australia.[80] A highly contagious research imperative, Google Scholar, logs 21,500 citations for 'Attitudes towards the inclusion of disabled children in regular schools' (10.30am, 29 January, 2009). People have turned over every rock in their search for and listing of negative attitudes: student teachers, college professors, non-disabled children, school administrators and ancillary workers, school governors and so the list grows. Most of this work is of questionable value and much of it is very predictable in design, execution and findings. There are examples of this work, such as that by Kathryn Underwood, that do move from the survey instrument to critical discourse analysis to reveal disjunctions and fine-grained narratives of experiences and beliefs that play out in subtle forms while shielded by liberal postulations.[81]

There remain two acute problems with much that travels in this research vehicle. First is the repeated construction of the disabled child as the problem and the object of others' attitudes – they remain the disruption to social equilibrium. Disability is further pathologized. This is most pronounced in research wherein hierarchies of attitudes according to category and severity of impairment are gathered. While this information may seem valuable, it sustains the legitimacy of defectology.

This is linked to the second issue that concerns the creation and adjustment of attitudes towards the disability. Attitude is conceptually decoupled from context. With the exception of work by Underwood[82] and Jordan,[83] few scales pursue their interrogation around the features of schooling that obstructs social cohesion across diverse populations. At the end of the day many studies arrive at a point of declaration of need for education to change attitudes. Changing attitudes becomes another job for the continuing professional development of teachers, principals, professors, aides, parents and students. Good business for the trainers; often the same researchers who identify the problem. Also at issue is the culture and processes of the research genre. The history and philosophy of science repeatedly points to incidents where the scientists, their preconceptions, knowledge and dispositions, laboratory designs, research methods and practices are clear obstacles to the unit of analysis. Is there a case in point here? Are the army of special education researchers who have turned their collective hand to surveying inclusive education in possession of the correct tools to apprehend and analyse an attitude – its complex social aetiology and processes of attachment?

Let us explore the operation of these dynamics at the everyday level. Stories are instructive. Disability studies, like feminist research and critical race theory, has mined narrative genre (story-telling) and sharpened the *phronetic* nature of social science research to unsettle the rules of the natural sciences.[84] Consider the following events.

Recollecting childhood incidents in a country town

Some years ago now my colleagues Len Barton and Felicity Armstrong invited me to contribute a chapter for a book they were editing on disability, education and human rights. Sitting, staring at a blank computer screen late at night I drifted along with the merged music of Keith Jarrett's piano and the gentle snoring of Winnie (my dog who used to venture from exile in her basket to underneath my desk when I worked late – it was our secret). I tried to summon my first encounters with disability. Mr. Seagrave, my Grade 6 teacher, read us *Reach for the sky*; Paul Brickhill's heroic saga of World War 2 fighter-pilot Douglas Bader's courageous battles against authority, Germans and impairment. The class did have a discussion where we named other disabled people who developed a determination to overcome the tragedy of their afflictions. We named them Helen Keller, President Roosevelt and I suggested Ray Charles. (I was particularly taken by him as he was banned in our house when my mother discovered that he was an 'addict'. Dad picked his moments to listen surreptitiously to Ray and to Dinah Washington, who also summoned mother's disdain.) This wasn't the first encounter.

I thought it was my neighbourhood associations with Jimmy, a boy who was in the cruelly and incorrectly named 'opportunity class' at Gray Street Primary School. Jimmy belonged to a large and poor family (derision piled upon derision) who lived two doors up in our street. He limped slightly and slurred when he spoke – people said he was slow. We spent hours; Jimmy, his brothers, Greg McLeod and me, together under large corrugated iron roofing sheets shielding ourselves from the 'yonnies' (rocks) we chucked at each other. In October/November we got to throw contraband firecrackers thanks to that inspired Westminster terrorist. Jimmy was one of us; a target for stones and fireworks, just like all of us. Come school time it was different. I didn't speak with Jimmy, didn't go near him, feigned not seeing his friendly signs of recognition. He wasn't as choosey as me. Admission of friendship would be a major social sleight in the society of Grade 1. Too great a risk to take. I was desperate for acceptance in a small-town sandpit.

It gets worse. I also remember that at around the same time, though we had moved house, we had to pass Mularatarong, a special developmental school, on our way to Gray Street. Two things are worth noting here. A special developmental school was for kids with worse disabilities than those who were in the special school. I didn't have categories to apply to make sense of that – I just knew it was bad. And it occurs to me that many special schools and centres in Australia were given Aboriginal names. I don't think that it was a sign of solidarity amongst oppressed people! We always crossed over and walked on the other side of the street from Mularatarong. When we were directly opposite the school we would run. Sometimes we would dare each other to cross the street to the same side of the road as those kids we never ever saw who were hidden behind the high ivy-covered fence. We were guided by our own fearful stories about special kids, all of them 'spastics'. We ran to limit the risk of catching IT from the unseen but threatening presence of the kids behind the divide.

These shameful admissions weren't the first encounters. A little more dredging summons Pauline. Before I started school my mother used to clean houses for some of the town's rich people and sell clothes hoists door-to-door. She did this with another lady. Both the women would take their pre-school children on their rounds with them. Sitting listening to Keith and Winnie, it took me a long time to remember the lady's daughter's name. I did remember that I had been told that she was Mongoloid and that was why, as an older child than me, she stayed at home a lot. Under strict orders we would play outside or sit still and amuse each other inside the posh houses if it was raining. Pauline was bigger than me and I was a bit scared of her. Mum said this was silly. One morning Mum and I went to Pauline's place to meet them on the way to the jobs for that day. The curtains were drawn. I waited at the gate. (It had a huge spring on it to keep it closed; this transformed it into a great ride by sticking your feet between the rails and gripping the top of the frame. The oil-thirsty hinge squealed.) Old enough to read ominous signs, I knew that all was not well when Pauline's Mum came to the door crying. The two women embraced and sobbed softly with each other. Pauline's mum went back inside and we walked on in silence for a time while Mum collected herself. She then told me that Pauline had been electrocuted in the bathtub the night before. Then, as now, I didn't know what to say when people die. Operating on my memory now I recollect Mum's words; directed as much to herself as they were to me, were something like: 'It's a tragedy, but a blessing.'

Trawling these stories I sense an intangible intelligence. The unconscious accretion of everyday knowledge formed the basis for understanding. This is the business of acquiring a common sense of the world, or at least the little bit of it that I inhabited. Many years later Mr. Seagrave leapt from the pages of Mike Oliver's *Understanding disability: From theory to practice*.[85] Oliver examines the tyranny visited on ordinary disabled folk by the disability heroes of popular culture. The expectation that all must strive to overcome personal tragedies is oppressive and denies the importance of disability as a viable identity.

Crossing the street and running to avoid the threat of infection, of catching what special kids had may be dismissed as the fantastical silliness of ignorant (naughty) children. It comes from somewhere. My guess is that I was not the only one who harboured these childhood fears of contagion. In fact scientists, years earlier, propagated respectable treatises on the contagion of feeble-mindedness and the need to protect the uncontaminated bloodstock by means of sterilization,[86] and permanent custodial care.[87] Eugenics has yet to be shaken loose of its grip. The early purifiers may have failed to conclude their project, but their legacy has endured and adjusted itself to new times.[88] Scanning the tables of contents of *Mankind Quarterly*, the journal of the Council for Social and Economic Studies published in Washington, DC, is chilling. Summoning the ghost of Arthur Jensen and echoing Herrnstein and Murray's controversial work on race, class and intelligence in *The Bell Curve*,[89] one of *Mankind Quarterly's* editorial board Richard Lynn declares in his website that he has proven the superior intelligence of Oriental people. New expressions of population hygiene have a firm foothold on the civic psyche. What responsible pregnant woman in the affluent world will not submit to amniocentesis to avoid the spectre of Pauline? The *Guardian* newspaper in the UK carried a report on research that might be able to save humankind from the autistic child.[90] We live as Hilary Rose has declared in an age of 'consumer eugenics'.[91] I will return to these issues.

Notwithstanding her threat to my early appreciation of jazz I do not think that my mother was uniquely evil; an isolated aberration of malevolence. She was the mouthpiece for a deep-seated social refrain; a disabled life is not a life worth living. Better off dead than disabled according to this calculus of human value.

Grown ups in a country town

For the second narrative I'm inviting you to travel west from the Australian city of Melbourne for 180 kilometres to the regional city of Ballarat. Teaching at the Ballarat College of Advanced Education, I offered a summer school in education policy for teachers undertaking postgraduate studies. One of the topics I selected as a policy case study was what was then referred to as integration following the publishing of the Collins Review of services for students with disabilities, *Integration in Victorian Education* (Victorian Ministry of Education, 1984). As a genuine treat I was able to invite my friend John Lewis to come and talk to the class about the subject of his PhD research, the history of special education in Victoria. A critical historian, John unsettled and enlivened the class with a real challenge to dominant views about the nature of special educational needs and educational responses to different children. He was probably the first person in their experience to issue serious challenges to the conception and measurement of the Intelligence Quotient.

It struck me that one of the more frequent contributors to classroom discussions had slunk back in her chair and sat quietly throughout. Enquiring about her welfare I realized that I was a poor reader of body language. She was angry and distressed. 'Good for you, John', I thought. Wrong tack, Roger. 'I recognized in the other students in that room today, my daughter's teachers', she spat. 'How so?' She then told me the story that follows.

She and her family lived in one of the tiny towns dotted along the road between Ballarat and Geelong. A few houses divided into as many streets, a general store, garage, pub, a primary (elementary) school, doctor's surgery and a police station. Her daughter who among many other attributes had Down's syndrome attended the primary school with her siblings and the gaggle of town and farm kids. Going to the local school was never questioned; there was nowhere else to refer and bus her to. She was a part of the community. Not selected first in the line-up to pick teams, but she was in the line.

Like so many other small schools the end of the year was marked with a school concert. This was the source of excitement and animated mealtime reports as casting and rehearsals commenced. It fell to my student, the mum, to make the costumes. Imagine first the pride of the parents as they sat in the audience awaiting the appearance of their excited and costumed child to sing with her class. Second, try to feel her surprise and disappointment when all of the children appeared on stage except for her daughter. Now imagine her sadness and anger when a benevolent and otherwise intelligent teacher told them that she kept her daughter backstage so that *she would not feel bad about looking different from the other kids.*

This is a remarkable, but not a rare story. Too many families carry and shed real tears over stories of the devaluing and rejection of their children. As I consider the story, I am interested in the gap in the knowledge and behaviours of the teacher and the parents, between the other children and the teacher. John Lewis's class is also memorable for a question that came from the floor from one of the teachers: 'What happens when I have a class where thirty kids require toileting?' My interjection was that the only place where this would happen was in a special school for the bladder disabled! John's considered response was more appropriate and strategic. 'Why do we loosen our grip on logic when it comes to disability?' We can hold onto his question while considering the next narrative.

A story of representations

19 August 1992, the day is typically crisp for late winter. The icy winds coming off the still snow-capped hilltops that surround the city quicken my step as I walk from a hotel to the new parliament building in Australia's compromise capital, Canberra. I say compromise capital, as it was a site chosen for a purpose-built seat of government and separate capital territory. In this way neither the colony of New South Wales nor the colony of Victoria was seen to be favoured in the new Federal arrangement of Commonwealth and State governments. The new building is unique as it is submerged beneath a grassy hill with a giant flag-post atop. Inside, the building offers the textures and colours of Australia's variegated landscapes; it has space and grandeur. No doubt some of the members missed the crusty charm, the memories and ghosts of the older more traditional parliament house that keeps watch on its flash replacement directly opposite across the fabricated Lake Burley Griffin.

As the Editor of the Australian Disability Advisory Council's Journal, *Australian Disability Review*, I have been invited to attend the Disability Discrimination Bill (1992), 2nd Reading. The House is unusually busy; the public gallery full with queues forming. The corridors and restaurants are abuzz and it is exciting to spot media, business and government personalities. This is a watershed day for Australian Human Rights history. The excitement however is not about legislative reform. Today is budget day and Treasurer Ralph Willis is doing the rounds of the press lock-in briefings. The second reading of the Disability Discrimination Bill is not that well attended, even the responsible Minister Brian Howe is called out intermittently; no doubt for cabinet readying for the day's real drama that will unfold in the evening when the Treasurer delivers his budget.

For the disabled women and men sitting in the gallery the reading of this proposed legislation is significant, the culmination of a long struggle for recognition and value. The debate is etched indelibly in my memory and reading transcripts seventeen years later I am surprised by the fidelity of my recollection of the details. Most memorable are the outrageous statements of members on both sides of the House. The Hansard record requires no embellishment; it is an astonishing and demoralizing read.

Graeme Campbell, an Australian Labor Party member from regional Western Australia, establishes the tone:

> It (the Bill) has very little to do with treatment of the disabled or the disadvantaged; it has everything to do with expanding the power of people such as Irene Moss and Brian Burdekin, who run the Human Rights and Equal Opportunity Commission. These people are in my view an abomination on society, and hopefully one day a government will have enough courage to sweep them away.... This Bill is a heyday for the social engineers, those people who have already done so much damage in society.

In his unstructured musing, he talks about the travesty of people not being able to read in Australia and condemns the teachers' union that 'fights for the State Government to spend millions of dollars removing asbestos from the roofs in schools, which poses no health threat whatsoever – and that has been scientifically proven – but it does not fight for remedial teachers'.

Warming to his theme, he goes on:

> But however much courage they ('handicapped people') display on some occasions, handicapped people can never aspire to be as efficient as somebody who is simply unafflicted. Therefore, they are going to be more expensive to employ because they are going to be less productive in some cases, although there are some cases in which I believe they are more productive. I have been told that there is quite a demand for employing blind people as telephonists. These positions are probably going to be made redundant, as technology advances, but it is an area in which they are very competent and efficient.
>
> ...prostheses should be available whenever they are needed. We should not stint on that at all. Australia could easily be at the forefront in the provision of this equipment. However, what has happened with kangaroo leather, which is the lightest leather in the world? When one talks about making orthopedic shoes, there is nothing comparable with kangaroo leather; it is by far the best. But do we have a manufacturing industry in this country utilizing this very valuable raw material – this renewable resource? The answer is: only to a very limited degree. Every attempt to do so is met with opposition. I have probably spoken for too long in this debate because I believe that my contribution will be welcomed by neither my Government nor the Opposition.

Wilson Tuckey, a Liberal Party (conservative) member must have been confused when he rose to reply to his government counterpart. For Mr. Tuckey the sole beneficiaries of the proposed legislation will be lawyers. Let's pick up his argument:

> A young man applied to this race club for and received indentures as an apprentice jockey. His master then discovered that he is totally deaf in one ear. Of course, a lot of things go on in horseracing, particularly in a race, including the fact that jockeys coming up behind tired horses call out for room. The master did not have any objection to this young man but he had a responsibility, as people get killed on racecourses, to refer the matter to the race club.
>
> The race club, quite responsibly, took the matter to experts. The young man was tested by ear, nose and throat experts who said, 'He has good hearing in one ear and bad hearing in the other ear. Unfortunately, in our professional opinion, this will affect his ability directionally to decide where noise is coming from – whether the jockey asking for room is on his right or his left.' That was the opinion of the experts. He was therefore told that he had no future in horseracing – that he could act as a strapper or as a track rider and gain a living in that area but that he would be a danger to everybody else in a race. The club had nothing against the young man, but it felt obliged to take this action in the interests of others....

Of course, the legal profession is a little short of work at the moment, so all of a sudden this young man went off to the Human Rights and Equal Opportunity Commission. The club did not wish to discriminate against him, but suddenly the race club is now up for thousands of dollars in legal fees while it defends the position that it has taken in the interests, as it sees it, of protecting the lives of other jockeys....

The Human Rights and Equal Opportunity Commission has got hold of it. It is funding the case and the club cannot win. I have had discussions with one of the participants about what the Human Rights and Equal Opportunity Commission might decide about someone riding in a race with only half-hearing and the disability that that creates for the person in that situation. I wonder whether, if it finds in the young man's favour, it will give an indemnity to that race club that, if anybody gets killed by this young man, it will pay the compensation. That is a pretty fair question. I see a couple of grinning advisers over there. I wonder whether they will answer that question.

It is tempting to let the story hang – to let you make of it what you might. I left the House in a state of genuine despair. I said to colleagues, 'How can these people claim to be our representatives and speak such nonsense?' Later it occurred to me that I was mistaken. I wanted them to represent a particular view; they were representative of the distortions and ignorance that is deeply embedded in the psyche of the polity. This was bar room, lounge room, boardroom, waiting room, locker room, and classroom conversation taken to the parliamentary chamber. The propagation of different knowledges of disability, of bestowed understandings is not astonishing. For so long as disabled children are segregated, our knowledge of the world will be seriously depleted and we will be condemned to what Jules Henry calls an education in social stupidity.[92]

I am tempted to provide other narratives of encounters with difference and diversity from my own biography. For example, in earlier drafts of this chapter I included an empty box and suggested that like other children growing up in my town, that could pass as the story of my encounters with Aborigines during my schooling. But this would lack precision. I was acquiring particular understandings about Aboriginal Australia through stories I picked up in school, on the street and from home. I came to know *The Australian Legend*.[93] Europeans rescued, so the white folklore unfolds, a great southern landmass from an uncivilized Aboriginal people. In fact, *terra nullus* was the name the Europeans gave to the continent prior to their occupation. These so-called savages put up little resistance, but their scavenging of the livestock that had driven indigenous fauna away, did threaten the livelihood of squatters. For their 'own good' Aborigines were press-ganged into Christianity and the children were separated from their families in order that they have better life chances. Dispossessed urban

Aborigines demonstrated their indolence, drunkenness and inability to care for family to what was becoming a white Australia.

My most vivid childhood image of Aboriginal people was of the young Aboriginal pugilists standing on the platform and beating the bass drum at Jimmy Sharman's boxing troupe tent that toured country town agricultural shows. Outside the tent there was a large stand, high above the ground where a clutch of young Aboriginal boxers would stand, one of them beating a bass drum; a summoning pulse. Jimmy, their white boss, would shout his challenges through a megaphone to the town's menfolk who were invited to get into the ring and fight a black guy.

Figure 3.1 Jimmy Sharmon's Boxing Tent at the town agricultural show (source: photo from www.jeffcarterphotos.com).

Figure 3.2 Jimmy Sharmon and his boy boxers.

Jimmy had a steady flow of challengers, and a paying audience, fuelled by a hostile fomentation of alcohol and racism. Frequently Jimmy Sharman's boys, according to folklore, took a dive to save the pride of the locals and to drum up further trade. At the time, though I could not read the semiotics of racism, I did know which group I was part of and who were the strangers in our town.

Henry Reynolds's book: *Why Weren't We Told?* attempts to counter the powerful white histories. His is a story of invasion, dispossession, genocide, colonization and cultural oppression. The knowledge I acquired did not speak about the hundreds of languages used by the different Aboriginal peoples spread right across the continent. The myth that they were nomadic was untested and suited the portrayal of the people as feckless. The rich history of agrarian and fishing communities was and remains largely ignored. The depiction of savagery obscured an understanding of a deeply spiritual and complex cultural life. The now prized art was dismissed as infantile. Indeed, the art is now sufficiently valued by European buyers to be forged. As counter-hegemonic knowledge began to replace the dominant wallpaper knowledge of my generation's childhood, there was a backlash. Conservative historians such as Geoffrey Blainey condemned what they dismissed as 'black armband history'. They found Prime Ministerial support in John Howard who stood firm in his refusal to issue a national apology, restore land rights and make reparation. Bestowed understanding, an admixture of fanciful folklore and official knowledge (Apple, 1998), is overt and covert in its operation. Herein lie the seeds of exclusion.

Before thinking about the political economy of exclusion, let us consider one more narrative. This is a story about disability and disablement that comes from the recorded experiences of Jean-Dominique Bauby (1997).

Of tourists and denizens

First published in France in 1997, *Le scaphandre et le papillon (The Diving-Bell and the Butterfly)* is a remarkable book. Following a 'cerebro-vascular accident' (Bauby, 1997: 12) on Friday, 8 December 1995 Jean-Dominique Bauby, then editor-in-chief of French *Elle* magazine, was consigned to a condition commonly referred to as 'locked-in syndrome'. This meant that he was unable to speak and completely paralysed, save for the movement left in one eyelid. Communication was achieved by blinking his left eyelid as people pointed to the letters of an alphabet arranged according to how frequently the letters were used in the French language:

E S A R I N T U L O M D P C F B V H G J Q Z Y X K W

Using this form of communication he wrote his slender yet weighty book that recorded his reflections on his changed life in 'Room 119 of the Naval Hospital at Berck-sur-Mer on the French Channel coast' (Bauby, 1997: 12).

'Calamity', writes Thomas Mallon (15 June 1997) of the New York Times Book Review, 'turns Bauby into a connoisseur of irony and eeriness.' There is a chapter entitled 'Tourists', some two and half pages long, which for me remains an indelible encapsulation of the worlds of disability and disablement and the distance between them.

Let me share two extracts from 'Tourists'. But first some background may be helpful. The hospital had been dedicated to the care and convalescence of victims of a tuberculosis epidemic after World War 2. Following that it has accommodated a mixed clientele comprising '...the aged, people who have suffered brain injuries that render them comatose, a cluster of morbidly obese patients whose substantial dimensions the doctors hope to whittle down' (Bauby, 1997: 39), and 'a battalion of cripples forms the bulk of the inmates'. This last group, the 'battalion of cripples' are the survivors of a range of accidents and injuries. Bauby calls them Tourists for they will pass through the hospital. The relationship between the people in the hospital is telling. Relationship may be an overstatement for it simply designates the fact that the Tourists and those who are permanent residents share the rehabilitation room where they take therapy and exercise.

Mallon is correct in describing Bauby's description of his observations as eerie. This eeriness is born of an attachment between Bauby's vignettes and threads of our own experiences and worlds. Observe his description of those with brain injuries:

> In one section are a score of comatose patients, poor devils at death's door, plunged into endless night. They never leave their rooms. **Yet everyone knows they are there, and they weigh strangely on our collective awareness, almost like a guilty conscience.**
>
> (Bauby, 1977: 39, my emphasis)

The unease between the categories of residents, whom he at one stage refers to as 'denizens' (p. 39), is amplified as the chapter climaxes.

> To complete the picture a niche must be found for us, broken-winged birds, voice-less parrots, ravens of doom, who have made our nest in a dead-end corridor of the neurology department. Of course we spoil the view. I am all too conscious of the slight uneasiness we cause as, rigid and mute, we make our way through a group of more fortunate patients.
>
> The best place to observe this phenomenon is the rehabilitation room, where all patients undergoing physiotherapy are congregated. Garish and noisy, a hubbub of splints, artificial limbs and harnesses of varying complexity, it is an authentic Court of Miracles. Here we see a young man with an earring, who suffered multiple fractures in a motorbike accident; a grandmother in a fluorescent nightgown, who is learning to walk after a fall from a stepladder; and a homeless man whose foot was somehow amputated by a subway train. Lined up like a row of onions, this human throng waves arms and legs under minimal supervision, while I lie tethered to an inclined board that is slowly raised to a vertical position. Every morning I spend half an hour suspended this

way, frozen to attention in a position that must evoke the appearance of the Commendatore's statue in the last act of Mozart's Don Giovanni. Below, people laugh, joke, call out. I would like to be a part of all this hilarity, but as soon as I direct my one eye towards them, the young man, the grandmother and the homeless man turn away, feeling the sudden need to study the ceiling smoke-detector. The 'tourists' must be very worried about fire.

(Bauby, 1977: 40–41)

2 Professional knowledge and a language of control

When Maggie X died, the (aged care) home decided that her savings of £450 was insufficient to pay for the funeral and asked the council to pay it. It refused and the owner of the home appealed to the Local Ombudsman. In his comments to the latter, the council Chief Executive wrote that 'without wishing to appear insensitive, one could argue that from a commercial viewpoint residents of a home are its income producing raw material. Ergo, from a purely commercial view, deceased residents may then be regarded as being the waste produced by their business'. Since, he continued the resident's body was 'controlled waste likely to cause pollution of the environment or harm to human health' the home had, under definition of controlled waste as defined by the Environmental Protection Act, 'a specific duty' to dispose of the remains. Disposal, under the definitions of the Act, was a 'business cost'.

(Doig and Wilson, 1999: 26)

No doubt your sensibilities are offended by the manner in which the Chief Executive of the council who, while 'without wishing to appear insensitive', has reduced Maggie X to industrial waste in order to recover cost for financial reporting. Stripped of her dignity, a new calculus is applied to Maggie, indeed to all aged-care residents, in order to shift her from one balance sheet to another. Maggie has been transformed from a resident to a unit of cost, from citizen to waste. Cost recovery is a squalid epitaph. For many this might be construed as a misplaced application of bureaucratic, legal and market discourses to assert vested interest. Reconciling a discourse of community engagement with technocratic market discourse tests the boundaries of spin. Establishing 'impossible alternatives'[94] is a political tactic that, in its repeated recitation, seeks to establish authenticity. In an age fuelled and propelled by competitive individualism, appealing to communitarianism may seem to stretch credibility. Co-opetition is a measure of civic responsibility. 'Equity and enterprise'; 'enterprise and fairness' are no longer discordant values.[95]

Speak with Iraqi academics living in exile, and they might tell you that people too easily become numbers – statistics of collateral damage. Language sanitizes and it shields us from recognition of the enormity of events and from our complicity. In this climate of linguistic dexterity the conflation of special educational needs with inclusive education in education goes unremarked. Teachers and parents have become familiar with the language of the DSM IV. We substitute terms such as ASD (Autistic Spectrum Disorders), ADHD (Attention Disorder/Hyperactivity Disorder), SLI (Speech Language Impairment) and EBD (Emotional Behaviour Disorder) for children's names. In so doing, the assignees – like Maggie – may more easily be detached from their humanity. They become an object for referral. There is also the development of a more contiguous relationship between the child and the professional expert. The classroom teacher may stand back while a bureaucratic solution is sought to that which extends beyond their expertise. As more children are being placed in these categories, the more we implicitly challenge the nature of schools and the provenance of the teacher. In the next chapter I will explore the politics of professional knowledge and language as a background to an examination of inclusive education policy.

4 Building a theory of inclusive education

I cannot say with certainty which of my motives are the strongest, but I know which of them deserve to be followed. And looking back through my work, I see that it is invariably where I lacked a political purpose that I wrote lifeless books and was betrayed into purple passages, sentences without meaning, decorative adjectives and humbug generally.

George Orwell (1946) *Why I Write*. London, Gangrel

There are a number of approaches one could adopt to write about the foundations of and futures for inclusive education. You will have observed that I have not opted for an intellectual compendium of inclusive education. Had I done so, this chapter may have come earlier in the book and would comprise another extensive annotated bibliography.[1] Its purpose would have been to chart the development of this field of scholarship and activism from a point we might call its inception to that point where I say, perhaps in exhaustion, I will deal with no more. The task would encourage me to exercise greater forensic and bibliographic discipline than you will find in what lies ahead.

Instead, this chapter explores the labyrinthine politics within inclusive education as it attempts to confront and make its statement about educational exclusion. A specific focus will be applied to that area which is conveniently referred to as special educational needs. It will demonstrate the multiple levels of political tension and the often-contradictory pressures that confront the quest to develop a theory of inclusive schooling.

On first considering the option to attempt a catalogue of inclusive education a number of challenges emerged that dissuaded me from the task. **First** is the Hegelian challenge.[2] How do we determine our starting point in the field? And, if we secure that starting point, where does one element of an argument conclude and another begin?[3] For inclusive education there is not so much a starting point but clusters of influence that have contributed differentially to the inception and growth of the field. Here I would list them, as they say, 'in no particular order', as follows:

- traditional special education and its antecedents in medicine and psychology;

- critical theory and the New Sociology of Education and in particular the application of this field by Barton and Tomlinson to provide a pioneering critique of the theories and practices of special education;
- disability studies and disability studies in education;
- post-structuralism, cultural studies and feminist theory;
- post-colonial studies, development studies and critical race theory;
- political theory;
- policy sociology;
- research into curriculum, pedagogy and assessment (including critical pedagogy);
- teacher education;
- social geography;
- studies in research methodologies.

Second, we come to the substantive field itself where researchers work under the banner of inclusive education. This work is very broad, suffering as it does from a *surfeit of meaning*,[4] and it needs to be unravelled. Glance back over the table of contents of past volumes of a journal such as the *International Journal of Inclusive Education* or the tables of contents of the many primers, handbooks or book series on inclusive education and you will soon encounter the scope of and the tensions within this field of educational inquiry. To give you a sense of what I am referring to let me summarize some of the groups of work within inclusive education:

- First, there is what I have called traditional, and I suppose, neo-special education. Here I refer to work that represents a rebranding of special education to align itself with the conditional forms of inclusive education that are promoted by education jurisdictions around the world.[5] Ellen Brantlinger has described the way in which traditional special education researchers have grafted inclusive education onto the titles and inserted a chapter on inclusion in the prescribed textbooks for their special educational courses.[6] These texts, and courses, maintain a categorical approach to what is, with no acknowledgement of irony, called special and inclusive education. The focus for this work is having students understand the special needs of children by becoming familiar with diagnoses and aetiologies of children's defects, disorders, illnesses and syndromes.
- Second, there is the rapidly growing collection of work that provides a critique of special education or its Trojan rendition – special and inclusive education. Within this field gather a range of sub-groupings. These groupings may converge around disability studies in education but feature distinctions according to divergent paradigms (for example, structural analysis based on the social model of disability; feminist and postmodern/poststructural analyses).
- Third, we can observe discussions of inclusive education according to constituent interests. Here I refer to writing that reflects work

dedicated to analysing exclusion and inclusion according to different identity groups including: race; gender; sexuality; class; traveller and refugee children; geographic isolation and so the list is developing in accordance with patterns of exclusion and oppression. The constituent interests may also become apparent around specific areas of educational interest such as curriculum theory, teaching and learning, educational leadership and administration, economics of education, assessment, classroom and school organization, educational sectors (early childhood, primary or elementary, secondary, higher education and vocational education).

Such a spread of interests, all self-identifying as inclusive education, requires elasticity rather than precision of definition. The British anti-racist education researcher Barry Troyna has contested the over-application of the term empowerment, which is used to a level of saturation in critical pedagogy by drawing on the works of W. B. Gallie, Murray Edelman and Fazal Rizvi.[7] For Gallie the properties of certain concepts render them as 'essentially contested'.[8] Edelman, observes Troyna:

> ...reveals how the protean form and contested nature of these concepts render them amenable, perhaps vulnerable is a better word, to various sometimes contradictory interpretations and uses.[9]

Rizvi suggests, 'without any agreed meaning with which to identify its salience', racism is an essentially contested concept.[10] Given the disparate and contradictory voices that have over time attached themselves to the concept or slogan of inclusive education we might reasonably suggest that it too is an essentially contested concept. Not surprisingly, '...endless disputes about proper uses'[11] have erupted and distract from the task of dismantling barriers to learning.

A means for considering contests in inclusive education may be found in the work of Edward Said. In the collection of essays, *Reflections on exile*, he offers his analysis of travelling theories to explain the degradation of political theories.[12] Using Georg Lukacs's theory of reification, Said illustrates the way in which '...theories sometimes travel to other times and situations, in the process of which they lose some of their original power and rebelliousness'.[13] In its original offering, reification theory presented a powerful critique of the discursive instruments of oppression. Lukacs had provided a set of conceptual tools for understanding specific sets of social relations as a lever for political agency.[14]

> ...the first time a human experience is recorded and then given a theoretical formulation, its force comes from being directly connected to and organically provoked by real historical circumstances. Later versions of the theory cannot replicate its original power;

because the situation has quieted down and changed, the theory is degraded and subdued, made into a relatively tame academic substitute for the real thing, whose purpose in the work I analysed was political change.[15]

By the time Lucien Goldmann in Paris and Raymond Williams in Cambridge had picked up and interpreted reification, 'the ideas of this theory had shed their insurrectionary force, (reification theory) had been tamed and domesticated'.[16] 'Stretched to adhere to changed political circumstances, the newfound elasticity subverted the original intent.'[17] In their popularization, travelling theories are often sanitized, generalized and popularized or they are entrapped within the fabrication of dogma.

Third comes a problem recently encountered by Julie Allan and myself when we were selecting and representing work across inclusive education for the research that is described in *Doing inclusive education research*.[18]

> In establishing our sample, we wished to avoid making a hardened taxonomy of the field because of our resistance to the ways in which such rigid categorizing fixes people and their work and our sense that we would, in any case, be inaccurate.... In spite of ourselves, and our good intentions, our sample of thirteen researchers located them at points on what appears to be a spectrum of research on inclusive education which went from what we termed traditional special educational research to critical research within a sociological framework.... While it was necessary at the outset for us to identify different research genres or traditions across the field, we were aware that the descriptions that we imposed on the research and the categories we constructed would, through the research itself, unravel.[19]

This is not simply coyness, a reluctance to get the categories wrong, misplace people's work, or cause offence. At issue is the reductive tendency of categorizing knowledge and researchers. The reader immediately attaches value to the categories notwithstanding the authors' insistence on the benign quality of their work. There is a profound irony here as this is akin to what happens to children who come to the attention of special education. Parts of their profile are selected to fit a diagnosis that results in an official label, the downward adjustment of teacher expectations and the setting of a rigid and restricted educational, and ultimately their social, trajectory. Ignored are all those qualities of the child and their community that make other options possible. The challenge is to discover a robust method for critically engaging with work across the field. In other words, there is a need to recognize the integrity of a range of work and not lose the potency of critique to take the field forward.

Others, including Skidmore[20] and Thomas and Loxley,[21] have represented earlier summaries and tabulations of the field I had offered (see Table 4.1).

More than a decade after compiling this *traveller's guide* to understanding disability I am ambivalent, less confident about the neatness I tried to impose. As a summation it is a starting point for debate, but little more. Superficiality allows misrepresentation and were I to provide an updated version I would undertake serious editing and elaboration. Most particularly I would want to revise the descriptions for category 4 and category 5. Specifically I would want to re-name category 5 as Disability Studies of which the Disability Movement is one part. The result may produce a reckoning that more adequately represents the voices of disabled researchers and their allies. It would still fail to represent the merging of areas and it may suggest irreconcilabilities that may or may not be the case.

Fourth, and most importantly, is the question of purpose and impact. Why would you bother attempting this task of cataloguing those works amassing within our field of inclusive education? What purpose does it serve? Sorting through, grouping and commenting upon the repository of textual materials may give a sense of progression and regression, of stasis and diversion in this field of research. It would certainly suggest the need for further, perhaps different, work to be done in the field. To pursue this as a clinical or detached exercise would provide little more than we can already retrieve from web search engines.[22] Worse, it would be a distraction from what many in this field of research see as the political purpose of their work. Ultimately comes the question: what is our (my) interest in inclusive education? Who is this research for? Here is where the politics becomes messy. What follows is not so much an attempt to tidy messiness as it is an attempt to identify the nature and levels of politics, and to capture struggles and tensions in the scholarship.

Confronting politics

The publication by Sally Tomlinson of *Educational subnormality: A study in decision making* in 1981 followed quickly by *A Sociology of special education* in 1982 may be described as an important political moment for special and regular education alike. Influenced by Steven Rose's critiques of IQ, and trained in the sociology of Weber, Marx, Bourdieu and C. Wright Mills, Sally was part of a small group of researchers in the UK to apply a sociological analysis to special education.[23] Segregated special education was largely untouched by the critical analyses of what was being referred to as the New Sociology of Education.[24] An interesting parallel is found in the frustration voiced by disabled activists, including Jenny Morris, at the omission of disability by early feminist researchers.[25]

Tomlinson reflects upon how she came to pursue a work that led her first to sit in the Bodleian Library at Oxford to '...read all eight volumes

Table 4.1 Competing perspectives on disability (Slee, 1998: 128–129)

Theoretical perspective	Brief description
1 Essentialist	Disability is located in the pathological impairments or deficiencies of individuals. This perspective has established its dominance over the taken-for-granted assumptions of special educational theory, which proceeds from diagnosis of individual defect as the baseline for intervention and remediation. The aim is to minimize difference within the project of normalization (Nirje, 1970). As Clark *et al.* (1995) point out, there exists no room for problematizing this perspective to suggest interactionist antecedents in the epidemiology of disability. The regular educational provision is accepted and special education assists in the identification and treatment of those whose pathologies 'naturally' exclude them from regular academic and social entitlements. Proponents of essentialism are merely responding to practical problems presented by the individual differences of children.
2 Social Constructionist	Presents disability as an oppressive and normative construct deployed against minorities enforcing social marginalization. This perspective is apparent in the work of Goffman (1961 and 1963) and implicitly lingers in the World Health Organisation construction of disability, impairment and handicap.
3 Materialist	This is enunciated by Paul Abberley (1987) who eschews the reductionist urge to locate disability within individual pathology or dominant social attitudes. According to proponents of this view, impairment can be identified as both historically and culturally specific, mediated through the organization of labour and the processes of material reproduction (Abberley, 1987; Oliver, 1990). Stories are then produced to explain disability as personal tragedy or a medical problem to be managed within the health system in order to locate and keep disabled people out of the labour market as dependent consumers. In purer expressions of this perspective, their destiny is leashed to the momentum of class struggle.
4 Postmodernist	These perspectives cast doubt over the limitations of class struggle and capitalist production narratives as an explanation of complex and fragmented experiences of disability across a range of identities. Postmodernist analyses provided space for other voices and expressions in describing and analysing disability. Consequently, feminist accounts (Morris, 1991 and 1992) insert women's voicing of their particular and diverse experiences and struggles. Corbett (1996), following Branson and Miller (1989), Fulcher (1989) and Shakespeare (1994), deconstructs the disabling language to reveal the politics of identity and difference.
5 Disability Movement	Devote less attention to the production of a coherent theoretical explication of disability in their eclectic quest for social change and the incorporation of disability rights in the mainstream political agenda.

of the *Royal Commission's report on the care and control of the feeble-minded, 1904–1908'* and then to consider the differential treatment of children from Asian and Afro-Caribbean backgrounds in English schools.

> In the 1960s when I was teaching in a primary school in Wolverhampton, many of my class were from Asian and Afro-Caribbean backgrounds and were regarded by the system as ESN(M) [educationally subnormal(moderate) – having moderate learning difficulties] and in need of remedial or special education, although English as a second language was also a factor. It occurred to me from that time that it was grossly unfair that children who had just entered a system were regarded as failures in that system and relegated to what I regarded, and still regard, as a non-education.[26]

She continues:

> It is astonishing the number of black adults who have been successful in adult life who have gone through this selecting-out process. In ILEA (Inner London Education Authority) in the 1970s, they were eight times more likely to be placed in special schools. Why it became a political issue, was that they were referred into schools for children with emotional and behavioural difficulty or into Pupil Referral Units.[27]

Len Barton recalls working with Sally Tomlinson at this time when they compiled the edited collections: *Special education: Policies, practices and social issues*[28] and *Special education and social interests*[29]:

> Viewing special education sociologically entailed us exploring questions of power, politics and social control. We were concerned with developing an approach to special education in which social interests rather than individual differences and deficits were to be a fundamental focus of analysis. Our critical concerns involved examining the nature and function of policy-making and implementation at national and LEA/school levels of the system. This included an analysis of key texts such as the Warnock Report and the 1981 Education Act and specific policy initiatives such as statementing and integration and the meaning and function of the discourse of special educational needs.[30]

Their critique considered the way in which psychological accounts of school failure narrowed to 'within-the-child' explanations and legitimized the untested assumptions within IQ. Barton[31] declared that Mary Warnock's notion of special educational needs[32] was a euphemism for the failure of schools to be able to educate all students. His declaration reveals the incorporation of the social model of disability into his analysis. The development of the social model of disability commenced, writes Mike Oliver, with the publication of the *Fundamental principles of disability* by the Union of the Physically Impaired Against Segregation (UPIAS, 1976).[33]

> This turned the understanding of disability completely on its head by arguing that it was not impairment that was the main cause of the social exclusion of disabled people but the way society responded to people with impairments.[34]

Accordingly, disability is not regarded as a pathological characteristic of a person. Rather it more precisely describes our collective negative reaction to human differences, our inability or unwillingness to include all members of a community. Individualistic models of disability such as we encounter in traditional special education narrows the analytic gaze to the pathology of the child and the aetiology of a disease, syndrome or disorder to explain the child and their experience of the world. This narrow gaze, according to the social model, deflects from the complex interactions between the social order and individual pathology. Inherently reductionist, disability is considered a personal trouble rather than a social issue for collective consideration and response.[35] People with impairments are blamed and/or pitied for their life trajectories.[36] Moreover, oppressive comparisons are drawn between the disabled person and popular disability heroes.[37] They become objectified targets for charitable, medical and bureaucratic intervention in an attempt to normalize them.[38]

This reductionism is manifest in at least two ways:

- 'Disability' is offered, and all too widely accepted, as an individual human characteristic. People are thereby reduced to limps, twitches or matched items on a psychiatrist's schedule of behavioural disorders. This is not dissimilar to a chilling phrase in a film made with a group of women from Iraq that I viewed recently. An Iraqi woman, now living in exile, spoke of family and neighbours who had perished and who continue to suffer the trauma of continuing conflict and the cancerous poison of depleted uranium that has infected the soil they walk on and the dust they breathe. 'People have become numbers', she said plaintively. Language is enlisted in the war effort. The killing of civilians is 'collateral damage'; they are casualties of 'friendly fire'. The use of depleted uranium in British and American weapons is not regarded as weapons of mass destruction even though we know that the lethal legacy will last for generations to come. Disability may more precisely be understood as the collateral damage of unequal social relations where impairment reduces human value and marks people out for subjugation.
- Disabled people become the objects of work for professional human services and, of course, researchers. As the professions amass and

specialize to capture subdivisions of the disabled, we are urged to 'look away' as they continue to do '*good*' to the *abnormal* (or to echo Bauman's term: *surplus population*). We will return to a discussion of professional intervention when considering inclusive education policy and practice in Chapter 5.

Tomlinson also challenged the benevolent humanitarianism that continued to shield segregated education from critical scrutiny.

> This all led to my awareness that there were vested groups in special education ... who have their own interests and are dedicated to 'doing good', but their actions do not necessarily do good to groups or to individuals. When this was pointed out, it incurred great hostility.[39]

These pioneering critiques of segregated special education and therefore of the structure of schooling in general, regular and special, are politically important and underscore the political project to which inclusive education ought to be inseparably attached. Let me explain this more clearly. From this point onwards a new argument was put onto the table that became increasingly difficult to ignore. Special education was not simply a technical and benevolent enterprise to teach and care for the so-called disabled, defective, disordered or disturbed child. Special education, as a subset of schooling in general, is a vital part of a political project to order and regulate the childhood population. Maintaining regular and special education involves decisions about the distribution of public funds. Decisions are made, based largely upon normative judgements about ability and disability, about the type and location of school placement. Make no mistake, these judgements and decisions also allocate life chances. Moreover, we cannot be confident of the decision-making validity and process.[40] Determinations are handed down by the state that overrides the wishes of individuals. These decisions: establish life trajectories that potentially limit opportunities; may separate children from their siblings, neighbourhood peers and communities; impact upon the nature and quality of the education they engage in; reinforce hierarchies that fracture communities and limit human potential; have profound economic implications; may put the interests of institutions above the interests of individuals; compromise our democratic ideal.

Over time, segregated and most recently co-located special schooling has been established or re-emerged in jurisdictions around the world, through the authority of medical and bureaucratic discourses,[41] as a reflection of a natural order of human difference; a precondition for the education of special disabled children. This is an erasure of the political origins of segregation. It is an act of historical omission that proscribes the terms of reference for the discussion of the education of disabled children. The original provision of segregated education for 'feeble-minded', 'retarded', 'crippled', 'blind', 'deaf' and 'mute' children can simultaneously be seen as the architecture of eugenics and the audacity of parents and advocates asserting the right to an education for their children.

All too often, special education is cast as a matter of parental choice, removing the fact that segregated education still symbolizes a more fundamental choice: the choice to establish the regular or neighbourhood school as a place for the education of non-disabled children. Where schools are encouraged to operate according to the logic of the market place and where there has been the narrowing of the curriculum to be measured through high-stakes testing and the publication of school performance 'league tables',[42] we have witnessed perverse effects. Schools have become particularly choosey about which students are likely to improve their inspection and examination performances. In this context disabled students become a threat and parents are counselled to look for more suitable educational settings or choices. Ironically we now witness the constant redefinition of the non-disabled child and the paradoxes this presents for segregation and exclusion.

Wading into a confused and confusing politics

It is important to acknowledge the complex politics behind the establishment of segregated special education. My purpose though is not to litigate the past and deepen antagonisms. The point is to understand the way in which present knowledge is infused by and carries a problematic politics in order that we are able to sustain change. Special and regular schools are historical artefacts. Like Janus, presenting different faces to different people, they survey, order and govern the childhood population. Their resilience is not singularly attached to educational purpose. The purposes of this bifurcation of schooling are social and administrative.[43]

There is a partial legitimacy in heroic portrayals of the establishment of special education as a radical or progressive claim of entitlement to educational provision for disabled children who were locked out of schooling. These children were banished to institutional care. They were believed to be ineducable and the accounts of the shameful conditions and treatments in these institutions hang like a guilty conscience over us all.[44] Many other disabled children were hidden in their homes for fear of the shame that disability would bring to the family. Of course in many cultures, including my own, religious and social obligation are blurred with fear and shame.[45] This is a story that tells of the establishment of special schools as a hard-fought struggle by parents, doctors and educators to establish the right to an education for disabled children. It was also an affirmation of the belief that disabled children could learn and be taught. Implicitly it highlighted, though devoid of due acknowledgement, the narrowness of the curriculum and pedagogic repertoire of the neighbourhood school. This story is also a narrative about the establishment of what over time was to become a more prodigious calibration of human difference and, implicitly of, a hierarchy of human value.[46]

The imperatives that drove the establishment of special education were not wholly innocent. As Scot Danforth[47] elegantly demonstrates in his depiction of the work of Samuel Kirk, such a narrative is incomplete. He writes of how as a graduate student in psychology in Chicago, Samuel Kirk met with a 10-year-old boy in the doorway of an Oak Forest institution for delinquent children. Having found that the boy was unable to read, Kirk commenced his clandestine lessons with the boy '...under a small corridor light, whispering so as not to be caught by the staff nurses'.

> There, in the least auspicious surroundings possible, the young man who later would be viewed as the father of the field of learning disabilities first encountered a child who could not read. The instructional moment would seem to be the most pure in its simplicity, an ... undistilled and genuine experience...
>
> Sitting alone on the floor with a child struggling to learn, communicating in hushed tones to preserve secrecy, neither supported nor fettered by the authorized curriculum and instructional procedures of the classroom, the young Kirk faced the pedagogical challenge in the raw.[48]

However, Danforth asserts that this picture fails to present the *symbolic complex* of the encounter. Though there was an absence of 'useful knowledge to inform teaching, he [Kirk] was far from conceptually naked in his first pedagogical encounter at the Illinois institution for the feeble-minded'.[49] Feeble-mindedness, in the world of Samuel Kirk, was a symbolic complex infused with a mix of authoritative science and popular sentiment. One does not require heavy tools for an archaeological excavation to unearth the science and sentiment of that time.[50]

John Lewis's studies of the expansion of segregated special and remedial education in the Australian state of Victoria are illustrative.[51] Tracing the development of the so-called science of measuring human intelligence, he describes the transformation of 'armchair conjecture into creditable science'.[52] The invention of craniometry and measurable intelligence, Stephen J. Gould[53] tells us, was bound up in the politics of racial supremacy and proved effective in fortifying claims of the latent criminality of the feeble-minded. The long-standing fascination with producing cranial indexes and graphic illustrations of the insane and feeble-minded as a diagnostic aide memoire for their detection by physicians and the public at large is seen in the works of Helvetius, Condorcet and Pinel's *Traite medico-philosophique* (1801) and in Lavater's *Physiognomic fragments* (1774–1778).[54] Just as Samuel Kirk was 'fully steeped in the then current scheme of educational and psychological notions about mental deficiency'[55] in the USA in 1929, the development of segregated education for disabled children in Victoria was propelled by an alliance of eugenics, the science of feeble-mindedness and measurable intelligence, and 'benevolent humanitarianism'.

Lewis traces a range of intellectual influences on key figures[56] in the development of segregated education in countries such as the UK and Australia. These include: Francis Galton who created a laboratory on heritable intelligence at the International Health Exposition of 1884 in London[57]; Jean Marc Gaspard Itard who developed instruction for deaf-mute and feebleminded children in France after his now legendary work with Victor the wild-boy of Aveyron in 1779; Edouard Seguin, a former student of Itard, who emigrated to the USA and later established schools for 'retarded children'; Johann Jacob Guggenbuhl who established a residential training programme for children 'with cretinism' in Abendberg in Switzerland; Samuel Gridley Howe who in October 1848 established a centre for educating children with mental retardation in a wing of the Perkins Institute for the Blind in Boston[58]; Alfred Binet who invented a paper and pencil test of Intelligence Quotient; and Lewis Terman and Henry Goddard who adapted this test in their work at Stanford University. In the incubus of the increasingly respectable eugenics movement,[59] a disturbing unity was struck between humanitarian calls for educational provision for disabled children and the fledgling field of special education, the latter insisting on segregation as a precondition of their professional practice.

As an aside we can report that the force of eugenics has lost little of its ardour.[60]

> But disease, death, and monstrosity certainly come together at one point: in the desire to kill. We should not hide from the fact that major disability, especially mental, generates such an urge to make it disappear that it must be called by its name. In embryonic form the desire to kill, to see dead, is extended to all those stricken. The practice in antiquity of doing away with deformed children originates in a sense of eugenics, in the will for a pure race, and thus reveals what lies in the human heart.[61]

Practices have certainly changed so that we now employ serum tests, ultrasound scans, amniocentesis and chorionic villus sampling to predict and terminate disability prenatally. Surrounding these practices are difficult and vexatious ethical debates that I will not rehearse. A more subtle form of population management, it has been argued, is achieved through the discourse of special educational needs and by offering parents the choice of a segregated schooling for their children.[62] Let us apply some detail to this claim. Over the past three decades there has been a rapid escalation in the calibration and categorization of the student population in order to identify and respond to the needs of children with special educational needs. The growth is most prominent in the area of behaviour, including children who are said to be located on the spectrum of Autistic disorders (ASD). Attention Deficit Hyperactivity Disorders (ADHD)[63] has taken on the dimension of pandemic across the developed world and is now emerging in wealthier sections of poorer countries.[64] I will consider the perverse effects of inclusive education policy in relation to student behaviour in Chapter 7.

Special education, like regular schooling, cannot be described as a benign practice.[65] It is a part of a confusing history of educational and social exclusion. Recognizing this politics is an important step in building a theory of inclusive education to inform decisions about children and their education. This is but one strand of the political complexity that infuses inclusive education.

The politics of inclusive education and 'ideological research'

Reaching back to the summer of 1999, I want to use a gathering of researchers at the University of Rochester in up-state New York to further pursue our discussion of the politics of inclusive education. Linda Ware[66] had volunteered to host the colloquium on inclusive education that had originated half a decade earlier in Newcastle-upon-Tyne through the efforts of Alan Dyson, Allan Millward and Catherine Clark.[67] The Rochester colloquium is personally memorable for a number of reasons.

At first light I went down to breakfast feeling travel-soiled and deprived of sleep. Greeting Tony Booth, who was already seated, I launched into my lamentations of privilege about the airlines having lost my luggage. 'Mine has gone missing too', he retorted. Keith and Pat Ballard from New Zealand joined us. They also had possession of an airline toiletries pack, but not of their suitcases. This seemed remarkable, four of us without our luggage. It must be an American thing. The infrastructure set in place to track luggage with wanderlust seemed to suggest this was the 'case'. Just then Len Barton from Sheffield joined us pleading that we excuse the absence of his usually affable demeanour. His luggage had not turned up at the airport.

In a show of lenience, Linda delayed the commencement of the colloquium so that she could take us all to the shopping mall to replenish our 'personal effects'. Julie Allan lent Keith Ballard a pair of her running shorts so that he could maintain his admirable fitness regimen. Were we becoming the interdependent community that our research advocated for schools? Though my paper carries a different title in the edited book generated from the conference, I didn't half feel clever about its original title: *Collisions in the baggage-hall of knowledge*. I had originally intended, as Orwell would have counselled, the title to signal political purpose to fuse politics and irony was a bonus.

To prepare for the colloquium Linda had distributed a now seminal paper in our field by Ellen Brantlinger. It is a scholarly provocation entitled: 'Using ideology: Cases of nonrecognition of the politics of research and practice in special education.' Our instruction was to read the paper and respond to it in our own colloquium papers. Linda also invited new-comers Tom Skrtic, Len Barton, Sally Tomlinson, Lous Heshusius, Jude MacArthur and of course Ellen Brantlinger, to join some of the original participants from the Newcastle colloquium. The list of participants announced an uncompromising political ethic. After all, I still remember the sudden intake of oxygen across the lecture hall in Cardiff when Tom Skrtic opened his keynote address at a World Congress of Special Educa-tion in Wales by announcing that two major threats to democracy were special education and educational administration. Special education com-promised democracy by excluding students from the right to be enrolled in their neighbourhood school, and educational administration provided the organizational rationale and infrastructure to do so. In other words, special education provided the means for exclusion of those increasing numbers of children considered to be disabled. The field of educational administration rationalized exclusion and, as I have argued in my critique of the school effectiveness research genre, gave us permission to 'look away'.[68] His remarks were as powerful and as unwelcome as Mike Oliver's announce-ment years later, immediately following the carefully crafted opening remarks of Her Royal Highness Princess Anne at the World Congress of Special Education in Manchester, that he was there 'to dance on the grave of special education'.

> Special education has no choice; it can begin to change itself from within or be swept away by the tide of history, which is washing over us all as we enter the twenty first century. It can be part of the struggle to produce a more inclusive world or it can continue to align itself with the forces of exclusion. The former strategy offers us all the pos-sibility of a decent future; the latter offers a few of us the illusion of a safe and stable world. I hope that special education is mature enough to make the right choice.[69]

Years later Julie Allan and I reminded Mike of his call to the dance-floor and of his need to put his dancing shoes back on.

Brantlinger's 'Using ideology' paper is politically unambiguous.[70] A sup-porter of inclusion, of its potential to contribute to more democratic forms of schooling, Brantlinger registers puzzlement at the absence of published responses to the series of critiques of inclusive education written by promi-nent US special education researchers. In 1994 Fuchs and Fuchs published a paper in *Exceptional children* entitled 'Inclusive schools movement and the radicalization of special education reform' which elicited a flurry of similarly polemical publications by eminent traditional special education researchers.[71] Selecting thirteen journal articles and five book chapters from these traditional special education scholars, Brantlinger undertakes an analysis of the quality of their 'science' and scholarship. The selected papers collectively condemn inclusive education as a political bandwagon that, lacking in empirical data to support its claims, is therefore profoundly ideological and devoid of scientific validity.[72]

To assist readers who are unfamiliar with the field, her analysis is introduced by a description of the rapid expansion of special education, the burgeoning identification of special needs students, discovery of new categories of disability, and the concomitant growth in the numbers of special educators and school counsellors to deal with this challenge in the USA during the 1950s and 1960s. At the same time the expansion of special education training, funded research programmes and research publications accelerated in universities and teacher education colleges. The sector was establishing itself as powerful and influential as it became increasingly

> ...occupied with tightening definitions of disability; determining eligibility for services; establishing 'due process' testing, classifying, and service provision routines; developing distinct special education pedagogy and curriculum; and designing a cascade of service delivery arrangements from special schools to self-contained classes to resource rooms to inclusion classes.[73]

Nonetheless, within the special education research community, a number of researchers including Lloyd Dunn, a former doctoral student of Samuel Kirk, questioned the efficacy and equity of segregated educational provision. For Dunn, segregated schooling and 'pull out' practices were: 'racially biased, instructionally ineffective and psychologically and socially damaging'.[74] Given the vulnerability of minority students and students from disadvantaged backgrounds, Brantlinger traces a number of emergent critiques highlighting the way in which special education and the classification and labelling of disabled children favours educational conservatism and the retention of inequalities in schooling. Affirming the medical model of disability, special education locates problems in learning within the child and thereby removes the school from the therapeutic gaze.

> This apparent overrepresentation can be interpreted in two ways: Either schools are neutral and kids are flawed, or something is amiss with schools. Those who support the status quo in (special) education buy into the first interpretation.[75]

The progress of education legislation in the US has not guaranteed the right of a disabled child to enrol in their neighbourhood school,[76] nor has it extinguished debate. Both Public Law 94–142 The Education of All Handicapped Children 1975 (EAHCA) and Individuals with Disabilities Education Act (IDEA) in 1990 rest on what I have called *clauses of conditionality*.[77] Concepts like *the least restrictive environment* and *the most appropriate setting* require professional interpretation, thereby authorizing special educational sovereignty over other sources of disability knowledge.[78] The Australian Disability Discrimination Act (1992) has several exemptions and caveats including the exemption of the Department of Immigration from its provisions. It also provides for the establishment of 'undue institutional hardship' to permit discrimination against the disabled person.

Applying a forensic intensity to her task, Brantlinger considers the selected critiques of inclusive education in terms of Mick Dunkin's *Types of errors in synthesizing research in education*.[79] The errors he refers to include:

- the exclusion of relevant literature;
- unexplained selectivity of sources;
- lack of discrimination between sources;
- wrongly reporting details;
- erroneously summarizing positions;
- suppressing contrary findings;
- stating unwarranted conclusions and generalizations;
- non-recognition of faulty author conclusions;
- consequential errors;
- failure to marshal all evidence relevant to a generalization.

The consequences of such errors can be dire, observes Dunkin, as syntheses of research are influential in regard to subsequent research, policy and practice.[80] According to Brantlinger, the risk is intensified by the seniority or prominence of the authors in their field.[81] Her analysis of the eighteen documents is presented in a series of tables that reveal the failures of the authors to adhere to their own minimum expectations for scientific research.

Brantlinger's paper should not be understood simply as a methodological challenge to the dominance of empiricism and experimental design in traditional special education research. While she does recognize and advocate the incorporation of post-positivism in research,[82] the paper progresses a political struggle about the purpose and form of schooling. In particular, it lays bare a deeply political struggle between the opposing views of disability studies and segregated education.

In challenging traditional special educators' conceptions of scientific research, Brantlinger confronts the dismissal of inclusive education research as ideological. She encounters what Pierre Bourdieu would regard as the repeated vagaries and misuses of the word ideology. Accordingly the authors[83] she cites use '*ideological*' as a pejorative dismissal of those they disapprovingly call full-inclusionists.

> It seems to convey a sort of discredit. To describe a statement as ideological is very often an insult, so that this ascription itself becomes an instrument of symbolic domination.[84]

In an interview with Julie Allan and I for a project on researching inclusive education, Dave Gillborn and Deborah Youdell declared that for some researchers ideology was like sweat; you smell everybody else's, but not your own.[85] One is mindful of Foucault's call for circumspection in considering ideology,[86] and as Zizek puts it: 'When some procedure is denounced as 'ideological par excellence' one can be assured that its inversion is no less ideological.'[87] Writers such as Barry Troyna have also encountered this struggle over the presence of ideology in research. Troyna confronted his detractors who denounced his notion of 'partisan research' as an oxymoron. He argued that racism had tended to 'be refracted through the lens of educational research' and that critical social research, in applying transparency and tests of scholarship, presented a form of integrity not apparent in the work of the so-called methodological purists.[88]

Although there was no direct response from traditional special education to Brantlinger's paper, the antagonism smouldered and later flared in the conservative special education journal *Exceptionality* in 2006. Herein Kauffman and Sasso employed lavish language to condemn the 'intellectually bankrupt' 'postmodern fashionable nonsense' of Deborah Gallagher and Douglas Biklen.[89] These exchanges underline the depth, continuity and heat of the political struggle.

On the other side of the Atlantic Ocean in England, the former Chair of the influential 1978 Committee of Inquiry into the Education of Handicapped Children and Young People, Baroness Mary Warnock took a *new look* at the impact of her committee's report (*Special educational needs*).[90] In her pamphlet published by The Philosophy Society of Great Britain in 2005 she declared that inclusion, '...though it springs from hearts in the right places', is the '...most disastrous legacy' of the 1978 Special Education Needs report.[91] In her writing, Warnock embraces a view of disability as the embodiment of individual pathological defects. Examples of vulnerable children with asthma, epilepsy, autism and Down's syndrome are offered to suggest a need for the reconstitution of small maintained schools employing stringent coding statements as a gatekeeper to build anxiety amongst parents. This heightened parent anxiety, she suggests, would lead them to regard the enrolment of their child in such a school to be a privilege.[92]

As Mel Ainscow observed prophetically the Warnock pamphlet had a deleterious effect on the progress of inclusive education, 'in the sense that it has tended to encourage some in the field to retreat into traditional stances'.[93] Warnock warmed to her topic in subsequent Forewords for books that hosted a rehearsal of traditional special educational political themes.[94]

> I profoundly believe that for many children, not only those with the most severe or multiple disabilities, special schools are their salvation. They can trust their teachers to understand their difficulties and they

can be free from the teasing and bullying that they fear from their fellow pupils (and this fear is more intense for those children who are not visibly or obviously disabled, such as those with autism in its various degrees). One of the huge advantages of a special school for such children is that it is small. In a small school, a child knows everyone and is known by all the staff. The staff, too, know one another and work in a collegiate atmosphere, where they can share their insights and their problems. Special schools are of course not cheap. But the policy of inclusion in mainstream schools should not be cheap either if it is to provide enough support for individual pupils to enable them to flourish. It is not enough that children with special needs in mainstream schools should be supported by teaching assistants; they need expert, trained teachers, who can teach them in small groups, or one-to-one. This is something that few mainstream schools can offer. What has been wrong with the policy of inclusion has been the idea that if some children with special needs can flourish in mainstream schools they all can.[95]

Warnock's language positions the disabled child both as the additional and the incomplete student. Their participation in the regular school is less valid than those students who have not been assigned a disability classification. They are the invalids. For a philosopher, Dame Warnock has strayed into difficult questions of entitlement and rights without due consideration.

To demonstrate Ainscow's proposition that the Warnock pamphlet encouraged the strenuous advance of conservative positions on special educational needs and segregated enrolments, let us consider the argument set out by Michael Farrell who contends that:

> ...at the heart of calls for the ultimate closure of special schools, lies a diminution of the importance of providing the best education possible for children, including children with SEN (special educational needs).[96]

'The danger', he goes on to argue, 'is that inclusion will come to be seen as more central to the work of schools than education.'[97] To support his proposition, he offers the example of a fire department that is more committed to multi-ethnic, sexuality and gender representation than to the requirement for fire-fighting knowledge and skills. Farrell's critique of inclusive education and its attachment to the human rights agenda pivots on what economists refer to as *bracket creep*. Here he refers to the inflation of the number of groups being identified as excluded or oppressed.

> Inflation strains credibility, leading people to ask how many oppressed groups can be found in a society before the bizarre situation is reached

where everyone is oppressed or excluded and there is nobody left to oppress or exclude them.[98]

Are you not struck by the irony of this line of argument? The steady expansion of categories of special educational needs is well documented and will continue. The imminent publication of an enlarged edition of the Diagnostic and Statistical Manual of Mental Disorders[99] guarantees it. This compendium of mental and behavioural disorders provides the schedules of symptoms and behaviours that govern children's 'achievement' of SEN status. Recent observers of the funding of SEN have chronicled a corresponding *category creep*.[100]

Let us return to Farrell's argument:

> Given this increasing lack of credibility, it can be argued that it is not being educated in a special school that might oppress pupils. The main oppression and exclusion that pupils in special school and their parents have to fear is that of political correctness seeking to force an over-zealous inclusion agenda even if it means denying the child a good education.[101]

Like other special education traditionalists' work cited by Brantlinger, such as Kauffman and Hallahan[102] and more recently Kavale and Mostert,[103] the correct observation is that children have been transferred from special schools and classes to ill-equipped and reluctant neighbourhood schools and classes only to experience marginalization in the mainstream. Researchers advocating inclusive education have long recognized this as a serious issue and argued that inclusion demands more than the physical movement of children from one site to another.[104] Using the maladministration of inclusive education to abandon the principles of democratic education and social inclusion reveals poor analysis as a shield for professional interest.

Following the debate generated in the media and the parliament in England by Warnock's *New look* pamphlet, Ruth Cigman edited a collection of papers that generally strike a conservative response to advocacy for inclusive education. Low, for example, calls for moderate inclusion. Ainscow observes that the '...distinction between SEN and Non-SEN children is a largely outmoded one'. This is a useful observation when considered in the context of Cigman's organizing questions:

- Included in what?
- Excluded from what?
- Excluded by whom?

In fact, we return to a fundamental proposition carried in this book: the administrative constructs of special and regular schooling hinder creative thinking about educational options and futures.

Who's asking? The politics of researching inclusion

Len Barton chose to respond to the Warnock pamphlet in an essay made available on the website of the University of Leeds' Centre for Disability Studies.[105] Let us turn directly to his objections:

> In trying to understand the claims of the author, we are left with the overwhelming feeling that this document is a mixture of important historical insights, but also a reflection of naivety, arrogance and ignorance on the part of the author. How have we come to this conclusion? In a document that claims to be offering a 'new look', one would expect some careful discussion of the ideas of those who represent an alternative perspective. Instead, we have no discussion of a serious nature with regard to such published material. This is particularly offensive when we recognise the central role that disabled people and their organisations have played in the struggle for inclusion. Not one serious reference is made to the extensive publications by disabled people supporting inclusive education.... Such voices are excluded from consideration. This does raise the question of whose voice is seen as significant and on what grounds? The position is made clear, in that we are informed that this is the voice of an expert, 'a prominent figure in education'. Nor is it any comfort to be told that those advocating inclusive education, and this we assume includes disabled people, have gone too far in their struggles for change, but that their efforts 'spring from hearts in the right place: a commitment to equal opportunities' (p. 40). This statement is rather trivial and patronising.[106]

Barton's response to Warnock's *New look* pamphlet raises another important strand of inclusive education politics: Who speaks for whom? Mike Oliver raises the issue of the representation of disabled people in research directly:

> When I began to read some of the things that able-bodied academics, researchers and professionals had written about disability, I was staggered at how little it related to my own experience of disability or indeed, of most other disabled people I had come to know. Over the next few years it gradually began to dawn on me that if disabled people left it to others to write about disability, we would inevitably end up with inaccurate and distorted accounts of our experiences and inappropriate service provision and professional practices based upon these inaccuracies and distortions.[107]

The majority of research into disability, according to Oliver, reflects the unequal power relations between the expert researcher and the disabled person who is an object of and within research.

> To put it bluntly, research has been and essentially still is, an activity carried out by those who have power upon those who do not.[108]

Moreover, '...disability research has been unable to shake off the methodological individualism inherent in positivist social research of all kinds'.[109] Within this dominant research genre disability is 'abstracted from the social world which produces it'.[110]

> Disability research, therefore, has reinforced the individual model of disability seeing the problems that disabled people face as being caused by their individual impairments.[111]

It has sought to 'classify, clarify, map and measure'[112] the dimensions of disability.

> The social relations of research production provide the structure within which research is undertaken. The social relations are built upon a firm distinction between the researcher and the researched; upon the belief that it is the researchers who have specialist knowledge and skills; and that it is they who should decide what topics should be researched and be in control of the whole process of research production.[113]

Drawing from Finkelstein, Oliver advises disabled people not to partake in research that does not fully involve them from the outset; *there should be no participation without representation*.[114]

I dwell upon Oliver's counsel from some eighteen years ago as it goes to the heart of the politics of inclusive education. The preponderance of research into inclusive education commences from the misrepresentation of disability as individual impairment and thenceforth sets out to 'classify, clarify, map and measure' these disabled people. This research will equip teachers and schools to meet the challenges of these additional children who are being redirected into the regular school. We witness subtle slippages where researchers investigate the attitudes of teachers, head-teachers or school principals, students whose tenure at the regular school is beyond question and parents of these regular school children in order to provide strategies for changing attitudes and smoothing the way for inclusion. Such attitudes research, spanning from the early work of James Ward and his colleagues to more recent work by Forlin, Loreman and Sharma, still commences from the individual disabled child as the problem and the focus of the work of inclusion. A better line of research may invite questions about how schools erect barriers to children from disadvantaged backgrounds, immigrant children, traveller children, children of colour, children with impairments and children who dissent. Moreover, we might choose to shed the expert *cloak of competence*[115] and invite the powerless and frequently over-researched minorities to speak authoritatively about their own experience.

Why research inclusion and exclusion?

Challenging the character and intent of research in inclusive education returns me to my critical roots. Marx's Thesis Eleven on Feuerbach is pertinent: 'The philosophers have only interpreted the world, in various ways; the point is to change it.'[116] Hence the point of research on inclusive education should be to build robust and comprehensive analyses of exclusion in order that we might challenge social and cultural relations as mediated through education in order to dismantle oppression and promote inclusion. This task differs radically from understanding the etiology and symptoms of syndromes and disorders in order to manage and teach different people more efficiently; no matter how well intentioned that pursuit might be.

Julie Allan's essay, *Inclusion as an ethical project*,[117] draws from the 'much neglected final phase' of Foucault's work on ethics to break the inertia that has enveloped inclusive education. This inertia, stemming from confusion over its meanings, from ideological jousting and from the reduction of inclusion to a technical problem to be fixed by policy, has effectively:

> Deflected attention from the radical changes that teachers must initiate, and that schools require, in order to create the conditions necessary for inclusive education...[118]

For Allan the ethical project places responsibilities on us all. Inclusive education is everybody's business. Each of us has to observe an underlying *telos* (goal) and set of principles to guide our choices and behaviour. Barton shares this ethical framework where our research and practice subjects ourselves to critical scrutiny:

> I think there has been an increasing desire and commitment to try to understand and work on the purpose of research that is other than merely confirming academic interests and concerns. I think disability studies for example and some of the issues in sociology of education have been a wonderful confirmation of this in the sense that I do believe increasingly that my interest is not only in understanding the world but to see some change and change me in that process. One of the interests has been clearly to try to understand the nature of discrimination in its many complex and contradictory forms.[119]
> (Barton, Interview Transcript, Montreal, Researching Inclusive Education project, 2005: 3)

In this essay, and in her book on the philosophers of difference (Foucault, Derrida and Deleuze and Guttari), Allan refutes claims by Shumway and

Rorty that Foucault's work is overly pessimistic, offering little hope for social change and, as Zizek suggests, *'portrays individuals as unlikely to resist'*.[120] As she observes, Foucault's position leads not to apathy, but to hyper-activism.[121] The challenge for Foucault is that of:

> ... shaking the habits, ways of acting and thinking, of dispelling commonplace beliefs, [and] of taking a new measure of rules and institutions.[122]

This is akin to what I described in a discussion with Jenny Corbett as our having to act as *cultural vigilantes*.[123] This sensational couplet was offered to suggest that inclusive education was not a technical or policy project where we simply identified, classified, managed and educated so-called special educational needs students. Inclusive education remains a political project where we seek to identify the complex ways in which barriers prevent students accessing, authentically participating and succeeding in education.

Accordingly our research agenda is enlarged to reveal the architecture of inequality and exclusion. Positivistic research that focuses upon the perceived defects of individuals obstructs the inclusive education agenda. The range of human differences is not as David Reynolds suggested to be seen as a risk to the fail-safe school. Schools are not surgical operating theatres, nor are they flight control centres.[124] These preposterous suggestions reverberate through the elaborate, costly and anti-educational accountability and target-enforcement measures that risk-averse governments have erected in the UK, the USA, Australia and New Zealand. Measures that prize test performance above teaching and learning. Schools must become what Tony Knight and Art Pearl describe as an apprenticeship in democracy.[125] The link between inclusion and democratic schooling is indivisible. Bernstein 'announced' the requirements for democratic schooling. In doing so he highlighted the importance of inclusion, hastening to distinguish between inclusion and absorption.[126] Alain Turaine expounds upon this point:

> In a world of intense cultural exchanges, there can be no democracy unless we recognize the diversity of cultures and the relations of domination that exist between them. The two elements are equally important: we must recognize the diversity of cultures, but also the existence of cultural domination ... The struggle for the liberation of cultural minorities can lead to their communitarianization, or in other words their subordination to an authoritarian cultural power.[127]

These are important distinctions. Just as Barry Troyna insisted that multicultural education that consisted of the token celebration of saris, samosas and steel bands was a liberal blancmange incapable of addressing racism in education, Bernstein and Touraine show that inclusion cannot be reduced to absorption, assimilation or popular cosmopolitanism. Troyna stipulates a need for anti-racist education to dismantle the exclusion of Black British and Asian students. In Queensland, Australia, the Aboriginal principal of the Cherbourg Aboriginal Community School insisted on a revivification of Aboriginal knowledge and culture under the rallying call and educational blueprint of *strong and smart*. Gay and lesbian communities assert their queer identity as a source of pride, an asset of diversity. Disabled activists and disability studies researchers confront us with new understandings of impairment and disablement that challenge narratives of defectiveness, cure, remediation and normalization. The deaf community and people with Asperger's syndrome demand recognition as distinct and valuable cultural groups. These are new times that challenge the core of regular and special schooling to form new theories and forms of schooling. For Touraine, schools are the seedbed for social composition. If we are to learn to live together schools must subvert the classical educational fare.

> A form of education centred on the culture and values of the society that provides the education in question is replaced by a form of education that gives a central importance to diversity (both historical and cultural) and to recognition of Other.[128]

We will revisit the relationship between democratic schooling, inclusive education and 'the irregular school' in Chapter 8. Indeed, democratic education will form the intellectual heart (both in telos and principles) of this book's consideration of futures for inclusive education.

5 It's what governments do – policy inaction

Every revolution evaporates and leaves behind only the slime of a new bureaucracy.

Franz Kafka

Oliver: ...Now it's freelance. We've been – what's the word? – Outsourced. The politicians dismantle communities, then complain that community no longer exists. They incubate the disease, then profess to be shocked when people catch it.

The vertical hour, David Hare

Introduction

Recently I attended a conference on inclusive education organized by Professor Athena Sideri from the University of Athens. As is often the case the most powerful and instructive presentations are not exercises in erudition, but offerings from the heart. A father of a disabled boy representing a parent advocacy organization in Athens spoke about his son's experience of schooling. The boy would set off each day, he told us, with a satchel full of dreams and hope. Sadly the school did not value the boy, or his dreams. His differences challenged the habituated teaching developed for the other children who are seen as normal. The boy would return home each evening with an empty satchel. Too often, schools empty children's satchels; their dreams are strewn in the dust. As I listened through headphones to the narrative being translated from Greek to English, there came a pause followed by the voice of a second translator. The first translator was so moved that she could not complete her task and she left the booth in tears. This story is remarkable and painful for those outside of education. But these painful episodes pass without remark in schools. They are always painful. Parents and children suffer quietly as they feel the dead weight of the collapse of their hopes and dreams.

Teachers often feel at a loss and are personally distressed about the difficulties experienced by disabled children in their classrooms. They struggle within the constraints of inadequate classroom spaces and exhausted educational practices designed for times long passed. Unreasonable policy impositions, competitive targets and narrowing notions of educational purpose restrict creativity, innovation and the attention required to educate children rather than teach to tests. Differentiated teaching where teachers commence the planning of their teaching from familiarity with the strengths of and challenges for the individual child[1] and assessment for learning where portfolios of work are accrued to gauge progress and build aspiration rather than pronounce sentence,[2] require a policy foundation built upon trust and knowledge of educational principles. For teachers the 'boy with the satchel' is a metaphor for risk. He has become the additional student to cope with, an educational Other,[3] who threatens performance audits, and introduces a layer of special educational needs bureaucracy. Herein lies the creation of a surplus population and organizational disequilibrium. Teachers are overtly and covertly encouraged by prevailing cultures and circumstances to enter into a condition of collective indifference.

As the educational crisis, which I will attempt to explain in Chapter 7, deepens, more children become surplus to the capacity of the school to deliver its targets. These vulnerable students are condemned to being the new special class of behaviour and language disordered. Linda Graham observes how in the Australian state of New South Wales one-third of special school places are now reserved for students who have been classified as emotionally disturbed or behaviourally disordered.[4] Added to this are the growing number of pupil referral units, behaviour units and numerous other alternative settings for difficult, disruptive, disengaged and disordered students. We are witnessing the steady expansion of a residual tier of schooling. Do you wonder how this has happened? I do. Do you not also wonder how (if) this might change? I do. On the outskirts of Amman in Jordan, a temporary camp was established in 1948 for Arab refugees. In 2010 the camp has all the trappings of dilapidated permanence. The people remain outsiders. Viewing this camp from a taxi window I was struck by how knee-jerk responses to crises quickly establish themselves as part of the policy landscape and how education too displaces and establishes camps for undervalued young people.

I am not suggesting that schools, governments and teachers deliberately set out to make life more difficult for some children. This is an effect of a complex arrangement of social structures and values, education policy ensembles, competing curriculum choices, attenuated approaches to teaching and assessment, inflexible school structures and resource allocation decisions. As we have already noted, Michele Moore argues exclusion is the consequence of sets of decisions.[5] We therefore could exercise an alternative set of decisions. It is equally possible to make a principled choice of inclusion.

This chapter continues our thinking about futures for inclusive education by interrogating its past. To understand this past we will move from looking at detached theoretical explanations to the application of these ways of thinking about inclusive education that are manifest in education policies. My examination of what is imprecisely referred to as special educational needs and inclusive education policy will draw from a number of resources, textual and anecdotal, from around the world. The point is not to make judgemental comparisons. To do so would be naïve and misleading. I do this instead, as Mel Ainscow observes, in order to make the familiar strange and the strange familiar.[6] That things may be done differently elsewhere invites new possibilities, or it may suggest warnings.

For example, much of my involvement in inclusive education in Australia has been spent in discussions about resource allocation on a quest to produce a different distribution calculus; a set of algorithms for government to expedite disabled children's education with their neighbourhood peers in the local school. These Australian discussions about resources as the precondition for inclusion were thrown into relief at a conference in Manchester where I was struck by the serene bemusement of colleagues from poor African nations and from the Indian subcontinent as they patiently listened to those from the rich countries of the West bemoaning their insufficiency of material resources and personnel. They would happily include 'these other' students, who are presently excluded, had they the requisite resources. Our African colleagues told us that they ask students to bring something with them to school to sit on. They have little that would count as educational materials. There are few books. They do not bother counting how many children there are for each computer. They are not fortunate enough to complain about bandwidth sizes. Science laboratories and sophisticated science equipment and materials are nowhere to be found. I remember a proud head-teacher showing us a classroom in a school in China. We gazed across the rows of empty desks and scanned the barren paint-thirsty walls and politely nodded our approval. 'This is our science lab', he declared pointing to the sink and tap at the back of the room. SENCOs (Special Educational Needs Coordinators), therapists, psychologists and behaviour experts are not thick on the ground. It is impressive that our colleagues commence from a different starting line. They have made a decision of principle to which they adhere. It seems there is a principle of welcoming all students and then working out how to do the best with what they have. There is no one to whom to refer or defer unwanted children. Of course, there is the danger of romanticism in my representation. I must also acknowledge the fact that some children are kept away from school by parents who feel the cultural or religious shame of having a disabled child. Others keep them home out of concern for their safety.

Moving back to more familiar ground to ponder this further, I am also cognizant of the difference in the quality of inclusive schooling between urban and rural schools and between schools that lie in demographically similar areas across Australia. Resources are important, but our notion of resource is worth testing. Can we countenance a social accounting to generate resources of hope?[7] We will return to this question in due course.

Reflecting on (inclusive) education policy

In this chapter we will selectively explore the progress of inclusive education across various jurisdictions in order to identify some challenges, conundra and opportunities for reform. Chapters 5, 6 and 7 construct our bridge into a more speculative consideration of futures for inclusive education and a more searching discussion of the irregular school. It would be too difficult in the space of two short chapters to complete an analysis of inclusive education policy across all jurisdictions. Neither do I undertake to give the definitive account of policy-making in any one jurisdiction. Rather, I want to collect experiences and anecdotes, and draw from research to identify these challenges and conundra. More specifically, I am interested in opportunities for thinking otherwise about inclusive education. In this respect, this book embodies and mobilizes hope; it is a call to action.

Like the terms *democracy* and *inclusion, policy* is a seemingly obvious but 'differently and often loosely used' word.[8] Mark Considine has depicted policy as a process, a dynamic response to the changing nature of the world and problems governments seek to address (or avoid).[9] In developing a set of sociological tools to explore policy processes and cycles, Stephen Ball has reflected upon the 'hyperactivism' manifest in the deluge of policy statements, memoranda, releases, texts, edicts, speeches, Acts and regulations that have been unleashed on schools by governments wanting to appear in command, on top of their game.[10] Predictably, this unremitting flow of policy promotes cynicism, resistance and fatigue.

> Therefore, policy is not treated as an object, a product or an outcome but rather as a process, something ongoing, interactional and unstable.... Policies are contested, interpreted and enacted in a variety of arenas of practice and the rhetoric's, texts and meanings of policy makers do not always translate directly and obviously into institutional practices. They are inflected, mediated, resisted and misunderstood, or in some cases simply prove unworkable. It is also important not to overestimate the logical rationality of policy. Policy strategies, Acts, guidelines and initiatives are often messy, contradictory, confused and unclear.[11]

Policy-making and administration is not simply what governments hand down for implementation by an obedient civil service, as early commentators on public policy and administration such as Thomas Dye[12] suggested. This view is static and misleading. Such an account is also too linear, and unidimensional. Ignored is the process of struggle that exists in the complex relationships between the setting of policy agendas, the production of a policy text (an Act, regulation, media statement, speech or descriptive brochure) and the translation of this policy artefact into practice (implementation). This messy and often contested process is what Ball refers to as the policy cycle.[13] Not all early policy definitions have been devoid of analytic prescience. Rizvi and Lingard draw on political scientist, David Easton,[14] writing in 1953 to lay the foundations for their 'eclectic view of critical education policy analysis'.[15]

> The essence of policy lies in the fact that through it certain things are denied to some people and made accessible to others. Policy ... consists of a web of decisions that allocates values.[16]

In their consideration of the allocation of values through education policy, Rizvi and Lingard describe a process whereby often competing or contradictory values such as equality, justice, autonomy, efficiency, accountability, competition and excellence are organized according to political priorities. It may be that equality is not completely jettisoned, they suggest; it is reassembled or reconfigured, rearticulated or subordinated to dominant economic concerns.[17] Lingard previously reported how the Disadvantaged Schools Programme (DSP) and the Participation and Equity Programme (PEP)[18] together with a range of other social justice initiatives in Australia had been disbanded and the funding reallocated to literacy projects to raise student achievement scores on national testing programmes. Rebranding equity as literacy improvement and dismantling innovative and engaging education programmes built on the requirements for redistribution and representation[19] for children from disadvantaged and minority communities was actually the subordination of equity to the demands of improving test scores on national and international league tables to leverage economic competitiveness.[20]

The propensity for policy to generate perverse subversions of its articulated aims is illustrated by the fact that in the drive to raise achievement through improving state profiles of students' achievement on nation-wide paper and pencil literacy tests in Australia some schools were reported, albeit anecdotally, to have persuaded Aboriginal and under-achieving students to absent themselves on testing days. This travesty is understood when we realize that a State's (province, county, governorate) overall test performance affects their share of Federal funding grants. Likewise, an Aboriginal community school principal once told me how he had been admonished by regional education officials because his school's literacy scores had gone down. What was not recognized by the regional administrators was the fact that the school had halted truancy and teachers had begun teaching students from where they were up to after years of interrupted schooling. The instruments of accountability in that state registered this as failure. To say that using blunt tools to work in complex settings would seem to be as the British hotelier of international repute, Basil Fawlty[21] explains to his work colleagues, '*A lesson in the bleeding obvious*'. The story of inclusive education is also the story of the reworking of a concept to render it compatible with the priorities of power. It is a story of the assignation of values; it is the story of those who are and those who are not valued.

Policy is, as Norman Fairclough presents in his analysis of the rhetoric of Tony Blair's New Labour, a quest for the elegantly simple, captivating and mobilizing narrative.[22] This is what he calls the 'mediatisation' of policy. Image eclipses logic. Repetition and the exclusion of alternative discourses or ways of thinking establish the boundaries of the policy agenda. Fairclough also reflects upon, as we have noted earlier in this text, a process of creating impossible alternatives: 'enterprise and fairness'. The amalgamation of 'inclusive and special education' is the embodiment of this absurd yet generally accepted artifice. Indeed, there are institutions of higher education in the UK that offer the degree: Master of Inclusive and Special Education. In Canada, there are Faculties of Education who proclaim their inclusive education credentials while hosting courses on *retardation*. The 'R' word is to disablism what the 'N' word is to racism.

This is not to deny the importance and more positive power of language in the production and politics of policy-making. During his time as the Deputy Director General of the Queensland Education Department, Allan Luke recognized the importance of providing the politicians, the bureaucracy and schools, with what he called organizing nodes. 'New Basics', 'Literate Futures', 'Productive Pedagogies', 'Partners for Success' were metaphors for educational strategies that were digestible for journalists, parliamentarians and public (see Table 5.1). The couplets acted like computer screen icons for carefully organized descriptions of the key elements of the QSE 2010 reform agenda.[23] Behind the organizing nodes for each area – New Basics, Literate Futures, Productive Pedagogies and Partners for Success – lies a series of accessible documentation and teaching resources together with more detailed research (see the websites listed in Table 5.1). The reform blueprint envisioned in QSE 2010 was translated into Education Queensland's strategic plan *Destination 2010*. A plan transmuted, as signified by diluted language,[24] over time by successive Directors General and Ministers unable or unwilling to resist conservative moves toward national (traditional) curriculum outcomes, increased emphasis on national testing regimes and the introduction of league tables. Language is a key to reform as it simultaneously prescribes and proscribes possibility.[25]

Policy-making has also been impacted by two other phenomena that demand attention if we are to understand the complexity of exclusion and inclusive education policy. First is the profound impact of globalization.[29] Second is the contiguous relationship between government and private financial interests.[30] In this discussion of education policy, globalization refers to the flows of capital, people and information, the contraction of

Table 5.1 Education Queensland 2010 Reform Agenda

Organising node	Reform description	Additional information
New Basics	New Basics was a rhetorical device referring to a large research project involving forty-nine government schools trialling major reforms including: (1) the thematic organization of knowledge content in response to key organizing questions; (2) investment in the systematic professional development of teachers to broaden their pedagogical repertoire; (3) the development of authentic assessment (rich tasks); (4) the development of professional learning communities with approaches to building educational leadership.	Education Queensland (2000). *New Basics Project Technical Paper*. Brisbane: Department of Education. http://education.qld.gov.au/corporate/newbasics/html/research/research.html
Literate Futures	'Literacy is the flexible and sustainable mastery of a repertoire of practices with the texts of traditional and new communications technologies via spoken language, print, and multi-media.'[26] Literate Futures signalled the intention of Education Queensland to expand its approach to literacy beyond phonics programmes and reading recovery to adopt the Four Resources model which encompassed: (i) Code Breaker (coding competence); (ii) Meaning Maker (semantic competence); (iii) Text User (pragmatic competence); (iv) Text Critic (critical competence). Literate Futures also introduced notions of multi-literacies to cohere with the languages of new technologies.	http://education.qld.gov.au/curriculum/learning/literate-futures/pdfs/lf-teacher-summary.pdf Muspratt, S., Luke, A. and Freebody, P. (1997) *Constructing critical literacies: Teaching and learning textual practice.* Cresskill, NJ, Hampton Press. Freebody, P. and Luke, A. 1990, 'Literacies programs: Debates and demands in cultural context', *Prospect*, 5, pp. 7–15.

Productive Pedagogies	Productive Pedagogies was a key element of the New Basics Research project, a recommendation from the Queensland School Reform Longitudinal Study (QSRLS) that received high profile political support from then State Premier, Per Beattie. Productive Pedagogies describes a common framework under which teachers can choose and develop strategies in relation to: what they teach; variable styles sequentially developed through strong evaluative frameworks; and responsiveness to the backgrounds of their students. Productive Pedagogies embraces four elements in building teaching approaches: intellectual quality; connectedness; supportive and caring environment; and recognition of difference. It draws from earlier work by Fred Newmann and Associates around ideas of 'authentic achievement'.[27] Such approaches are grounded in a measure of educational rigour not reflected in the ill-conceived targets in other jurisdictions such as England and the economists frameworks established by OECD.[28]	http://education.qld.gov.au/corporate/ newbasics/html/pedagogies/pedagog.html Queensland. Dept. of Education (2001) *The Queensland school reform longitudinal study.* Brisbane, The State of Queensland (Department of Education).
Partners for Success	Partners for Success is the department's key strategy targeting the education and employment needs of Aboriginal and Torres Strait Islander students in Queensland. Its priority areas of attendance, retention, attainment and work force capacity drive planning and are the basis for measuring performance. Launched in 2000 in thirty-eight trial schools and communities, mainly in rural and remote locations, Partners for Success was developed as a direct response to the Review of Education and Employment Programs for Aboriginal and Torres Strait Islander peoples.	http://education.qld.gov.au/schools/indigenous/ strategies/part-for-success.html Sarra, C. (2003) *Young and black and deadly: Strategies for improving outcomes for indigenous students,* Deakin West, ACT, Australian College of Educators.

time and space (distance) and the complex interplay of domination and subordination in the formation of new communities of interest. In particular I am interested in the global movement of education policy discourses and in the operation of various agencies that support and transport those powerful discourses. Here I refer to the global policy convergences around the commodification of education and schooling and the reconfiguration of public (state) education under the rubric of the marketplace. Kahn and Minnich write of the threat to democracy in the 'white flight' from neighbourhood schools and the systematic privatization of public education following desegregation in the USA:

> Privatisers then and now do this: They claim a public system is failing, disinvest and otherwise make sure it does fail, create or support private alternatives, and justify the shift from public to private by saying, 'We had to do it because the public system was so terrible. And if subtler methods such as disinvestment seem too slow, and they can get away with more, sometimes what was public is outright sold to private buyers. In the South, (white) school boards sometimes closed a school and then sold it for next to nothing to a segregation academy.'[31]

On the basis of his extensive evidence and analysis of new forms of education organization as the private and public become increasingly blurred, Stephen Ball contends that, 'we should see privatisation as part of a much larger canvas of social changes'. He continues:

> Privatisation is an ongoing but unstable process which encompasses changing relationships between the state, capital, the public sector and civil society and which connects the grand flows of the global economy to the re-working of the textures of everyday life, for students and teachers (and researchers), and families ... within this new episteme, education is increasingly, indeed perhaps almost exclusively, spoken of in terms of its economic value and its contribution to international market competitiveness.[32]

Ball leaves his readers with sombre and sage advice:

> We need to struggle to think differently about education policy before it is too late. We need to move beyond the tyrannies of improvement, efficiency and standards, to recover a language of and for education articulated in terms of ethics, moral obligations and values.[33]

He is not alone in this view. Addressing the Conference of Commonwealth Ministers of Education in Edinburgh in 2003, Amartya Sen used the occasion to remind the Ministers of Adam Smith's counsel that education was far too important to be left to the capriciousness of the marketplace.[34]

Globalization, as Rizvi and Lingard reflect, has been an incubus for and the carrier of the neo-liberal social imaginary. Agencies such as the OECD, the World Bank, UNESCO and the International Monetary Fund have reified a particular form of economic organization and with it the type of education organization and culture that will produce the new cosmopolitan workforce for the knowledge economy. Education is now cast as the means for producing global citizens with knowledge, skills and dispositions that value mobility, flexibility and competition commensurate with a mercurial and, as we have recently witnessed in the crisis of banking and capital, cannibalistic marketplace. This echoes Sennett's depiction of the culture of new capitalism. While nations of contrasting states of economic development and political persuasion scramble to enter the OECD Programme for International Student Assessment (PISA) and the Trends in International Maths and Science Study (TIMSS) testing competition, the list of student casualties from the high-stakes testing culture grows.[35]

Two American academics, Dale Johnson and Bonnie Johnson,[36] describe how they took a one-year leave of absence from their university in the summer of 2000 to teach third and fourth grades in a school in a disadvantaged community in Louisiana. The school, which they call Redbud Elementary School, provided these two teacher education professors 'with real life opportunities to see firsthand the effects of the accountability movement on life in school'. A number of themes emerged from their daily journal entries:

- The grinding effects of acute poverty on all aspects of life including education.
- The negative consequences of the continuing drive for accountability in the schools.
- The unreasonable demands placed on teachers that stifle their creativity and enthusiasm and hasten their exodus from the profession.
- The rising growth of for-profit ventures feeding off the accountability movement.
- The developing alliances between policy-makers and profiteers.
- The regressive and disproportionate impact of high-stakes testing on America's most vulnerable and minority children.[37]

This is the long shadow of the 'spectre of uselessness'.[38]

The sound and logic of policy: timbre and pitch revisited

In 1984 in the Australian state of Victoria, the Victorian Ministerial Review of Educational Services for the Disabled chaired by then Deputy Director General of Education, Kevin Collins published the report of its findings, *Integration in Victorian education*.[39] Readers may be puzzled at my return to what some may now consider antiquity or policy pulp.

However, this report represents a remarkable departure from previous comparatively conservative reports such as the often-cited 1978 Warnock Report: *Special educational needs* in England,[40] or the caveat-laden Public Laws governing the education of disabled schoolchildren in the USA.[41] It also strikes a more progressive posture than subsequent reports such as the deceptively entitled report from the Ontario Ministry of Education's 'working table' on special education commissioned in 2005 by Minister Kennedy. The report from the 'working table' was presented under the enticing title, *Special education transformation*[42] in May 2006 to the new Education Minister Sandra Pupatello. The authors of the *transformation* report were Brock University professor Sheila Bennett and the parliamentary assistant to education (now Minister for Education) Kathleen Wynne. Asked to speak at a meeting of senior education personnel by Deputy Minister Ben Levin, I rather uncharitably described *Special education transformation* as 'a sheep in sheep's clothing'. I had borrowed this phrase from a former Australian Labor Party Prime Minister, Paul Keating. He had used it to describe the Liberal Party (conservative) Prime Minister, John Howard.[43] Written some twenty-one years later, the language of the Ontario report reverberates the form and tone of traditional special education with occasional references to inclusion. It is little more than a variation on the theme of a continuum or cascade of provision.[44] It also safeguards segregated schools as a representation of parental choice, albeit with an attempt to rein in the dramatically escalating total expenditure on special education needs across the province.[45]

Unlike the Warnock Report or the Ontario Report, the Collins Report adopts what its principal policy analyst and author, Gillian Fulcher, describes as a democratic discourse.[46]

> In contrast to the British policy, Integration in Victorian Education is politically far from equivocal, and though it too draws on some opposing discourses or frameworks, it has a predominantly democratic discourse (its guiding principle is that every child has a right to regular education) and a clear critique of the historically established professional control of special education practices.[47]

Within the report, there is an unambiguous statement of what (and *who*) is valued. This is set out in a definition and set of Five Guiding Principles (see Tables 5.2 and 5.3). *Integration in Victorian education* (the Report of the Ministerial Review Committee of Educational Services for the Disabled) rejected the utility of the medical model of disability that infuses special educational knowledge, language and practices for advancing either the rights or the education of 'disabled' schoolchildren. By adopting a distinctively democratic or rights-based discourse, the report predated later human rights legislation by proclaiming the right of *every child* to be enrolled in his or her neighbourhood school. It set an expectation for participatory decision-making that redressed the prevailing imbalance in the power relations between an array of expert professionals and parents in making decisions about their children.[48] This was a profound distancing of the report and its recommendations from the discourse and epistemic edifices of expert professionalism that characterize the theories and practices of special education.[49]

> The Report's dominant objective was democratic: to restore parity of treatment in the educational apparatus for those children tagged disabled. This democratism underpinned the critique of professionalism (assessment, placement, 'in the child's best interests' etc.)...[50]

Privileging parents in a more democratic process of collaborative decision-making about their children's education was consistent with the rhetoric of devolution struck in the State of Victoria Education Department's Ministerial Papers 1–6.[51] *Integration in victorian education* was intended to herald the systematic repatriation of resources from a binary system to enable the education of all children in their local school. In other words, the extensive resources dedicated to the separation of children from their peers would be reinvested in building the capacity of regular schools and teachers to provide an education for the actual population of their neighbourhood rather than their preferred population. Or so it was thought. While entirely predictable, as Skrtic observes,[52] the resilience of traditional special education and professional interest, were seriously underestimated.

The principal author of the Victorian State Government's Report on the review of educational services for the disabled, Gillian Fulcher, went

Table 5.2 Integration in Victorian education definition of integration

	Integration refers to a two-fold process:
1	a process of increasing the participation of children with impairments, disabilities and problems in schooling in the education programs and social life of regular schools in which their peers without disabilities participate; and
2	a process of maintaining the participation of all children in the educational programs and social life of regular schools.[53]

Table 5.3 Integration in Victorian education – five guiding principles

1	Every child has a right to be educated in a regular school.
2	Non-categorisation.
3	Resources and services should, to the greatest extent possible, be school-based.
4	Collaborative decision-making processes
5	All children can learn and be taught

on to analyse the processes and impacts of integration policy in her book called *Disabling policies*.[54] First published in 1989, it is an extraordinarily important text for researchers of disability studies in education and policy sociology alike. At the outset Fulcher establishes the specific concern of her text: 'how we can develop a better deal for those schoolchildren who are (in increasing numbers) called "disabled" or handicapped, and for their teachers'.[55] After all, this had been the intention of the report, *Integration in Victorian education*. However, as Fulcher reminds us, in the first pages of her text, what had been a very well-intentioned report had foundered upon the conflicts in its committee work, and in interpretation and implementation across the various arenas in Victorian schooling.

The conflict generated by the report was 'vigorous, marked and prolonged: it continues'.[56] Fulcher describes in a number of accounts how ten minutes before the presentation of the report to the Minister the representative from the technical and secondary teacher unions lodged Extension Note 2 in the report to make clear that the term 'problems in schooling' did not represent problems of the school, but a reflection of the deficit of the child. In this way 'problems in schooling' paradoxically became the largest category of children for whom integration funding was sought. More cruelly, that descriptor was frequently applied to children in regular schools as a new professional marker of difference and covert exclusion.[57] 'Problems in schooling', a legitimized (i.e. the school could claim money to integrate these students) and catchall diagnosis for disengagement, disruption and failing children caught on. It became a means for controlling, to borrow from Michel Foucault, the not so docile bodies in the classroom.[58] Elsewhere I have written about the impeccable timing of this new diagnostic category (it predated the rise of attention disorders) and the changes to Regulation XVI – School Discipline in the state of Victoria.[59]

A parent representative on the review committee also had an Extension Note inserted to argue that Enrolment Support Groups comprise even numbers of parents and professionals.[60] Conflict does continue, though the report itself has receded into the obscurity of library shelves and policy pulp. We shall consider conflicts in subsequent inclusive education policy debates that echo the central themes of this struggle as it played out in Victoria through the 1980s:

- democratic decision-making versus expert authority and professional interest;
- contradictory understandings of disability and disablement;
- struggles over who schools are for (which students belong in regular classrooms and which students are seen as additional or surplus population);
- contests about the allocation of resources;

- debates about the limits of the professional role and responsibilities of classroom teachers;
- ambiguity about the notion of regular and special curriculum and pedagogy;
- disagreement about the organization of a school; and most importantly
- agonisms over a statement of values.

I returned to this report and to its principal author's later reflections upon it,[61] with purpose. There are two aspects of Fulcher's reflections on the report and the controversies surrounding its production in committee debates and its reception across policy arenas that I would like to highlight:

- policy as an agent of social theory;
- language matters.

Policy as an agent of social theory

The production of *Integration in Victorian education* demonstrates conflicts over professional and democratic discourses at all levels of policy (written, stated and enacted) following Macdonald,[62] and across all arenas of the Victorian education policy apparatus. The descriptions of the policy processes and contetsts in Fulcher's work illustrate her proposition, as I have already observed, that policy is made, contested and remade at all levels. In this respect her work coheres with Ball's policy sociology and notions of policy cycles. Her view is 'that policy cannot be theorized in terms of intent ... policy is political practice: it is always the outcome of political states of play and struggle'.[63] In other words, it is theoretically flabby to attempt to explain failings of policy as a problem of its implementation. Policy consists of practices at all levels of its development and implementation and should be made and analysed as such.

In extant studies of policy she highlights: '...the almost non-existent discussion about the relationship between policy and the social theory which guided it.'[64] Accordingly, it is necessary to acknowledge different ways of understanding, talking about and responding to disability and difference. While not trying to sound pompous, our concern here might be described as both ontological and epistemological. I employ these terms to re-emphasize the all too often ignored point that the phenomenon of disability can be understood in very different ways and as a consequence the kinds of knowledge about it will vary and, most importantly, result in different responses to people who are considered or made disabled.

In essence, ontology refers to that branch of philosophy that considers the nature of existence or phenomena. What is disability? Epistemology is a closely related branch of philosophy. Here the investigation concerns the nature of knowledge itself; how explanations and understandings of phenomena are formed, deployed, gather authority and take hold. Policies are not detached, neutral or benign but are constituents of and agents for ways of understanding, maintaining or changing our world. In this respect they are discursive practices that represent particular forms of understanding and interacting. Therefore, as policy analysts such as Ball, Rizvi and Lingard and Fulcher instruct, it is inevitable that policy is characterized by contest and struggle given the competing views of the world that policy actors will have.

Drawing from Foucault's notion of discourse and from the emergent disability studies of the time Fulcher traces a range of representations of disability (see Table 5.3). Accordingly she describes four discourses on disability:

- medical discourse;
- charity discourse;
- lay discourse; and
- rights discourse.

As we noted in Chapter 4 (see Table 4.1) there have been various representations of ways of understanding, talking about and responding to disability. In their work Thomas and Loxley also refer to Martin Soder's presentation of four disability paradigms:

- the medical/clinical perspective;
- the epidemiological approach;
- the adaptability approach;
- the social constructionist approach.[65]

Soder points to an 'epistemological error' in the fourth category by challenging the over-optimistic belief that structures and meanings can be changed by the power of reformist thinking and agitation. Skidmore suggests otherwise. For him, the limitations of sociological accounts of disability reside in their fatalism and the failure to identify credible alternatives supported by evidence.[66]

Perhaps both authors are, in part, correct. Deconstruction, a popular post-modern pastime that allows academics to be playful with language and ideas, can ring hollow in the absence of an attempt to offer propositions or questions that address these most urgent matters of oppression. We need to be vigilant in our quest for paradigmatic purity that we do not lose sight of the nature and impacts of the problem. As Ivan George Morrison puts it: 'I cleaned up my diction and had nothing left to say.'[67] Many, including Raymond Williams, Stuart Hall, Edward Said and Anthony Giddens have warned of the drift of critique into dogma and the forfeiture of analytic sharpness. Paul Gilroy's stark observation that the consignment of the phenomenon of race to the dustbin of history by the discovery of DNA is insufficient to dismantle what he refers to as raciology, and reminds us of the enormity of the task of the project of educational reconstruction.

> Raciology has saturated the discourses in which it circulates. It cannot be readily re-signified or de-signified, and to imagine that its dangerous meanings can be easily re-articulated into benign, democratic forms would be to exaggerate the power of critical and oppositional interests.[68]

In Chapter 4 I expressed my dissatisfaction with attempts to explain the world through the imposition of ordered descriptive categories. Thomas and Loxley register their misgivings about 'theory-shaped critique'.

> Art, theory and research are all examples of artifice: the attempt to draw a narrative, a theme out of the 'monstrousness' and 'abruptness' of life. The theory of our educational scholarship and this applies espe-cially to special education, seeks order.... The disciplines in which theory is framed encourage attempts at explanation in a social world which is singularly lacking in order or intentionality.[69]

Distancing themselves from 'models, theories and intellectual castles' which they argue 'have helped little in understanding in improving learning'[70] and can as Foucault suggests prove a hindrance to understanding, they move to what they describe as an *atheoretical* position. Herein they adopt Bourdieu's notion of theory as a temporary construct – a thinking tool to deal with contingency and change. They are drawn to his predilection for an ensem-ble of concepts to assist the jobbing sociologist.[71] Like Dewey, they propose *small thinking* that embraces specific enquiries that draws them to the par-ticularity of human experience as a field for analysis. Stories become important in meaning making and in the process of constructing scenarios for change. In this respect narratives become research tools[72] that bring together events and emotions in a process that Ricoeur calls 'emplotment'. I hope that I have not done violence to Thomas and Loxley's refreshingly iconoclastic book in my rendition of some of its themes? Theirs is an important contribution to the field that endorses intellectual eclecticism.

In this there is an important alliance to be struck with Gillborn's description of the tools of Critical Race Theory (CRT). Some of the key themes of CRT that intersect with our interests in inclusive education are best summarized by Gillborn himself:

> CRT does not offer a finished set of propositions that claim to explain all current situations and predict what will occur under a certain set of

conditions; rather it is a set of interrelated observations about the significance of racism and how it operates in contemporary Western society ... CRT is very much a work in progress: CRT is neither dogmatic, exclusionary nor inflexible.[73]

'CRT', as Gillborn explains through the fictitious agents, the Professor and Steve, whom he uses incisively in *Racism and education: Coincidence or conspiracy?*, as they wend their way home from the 'Dog and Duck' (one of George Orwell's favourite drinking spots), is 'very much alive and changing', it's orientation is not cerebral – it is passionate about activism and it is interested in the intersections between race and other forms of exclusion and oppression such as class and gender.[74] Here we return to our earlier discussions and to Julie Allan's depiction of inclusive education as an ethical project[75] and to Stephen Ball's call to recover 'a language for and of education articulated in terms of ethics, moral obligations and values'.[76]

Following on from our discussion of disability and the meanings we attach to it is the second observation that I wish to highlight from Fulcher's *Disabling policies*: namely, her determination to demonstrate that 'language matters'. She describes the discrepancy between 'the literature (on education policy-making) and the political reality (she) saw'.[77] Most models of education policy-making available to her at that time failed to reflect the existence and intensity of struggle in the policy process, merely offering loose explanations of gaps between policy (theory) as government decisions and practice as the work of implementation by bureaucracies and schools.[78] The struggles and contests in integration policy in Victoria were waged across the education organization and the community at large through the deployment of language as 'an instrument of power'. 'I saw that *how* language is used *matters*. It was the instrument of power.'[79] To illustrate her point, she describes the way in which the term integration which had been offered as a force for democratizing education for children who were disabled by the processes of schooling became a means for identifying children with disabilities, impairments and problems in schooling and delaying their admission to school until additional resources were found for teachers in classrooms. It is important to acknowledge that following disputes over the right of every child to be enrolled in its neighbourhood school, there was increased teacher union agitation and the Minister acquiesced by inserting a caveat to explain that while students would be enrolled in their local school, their admission to that school could be delayed until the resources required for their education were forthcoming to the school. This influenced the way in which the resources required for integration were calculated. Unsurprisingly it was an inflationary influence. The higher the claim, the longer the delay. Harry Daniels has also alerted us to the corrupting affect of linking diagnosis and resource distribution.[80]

We noted how the report's identification of students with 'disabilities, impairments and problems in schooling' led to the discovery of a new category of educational defect: the child with 'problems in schooling'. Consequently the target population for integration was not only children in segregated schools, but also children who were difficult to manage in the regular school. Paradoxically the ranks of the disabled were swelling as teachers and guidance officers (school psychologists) diagnosed more of the regular school students being in need of integration support. At the time, I remember my colleagues John Lewis, Sandy Cook and Brian Sword who had a large research grant to track the implementation of integration, referring to the 'limp and twitch hunt' that was mounted across state schools in Victoria at the time. Ironically, integration effectively reduced the tolerance of schools to difference as they sought to calibrate and categorize their students in order to apply for a new source of funding.

The *integration child* was a marker of separation and exclusion. It was a public assignation to the ranks of a surplus population in need of expert intervention and paid minding through the support of an integration aide. In too many instances the purchase of the integration aide was a down payment on collective indifference. The teacher should attend to the legitimate regular school children while the aides would do what they could to translate lessons and see to it that the child didn't impinge on the learning of others. This was certainly not the case for all, but it remains a common feature of what people now call inclusive or special needs education. Of course this is a global phenomenon that we will explore further – people in education in England feel little, if any, discomfort in talking about EBD and SEN children; in New Zealand they talk of their ORRS kids; in Queensland disabled children, up until about six years ago were administered through the 'low incidence unit' (an offensive and imprecise way to speak of children as the number of 'incidents' was swelling exponentially). As in other parts of Australia these children were discussed as special needs children, behaviour problems and more poignantly as 'integration kids'.

Some six years after the publication of *Integration in Victorian education*, a conference was convened in Melbourne at which senior civil servants from the states and territories were invited to describe the state of play in their jurisdiction with regard to integration. I remember one state representative declaring that they were so appalled by the negative impact of labelling on the educational and social progress of children that they abolished the use of the polyphony of diagnoses and acronyms used to categorize 'special children'. Accordingly they thenceforth referred only to group A and group B children! I laughed into the silent reception of this absurdity and wondered why I was the only one laughing. Notwithstanding the stockpile of research on streaming, setting and banding from Rosenthal and Jacobson's classic *Pygmalion in the classroom study*[81] and Good and

Brophy's *Looking in classrooms*,[82] to more recent research reviews by Slavin,[83] Harlen and Malcolm[84] and Ireson and Hallam[85] that collectively cast doubt on its educational and social value, teachers continue to establish hierarchies in and across classrooms. Moreover, in recognition of the social and psychological impacts of streaming, they also pursue this policy through diversions such as naming classes by colours, animals or points of local significance. As Ted Sizer counsels, the children are watching.[86] They know the real meaning of the euphemisms we use to deflect from the practice of streaming. They soon work out if blue is better than red. They know the difference between Year 5 Kangaroo, Year 5 Koala and Year 5 Road-kill.

My point, though drawn out, is very simple. How we describe the world reflects certain understandings and it determines how we reproduce that world. In effect then, the special child is the problem. After all, it is they who have the defective pathology and are seen to be in need of integration. Removed from the analytic gaze is the role of the complex amalgam of factors in schools that more or less disable or enable children. We also fail to acknowledge that we are accepting uncritically an expert medical view of disability and in so doing denying the voices of disabled people and their contribution to a very different and potentially emancipatory (for all) view of the world.[87] Len Barton declared that Special Educational Needs is a euphemism for the failure of schools to educate all children.[88]

A story that reflects the ineptitude that surrounds people's attempts to pursue inclusive education comes to mind. It is drawn from the time when I worked at the Queensland University of Technology. Upon the conclusion of one of my lectures to a cohort of initial teacher education students, the students roused themselves from their slumber and moved out of the theatre. A young woman called Becky approached me with another girl whose arm she held. Becky told me that things I had been talking struck a chord with her experience of school as a young disabled woman. We had a number of conversations and I asked her to write about her experiences as the world needed to know her story and comprehend her way of understanding disablement. Amazingly she told me of how when she was diagnosed with macular degeneration and rapidly lost her vision in primary (elementary) school, the school felt that it was faced with the decision about whether to integrate her or send her to a school for the blind. She said that it seemed obvious to her that going to unfamiliar surroundings would add to her difficulty in getting around school. Being with people and teachers who didn't know her, she thought, would set her learning back. Her mother shared this view and believed that in fact Becky would have to know more and do better than the other kids to prove her value to an unaccommodating world. She therefore thought that the more specialized and restricted curriculum offerings at a special school were not sufficient to meet that challenge. The primary school was unconvinced and advised a psychologist to give Becky an intelligence test to see if she could be integrated. Becky put it bluntly: whose intelligence was in doubt! It was a sight-based test and they had to read it all out to me, describe pictures and try to make allowances for time. The science and the rigour of the Intelligence Quotient had stumbled.

The story may well seem apocryphal and is, I dare say, distorted by my repeated telling. What amazes me is that when I do relate stories like the ones throughout this book to groups of people, different but similar stories are returned to me with force. What should be extraordinary tales are not. People with tearful eyes tell of their children's 'emptied satchels'. The stories are too frequent to ignore, too painful to dismiss as misplaced sentiment. This is the politics of everyday exclusions – this is education policy at work.

6 From segregation to integration to inclusion and back (a policy reprise)

> He is walking in one of those leafy suburbs of London where the presence of a man like him still attracts curious half-glances. His jacket and tie encourage a few of the passers-by to relax a little, but he can see that others are actively suppressing the urge to cross the road. It is painfully clear that, as far as some people are concerned, he simply doesn't belong in this part of the city.
>
> Caryl Phillips, *In the Falling Snow*

Introduction

This chapter continues the discussion of education policy and will expose the way in which policy frequently failed to embrace and mobilize new ways of thinking about children, difference, learning and schooling. An interview with Michel Foucault was conducted in 1983 and later published in the *University of Brussels review*,[1] with the title: *What is called 'punishing'?* In that interview, he reflects upon his reasons for writing *Discipline and punish: The birth of the prison*. In doing so he makes some telling remarks about institutional change.

> ...but I think that when one engages in a project of transformation or renovation, it's very important to know not only what the institutions and their real effects are, but also what type of thought sustains them: What elements of that system of rationality can still be accepted? What is the part, on the other hand, that deserves to be cast aside, abandoned, transformed, and so on? It's the same thing that I had tried to do with respect to the history of psychiatric institutions.

Commencing this chapter in the middle of our consideration of policy is an acknowledgement of a rhetorical shift from integration to inclusion. It is a reminder to continue to expose networks of events, theories and practices that sustain exclusion, so that, following Foucault, we can come to understand 'the system of rationality' that ventilates exclusion. Put simply, there have been clear adjustments to language to suggest a more inclusive approach to education, but the 'system of rationality', or the way we think, is remarkably static.

The shift from integration to inclusion may be regarded by some as momentous, by others as a continuation of old practices under the veneer of a new lexicon.[2] Integration policies are best described by using Bernstein's term absorption.[3] For Bernstein inclusion is a fundamental right and requirement for a democratic education. He is meticulous in explaining the complex properties of inclusion and warns against absorption or assimilation as a proxy for inclusion.[4] His warnings underline the critiques across the disability movement of what Wolf Wolfensberger originally referred to as theories and practices of normalization prior to settling upon the more innocuous term, Social Role Valorisation (SRV).[5] In this respect Bernstein and also by implication Oliver, in his critique of SRV, are in agreement with Touraine.[6] He dismisses liberal communitarianization as a conservative force that undermines democracy. As Touraine says as we observed earlier in the book:

> The struggle for the liberation of cultural minorities can lead to their communitarianization, or in other words their subordination to an authoritarian cultural power.[7]

Inclusive education, as demonstrated by the shortcomings of integration in Australia and mainstreaming in the USA, is not achieved through charitable dispensations to excluded minorities. It is not about the movement of people from their tenancy in the social margins into unchanging institutions. Doing so redraws the boundaries for the containment of marginalized people. Structural violence is deepened. Integration requires the objects of policy to forget their former status as outsiders and fit comfortably into what remain deeply hostile institutional arrangements. There is an expectation that they will assume an invisible presence as they accept the dominant cultural order. McLaren suggests that neo-liberal assimilation is organized around a degree of social amnesia:

> Diversity that somehow constitutes itself as a harmonious ensemble of benign cultural spheres is a conservative and liberal model of multiculturalism that, in my mind, deserves to be jettisoned because, when we try to make culture an undisturbed space of harmony and agreement where social relations exist with cultural forms of uninterrupted accords we subscribe to a form of social amnesia in which we forget that all knowledge is forged in histories that are played out in the field of social antagonisms.[8]

Inclusive education therefore requires that we seek understandings of exclusion from the perspectives of those who are devalued and rendered marginal or surplus by the dominant culture of the regular school.[9] Giroux refers to these people as 'disposable populations', the casualties of neo-liberalism. His forthright prose returns us to the political economy of exclusion and to the architecture of collective indifference:

> The varied populations devalued and made disposable under neo-liberalism occupy a globalized space of ruthless politics in which the categories of 'citizen' and 'democratic representation', once integral to national politics, are no longer recognized. In the past, people who were marginalized by class and race could at least expect a modicum of support from the social state, either through an array of limited social provisions or from employers who recognized that they still had some value as part of an army of unemployed labour. This is no longer true. Under the ruthless dynamics of neoliberal ideology, there has been a shift away from the possibility of getting ahead economically and living a life of dignity to the much more deadly task of struggling to stay alive.[10]

Education jurisdictions, as I have argued throughout this book, are complicit in the task of calibrating and categorizing young people for social futures or social endings. Inclusive education is not a technical problem to be solved through an ensemble of compensatory measures; be they adjustments to the curriculum, the physical arrangement of the school, the form of the test and the provision of assistants to interpret, as best they can, the teachers' instructions. Such approaches, as we will see in this chapter, fail to challenge the architecture of exclusion. Inclusive education ought to declare itself as a far more radical and creative enterprise. It is simultaneously a tactic and an aspiration. It is also a statement of value.

Norwich registers his concern that stipulating inclusion '...as a universal concept representing a "pure" value, that accepts no degrees, conditions or limits, leads to a conceptual dead end'.[11] In return he offers what he calls a dilemmatic approach to confronting the difficulties of pursuing inclusion in the area of disability that is carefully constructed through a reconsideration of the legal, political and philosophical frameworks presented by Martha Minow,[12] Robert Dahl,[13] Isaiah Berlin,[14] Goodhart[15] and Stocker.[16] Also enlisted, through the interpretation of Terzi,[17] is Amartya Sen and Martha Nussbaum's conceptualization of a capability approach to addressing difference and inequality.

> The capability approach argues that equality and social arrangements should be evaluated in the space of capabilities, that is, in the space of the real freedoms that people have to achieve valued functionings that are constitutive of their well-being.[18]

In *Rationality and freedom*, Sen outlines a different notion of poverty and deprivation that addresses the capability or '...lack of opportunity that one has to lead a minimally acceptable life, which can be influenced by a number of considerations, including of course personal income, but also physical and environmental characteristics'.[19] This may include variables such as access to an education that leads to viable social destinations or access to health care. He revisits the idea of capability and freedom with specific reference to disability in *The idea of justice*. Herein, he examines the 'earning handicap' and its magnification through the 'conversion handicap'.[20] Citing Kuklys's[21] study of poverty in the United Kingdom in 2004, he reveals that while 17.9 per cent of individuals lived in families with incomes below the poverty line, 'if attention is shifted to individuals in families with a disabled member, the percentage of such individuals living below the poverty line is 23.1 per cent'.[22]

> This gap of about 5 percentage points largely reflects the income handicap associated with disability and the care of the disabled. If the conversion handicap is now introduced, and note is taken of the need for more income to ameliorate the disadvantages of disability, the proportion of individuals in families with disabled members jumps up to 47.4 per cent, a gap of nearly 20 percentage points over the share of individuals below the poverty line (17.9 per cent)...[23]

Herein we observe the intersections of disadvantage, the multiplier of inequality and the capability concept of equity. Justice is not achieved by the identification of merit through a liberal education and the advancement of deserving individuals. Recognition of disadvantage and injustice, followed by the redistribution of resources are key tactics for reducing exclusion. The inevitability of compromise embodied in a dilemmatic approach to inclusive education is a conservative option that will not alter the relations of inequality. Daniel Dorling takes this argument further by proposing that present articulations of elitism in education and social organization have established a view that exclusion is inevitable, necessary and unchangeable.[24] Acknowledging Crawford's Canada-based research that suggests that segregated special education makes transitions to the paid workforce less likely,[25] we are compelled to rethink neo-liberal assertions about placement in segregated special education as a question of choice or a humane response to the unsympathetic culture of the regular school. Neither option is tenable; choice will only exist through the radical reform of the regular school so that inclusion becomes a viable option.

Norwich's application of a dilemmatic approach to questions of disability and difference in education has a number of useful elements to build strategies for change, but at its heart (perhaps by omission) there seems to be a conservatism born of insufficient interrogation of the foundations of special educational needs and the structure and cultures of schooling.

From integration to inclusion

Important distinctions were made when in the latter part of the 1980s the practice of integration was declared to be 'inherently assimilationist'.[26] Jenny Corbett and I reflected upon the shortcomings of integration policy at the time:

> Central to our vigilance is the continuing need to guard against the conceptual and practical reduction of inclusion as this decade's version of integration. Integration is inherently assimilationist. It holds firm to a traditional notion of ideal types, both of people and institutions. According to this model the emphasis is upon deficit, diagnosis, categorisation and individual treatment.[27]

We distinguished inclusive education from integration by suggesting that the former is a project of political struggle and cultural change, and that the latter while generating political tensions did not challenge the dominant culture.

> The challenge for the integrationist is how to regulate the flow of different students:
>
> - what streams they go into in the regular school;
> - what additional resources will be required to contain these defective and difficult students in the regular school (albeit at the margins); or
> - what special settings will they occupy outside of regular educational provision.[28]

Inclusive education was, and remains, for many activists and researchers an attempt to insinuate a democratic discourse and approach within educational decision-making. Alternative understandings of disability and school failure dislodge the traditional special educational theory and practices that emphasized defect, expert diagnosis and remediation. Difference is not only seen as natural, it is promoted as an educational and social asset. The beneficiaries of inclusion therefore are not just those we have deigned to bring into the school. Rejecting pity and charity, inclusive education makes everyone more socially knowledgeable and teaches us that injustice is not a feature of the laws of nature. Injustice and exclusion are constructed and sustained by the choices of powerful people. Inclusive education is therefore not a formulation of ideas about special educational needs; it is a theory of and tactic for education and social reform.

The agenda is therefore bold. Inclusive school cultures require fundamental changes in educational thinking about children, curriculum, pedagogy and school organization.[29] The notion that inclusive education is about placing disabled children in unchanging regular schools is reductive. The evidence of permanent school exclusion in England is abundant.[30] While there has been success in holding the apparent volume of exclusions static over time to meet targets, exclusion is opaque. The expansion of alternative provisions for difficult and disruptive students points to hidden exclusion. In his 2009 report to the Brown government in England on special educational needs and parental confidence in the system, Brian Lamb reveals pupil referral units (PRUs), in which 75 per cent of the students have a statement for emotional disturbance or behaviour disorders, to be little more than a de facto segregated special school. Because the goal of transition back to the regular school is unlikely, the PRU represents a form of exclusion. Permanent exclusion, suspension, in-school exclusion and 'unofficial exclusions' show the intransigence of disaffection. Considering the enduring disproportional rates of exclusion for Caribbean boys in England from Tomlinson's[31] work some thirty years ago, to more recent work by Gillborn,[32] structural racism becomes more apparent. Black Caribbean students, reports Gillborn,[33] were six times more likely to be excluded than White students in England in the 1990s. On the basis of more recent OfSTED and DfES reports on the exclusion of black pupils he concludes that:

> ...there is compelling evidence that the over-representation of African Caribbean students in exclusions is the result of harsher treatment by school, rather than simple differences in behaviour by students.[34]

Inclusive education calls on our ability to recognize and understand the mechanics of exclusion. It then invites us to work, bit-by-bit, towards reconstructing ourselves, and our approaches to education consistent with changing contexts and changing populations in new times.

In the past two decades, there has been a simultaneous abandonment of the usage of integration as a policy descriptor across education jurisdictions globally and the adoption of the term inclusive education. The changing of the language of policy has received impetus from a number of sources. Supranational organizations such as UNESCO, UNICEF, OECD, the World Bank and the Asian Development Bank have increasingly developed Education For All (EFA) programmes under the rubric of inclusive education. Human Rights Conventions including the Convention on the Rights of Persons with Disabilities and the passing of anti-discrimination and Disability Rights legislation in countries around the world have impacted on education jurisdictions. Let us briefly consider these two catalysts for change in reverse order before examining a series of key issues in inclusive education policy.

Making education policy inclusive in an era of human rights?

For Alain Touraine,[35] 'The clearest manifestations of a society's spirit and organization are its juridical rules and its educational programme.' Globally, as Reiser,[36] Norwich[37] and Artiles and Dyson[38] have noted, there has been a progressive movement to combat discrimination and exclusion of disabled people through the ratification of international human rights conventions and national anti-discrimination legislation. The Convention on the Rights of Persons with Disabilities was adopted by the United Nations General Assembly in New York on 13 December, 2006. There are now 144 country signatories to the Convention, with eighty-eight signatories to the Optional Protocol that sets out the provisions for individuals to appeal against matters of discrimination to the Committee on the Rights of Persons with Disabilities. Of the signatories to the Convention there have been eighty-four ratifications and fifty-two ratifications of the Optional Protocol.[39] Article 24 of the Convention sets out the provisions of the agreement for education. It needs to be acknowledged that some country signatories, including the UK, have applied their ratification with 'reservations' about certain sections of the Convention, including Article 24 concerning education and persons with disabilities.

Of course many of the signatory nations have their own human rights and anti-discrimination legislation, which includes provisions to apply for discrimination on the grounds of disability. Like the UN Convention, anti-discrimination legislation carries caveats and exemptions. For example, the 1992 Australian Disability Discrimination Act (DDA) exempts the Department of Immigration from its provisions. This is interesting when considered against the backdrop of Australia's immigration history. The European colonizers systematically practised genocide against Australia's indigenous people. Following more open forms of genocide, cultural genocide was applied through the separation of children from their families and the encouragement of inter-breeding in the belief that Aboriginality could be systematically eliminated through this form of marginalization or eugenics.[40] Posturing as a fortress island on the Asia-Pacific rim, the first federal government of the Commonwealth of Australia established the Immigration Restriction Act (1901).

It is important to recall that South Africa modelled its infamous Apartheid laws on Australian colonial governments' Natives Protection Acts. Indeed, the state government of Queensland passed its own legislation to deport Pacific Islanders who had been forcibly brought to the sugar plantations as a cheap labour supply. The labour movement was very slow to relinquish discriminatory stands against the immigration of non-white people to Australia. Immigration policy was enforced through a dictation test, that could be administered in any language, to select suitable 'New Australians' and expel others. Though there were relaxations, restrictions on immigration to Australia on the basis of skin colour endured until the passing of the Racial Discrimination Act in 1975. Over the years such practices quite properly brought international condemnation. There would be widespread, though not universal, outrage if a colour ban were applied now. Not so for the blocking of disabled people seeking to immigrate to Australia. This does not register as a matter for scrutiny.

Parallels can be found in disablist teacher industrial organizations' reservations about inclusive education on the grounds of teachers' working conditions or student welfare. There was a lengthy delay reaching into a second decade when attempting to establish national disability standards required by the DDA for education in Australia. Struggles over finance ground the will of governments to a standstill and lay bare the limits of teacher associations' commitment to equity. In public policy and industrial relations inclusion is a burden rather than an aspiration. The costly and elaborate infrastructure of exclusion is sustained and described as choice or a 'range of placement options'. In effect, this simply allows us to 'look away' as some children are inducted into a residual education.

It remains a major achievement to secure disability discrimination legislation against which matters of discrimination on the grounds of disability may be tested at law. The drafting and ratification of disability discrimination legislation represents the culmination of long and costly battles by disabled people and their allies to secure rights of participation in community life. Indeed, the history of disabled children's participation in regular schooling is a history of political struggle and litigation to extend provisions in education legislation and regulations.[41]

Anti-discrimination legislation does not in or of itself constitute a culture of inclusion, even where compliance is achieved.[42] Too frequently, 'clauses of conditionality'[43] within the legislation can be applied to create exemptions and subvert the spirit if not the letter of the law. In Australia, the clause 'undue institutional hardship' in the provisions of the DDA is often invoked to deny the rights of access and participation in schools. The UK, though a signatory to the United Nations Convention on the Rights of Persons with Disabilities, registered its reservations on key sections of Article 24: Education where there were deemed to be resource implications. My point is not to suggest that extraordinary circumstances may not make inclusion difficult and expensive. The point is to reflect the expansive room for interpretive latitude.

The imagination and creativity applied by education leaders to maintain institutional rigidities is sometimes staggering. I can report an instance where a principal of a small rural school in Australia attempted to prevent the enrolment of a student who used a wheelchair. In the event of a bomb scare and the enforced evacuation of the school, he argued, other children would be held up behind this child in the corridor. This case ought to be straightforward at law, and more importantly as an ethical issue. Sadly it is an instance where a school will expend valuable resources in its fortification from the threat of the dangerously disabled child.

To underline this point, I recall being asked to be an expert witness for a school in a disability discrimination case. The school had excluded a child with Down's syndrome on the grounds that because the child walked home alone and was unattended until his sole parent returned from her job in the evening, the school's duty of care was compromised. I informed the school that I would much prefer to assist them in finding ways to support the parent so the child could remain at school than deepen their struggle against the usual rights of access and participation and intensify the hostility on both sides. My status as an expert was withdrawn.

When we move into normative questions about cognitive abilities and behaviour it becomes much more complicated and emotionally and financially destructive. Presently, the burden of proof of discrimination on the grounds of disability rests with the 'heroic complainant'.[44] The case of *Alex Purvis* (on behalf of Daniel Hoggan) v. *The State of New South Wales* (Department of Education and Training) is illustrative of the vicissitudes of seeking redress under the provisions of disability discrimination legislation.[45] Mr and Mrs Purvis claimed their foster-child Daniel who had residual intellectual disabilities, a visual disability and epilepsy from a brain injury during his infancy, had been subject to discrimination on the basis of his disabilities. After completing his primary (elementary) schooling in a regular school, the Purvis family applied for admission to South Grafton High School in the Australian state of New South Wales. The school rejected the application. Mr Purvis filed a complaint with the Human Rights and Equal Opportunities Commission (HREOC).

Following a period of conciliation between the school, the regional authorities from the New South Wales Department of Education and Training, the family, the teachers' union and HREOC, Daniel was enrolled in the school at the commencement of 1997. Daniel was suspended five times in his first year of high school on the grounds of violent behaviour and was excluded from the school at the end of the year. Mr Purvis lodged an official complaint with the HREOC, which heard the complaint over a period of twenty-three days in 1999. Commissioner Graeme Innes adjudicated that the New South Wales Department of Education and Training had been in breach of the Disability Discrimination Act (1992) (Commonwealth) on the 13 November, 2000.[46] The New South Wales Department of Education and Training appealed to the Federal Court under section 5(1)(f) of the Administrative Decisions (Judicial Review) Act 1977 (Commonwealth). The judge, believing that HREOC had 'erred' set aside decision and remitted the case back to HREOC. Mr Purvis appealed to the Full Court of the Federal Court and the appeal was dismissed. Mr Purvis then appealed to the High Court of Australia. In a 5–2 split decision handed down on 11 November, 2003 it ruled against the appeal.

Of course this report on the Purvis case is necessarily brief and trimmed of detail. The point of highlighting it is to establish the complexity and the considerable emotional and financial costs associated with attempts to test a society's spirit and organization through juridical processes.[47] This is amplified when we learn that a requirement of the implementation of the DDA (Australia) (1992) (Commonwealth) was that State and Commonwealth departments of education were to draft and implement 'disability standards'.

The main purpose of the Disability Standards for Education 2005 is to clarify the obligations of education and training service providers, and the rights of people with disability, under the Disability Discrimination Act 1992 (the DDA). The Standards were developed in consultation with education, training and disability groups and the Human Rights and Equal Opportunity Commission.[48]

The DDA was enacted in 1992 yet it took some *thirteen* years for the Commonwealth and State Education jurisdictions to agree on and publish the Disability Standards for Education. At the heart of the considerable delays were anxieties about the locus of the burden of cost for the 'just and secure society'.[49] At best the juridical system reflects an ambivalent spirit despite rhetorical flourishes of safeguarding the just society.

A postscript

The 'Purvis Case' is frequently cited. It has established a precedent for exclusion. By referring to this family's difficult struggle against the state as the *Purvis Case*, we seem to objectify and diminish the human dimension of the real people involved. And here I refer not just to the complainants. Trying to maintain family and work as you struggle through the costly legal system is, to say the least, onerous. There are numerous casualties in testing the provisions of protective legislation. It simultaneously fractures and unites communities. And what is the nature of a victory if one is secured? The entry into an institution where one is not wanted is the prize. This is absolutely right and the point of the law, but it remains a pyrrhic prize nonetheless. The law does not in and of itself make an inclusive culture, but it remains an important tactical step and a force for changing community understanding as has been demonstrated elsewhere through disability discrimination law.[50]

Why do I highlight the Purvis complaint? I had been invited by a friend in the New South Wales Education department to run a workshop on school discipline. At the end of the day, Dimity Purvis approached me to tell me of their struggle to retain their son Daniel's enrolment in his school. 'Is it a case of discrimination?' she asked. I thought that it was. There were successive phone calls from the Purvis's, each time asking if I thought they should pursue a challenge first through the Education Department and then through the Human Rights and Equal Opportunities Commission. I lost contact with them, but from time to time heard about their unfolding legal saga. I last saw them before the final judgement. They remained hopeful, but were visibly weary. I felt culpable for putting them through such emotional and financial difficulty.

How would I respond to them knowing what I now know about the pursuit of justice through law? The law and justice should not be conflated; they are altogether different propositions. Perhaps I would counsel in the same way, but I think that I would also try to look for other ways that avoid the legal processes to stake a claim where possible. However, all parties were convinced before embarking on this tempestuous legal journey that all other options had been exhausted. This case is testimony to the truth in Touraine's stark observation that our juridical rules and educational programmes are the litmus test of the spirit of a society.

Language and inclusion after the Salamanca Statement and Framework for Action on Special Needs Education

Representatives from 155 countries and 150 organizations met in 1990 at the World Conference entitled *Education for all* in Jomtien, Thailand under the aegis of the United Nations Educational, Scientific and Cultural Organisation (UNESCO), the United Nations Development Programme (UNDP), the United Nations Fund for Population Activity (UNFPA), the United Nations International Children's Emergency Fund (UNICEF) and the World Bank. The participants at the Jomtien EFA Conference pledged to harness international resources to universalize basic (primary) education and reduce illiteracy by the year 2000. Six education goals were established:

- Expand and improve comprehensive early childhood care and education, especially for the most vulnerable and disadvantaged children.
- Ensure that by 2015 all children, particularly girls, those in difficult circumstances, and those belonging to ethnic minorities, have access to and complete, free, and compulsory primary education of good quality.
- Ensure that the learning needs of all young people and adults are met through equitable access to appropriate learning and life-skills programs.
- Achieve a 50% improvement in adult literacy by 2015, especially for women, and equitable access to basic and continuing education for all adults.
- Eliminate gender disparities in primary and secondary education by 2005, and achieve gender equality in education by 2015, with a focus on ensuring girls' full and equal access to and achievement in basic education of good quality.
- Improve all aspects of the quality of education and ensure the excellence of all so that recognized and measurable learning outcomes are achieved by all, especially in literacy, numeracy and essential life skills.[51]

Taking a lead from the Jomtien proclamation on Education for All (EFA), the World Conference on Special Needs Education: Access and Quality, held in the city of Salamanca in Spain in June 1994 brought together delegates from ninety-two governments and twenty-five organizations. The conference culminated in the production of the now famous Salamanca Statement and Framework for Action on Special Needs Education.[52]

We believe and proclaim that:

- every child has a fundamental right to education, and must be given the opportunity to achieve and maintain an acceptable level of learning;
- every child has unique characteristics, interests, abilities and learning needs;
- education systems should be designed and educational programmes implemented to take into account the wide diversity of these characteristics and needs;
- those with special educational needs must have access to regular schools which should accommodate them within a child-centred pedagogy capable of meeting these needs;
- regular schools with this inclusive orientation are the most effective means of combating discriminatory attitudes, creating welcoming communities, building an inclusive society and achieving education for all; moreover, they provide an effective education to the majority of children and improve the efficiency and ultimately the cost-effectiveness of the entire education system.[53]

The Salamanca Statement has become a linguistic and policy touchstone enlisted to support both those who argue for what is spuriously referred to as 'full inclusion' and also those who frame conditions around the location and duration of inclusion.

Full inclusion is, however, a spurious proposition. Cascade models as devised and legitimated in the rationality of traditional special education[54] reinforce the conditional tenure of the defective child as they are granted dispensation to be present for selected activities and classes. One is included or one is not included. Fractions of inclusion time or place are vulgar fractions. This lexical contortionism comes from the same stable that offers us 'reverse inclusion'[55] as a progressive educational proposition. Reverse inclusion refers to the practice of placing so-called normal children in a special class with disabled students. At one level they may be correct – children who are escorted to the segregated setting to do their community service may learn about exclusion. I am more inclined to believe that the blanket of benevolence in which such initiatives are wrapped smothers critical engagement.

In a similar vein, attempts have been made to teach students about disability by blindfolding and leading them through obstacle courses, or by consigning them to a wheelchair for a day. These experiences, it is claimed, foster understanding of what it means to be a disabled person and thereby builds tolerance. There are problems with this approach that fosters a superficial engagement and weak analysis. First, we ought to reconsider the concept of tolerance and the unequal power relations from which it proceeds. Second, the vicarious discomfort of bumping into a wall or finding one's progress impeded by a narrow doorway or a set of steps means very little if it is not connected to analyses of the structural violence of disablism and the way in which particular kinds of knowledge or systems of rationality establish injustice as the natural order. These 'feel good' activities are most frequently consistent with the neo-liberal delusion that Barry Troyna identified in the practice in schools of holding samosa, sari and steel band days to celebrate ethnic difference on the one hand, and failing to engage with the institutional racism that produce unequal educational outcomes.[56] Deflection from the minutiae of racism and disablement in the structures, practices, policies and cultures of schooling compromises claims of inclusiveness. These activities are often self-serving nonsense. To tolerate is not to include. Structural violence requires confrontation and direct retaliation. I will return to the ongoing problem of language in inclusive education shortly.

Following Daniels and Garner,[57] Artiles and Dyson claim that the extraordinary power and worldwide influence of the Salamanca Statement comes from its 'ability to deal in absolutes'.[58] They track a progression of the logic of the statement from a reliance on declarations of human rights to assertions about the uniqueness of individual needs 'and thence into assertions that education systems should be designed around uniqueness', and 'that children with special educational needs must attend regular schools'.[59] The regular school will then, it is assumed, deliver educational and social benefits. Where the Statement is wanting is in the provision of detail to suggest the kinds of reforms required for regular schooling to become more inclusive. As Norwich reminds us:

> Though the Salamanca Statement about inclusive education makes strong statements about inclusive schooling, it only asserts the fundamental right to education, not to an inclusive education.[60]

The Salamanca Statement, and the successive activity under the Education For All banner, provided an overdue platform for educators, civil servants, activists and researchers of many hues to adopt a general acceptance of the discourse of inclusive education. We celebrate and struggle with the consequences of this.

Talking of words. The building blocks for a system of rationality

In his *Poem for a dead poet*, Roger McGough wryly muses on the achievement of a departed wordsmith:

He had a way with language
Images flocked around him like birds,
St. Francis he was,
Of the words. Words?
Why he could almost make 'em talk.[61]

In the sphere of public policy, words are instruments tactically employed in the service of power. They are made to talk in particular ways for specific ends. The celebrated economist John Kenneth Galbraith wrote an essay entitled *The economics of innocent fraud* shortly before his death at the age of 98 in 2006. The essay excavates the foundations of managerial authority. Notwithstanding the solemn title, Galbraith playfully admits that: 'A marked enjoyment can be found in identifying self-serving belief and contrived nonsense.'[62] My interest in his essay was aroused by his description of the process of what he calls *innocent fraud* whereby capitalism underwent name changes to assign itself a benign face to maintain the confidence and cooperation of the masses. While '*free enterprise*' was short-lived, '*the market system*' is applied as a description for capitalism to build a sense of independence and consistency with notions of the common good. Though the form of economic operation has undergone adjustment over time, the assumptions and values of capitalism still apply:

> One must accept a continuing divergence between approved belief – what I have elsewhere called conventional wisdom – and the reality. And in the end, not surprisingly, it is the reality that counts.[63]

The discursive dexterity of vested interest renders something into that which it is not. Then public naïveté and 'innocence' fuse to accept the 'fraud'.[64]

7 Building authority, dividing populations and getting away with it (exposing a system of rationality)

> It is about a way of seeing that requires humility, so that one can recognize sameness of self in the other. It is about the mutuality that can exist between us, if we so choose.
>
> James Orbinski, *An imperfect offering: Humanitarian action in the twenty-first century*. Toronto, Anchor, p. 4

In this chapter I will suggest that shortcomings in inclusive education policy-making may be attributed to two major shortcomings. First is what has been characterized as its alleged lack of conceptual clarity.[1] Second, and this emanates from the lack of stipulation and absence of conceptual clarity, is the opportunity thereby provided to deploy inclusive education for various and oftentimes contradictory ends. Let me offer a general explanation for this before attempting to demonstrate it through the detail of policy issues.

Fighting on all fronts

Many scholars and activists dedicated to inclusive education as a political struggle against unequal power relations that oppress marginalized people offer a shared view that inclusive education is not solely concerned with the education of disabled children and adults, though it found its voice from the desire to build a critique of special education knowledge and practices.[2] In an interview with Julie Allan and myself, Len Barton describes the motivation of inclusive education research in the following terms:

> One of the interests has been clearly to try to understand the nature of discrimination in its many complex and contradictory forms. That is something I have become increasingly sensitive to and aware of. These issues are profoundly multifaceted and therefore demand a range of perspectives to try to grapple with some of the concerns that are involved. Issues about the nature of discrimination, issues about the question of change...[3]

Inclusive education should never be default vocabulary for Special Educational Needs. The moment we allow inclusive education to be special education for new times is the moment we submit to collective indifference. This is the point at which the focus on the school, the curriculum and the practice of classroom teaching and learning fades and is replaced by old and powerful notions of defective children. Simultaneously, the classroom teacher is encouraged to think of inclusive education as an additional part of their classroom practice that is best achieved through the enlistment of specialists and teacher aides. In times where narrow conceptions of standards have compromised the educational imagination, these additional children threaten the achievement of school performance targets and they become the conspicuous casualties under friendly accountability fire. Their care and educational support becomes a means for schools to have them removed from the figures that count. Alison Kearney is incisive in depicting the New Zealand rendition of this process. Her research gathers evidence of the general 'perception that disabled students are less entitled to human rights than non-disabled students'; of a lack of accountability across the New Zealand education system in matters of disability, a belief that inclusive education should be predicated on issues of funding, prejudice and the intersection of race, class and disablement.[4]

The following tale may be apocryphal. Nonetheless, it is an application of Ken Kesey's epigram in *One flew over the cuckoo's nest*, namely that, 'This is the truth even if it didn't happen.'[5]

A teacher in London once told me that OfSTED inspectors came visiting the PRU she worked at. There is a published schedule detailing the review criteria to guide inspectors in their evaluation of the performance of these second-tier education facilities. She says a student, when greeted by an inspector in the corridor, quipped, 'You're the reason we are here.' The story may be an elaboration of events. The message stands; is the so-called EBD (Emotional and Behaviour Disorder) student a metaphor for ESLTI (English School League Table Insurance)? In other words, to what extent do we use categories of emotional and behaviour disorders to evacuate those students who threaten a school's standing on performance measures such as nationally published school league tables?

If inclusive education is not special education, what is it? It is a general struggle against failure and exclusion. Engaging in this struggle we quickly encounter data that makes apparent a growing list of vulnerable students in need of additional educational assistance. Indigenous and first nations students, immigrant minorities, students whose first language is not the language of the curriculum, traveller and refugee children, gay, lesbian and transgender children, children from poor neighbourhoods and families, children whose schooling is disrupted by chronic and long-term illness, children living in geographic isolation, disabled children are all vulnerable. Add to this the fact that absenteeism, both reported and hidden truancy, increases as more students are expected to attend school than has ever previously been the case, and the question of student vulnerability is amplified.

As Foucault reminds us, power is not linear but is better likened to the complex structure and flows of capillaries that carry blood around the body. It has become popular now to apply a botanical analogy, suggested by Deleuze and Guattari, of the rhizome that 'moves and grows (underground) in messy and unpredictable ways'.[6] Students assert their agency in forging identities that are more acceptable than those that the school enlists to maintain control.[7] Here, I am not calling up romanticized notions of student resistance,[8] but reminding myself of the enduring utility of John Furlong's carefully argued case for reassessing student disruption through an appreciation of the way schools form student identities some of which offer respect and others that do not. It is hardly surprising that students then negotiate their own identities within their networks to forge respect through alternative routes. This draws us into the pervasive incidence of student withdrawal from schoolwork as a way of avoiding a spoiled academic or a special educational needs identity.[9]

Inclusive education policy is a grand reform movement, simultaneously taking care of business for particular groups and individuals by scaffolding their education, while establishing the belief that inclusion is everybody's business. Inclusive education is code for educational reform at all levels. A new social imagination and congruent vocabulary is required that delivers us from the fortification of outdated traditions and practices of schooling.

Inclusive education policy – a new conservatism?

Our discussion is close to crossing from a consideration of educational foundations to a discussion of educational futures and an agenda for change. Before we take this step, and holding onto our desire to identify the underlying rationalities that support exclusion, let us consider some general policy constraints that obstruct educational opportunities for an increasing number of children and young people. These constraints will be considered under the following headings:

- Policy reductionism.
- Policy disconnection.
- Policy resources.

Policy reductionism

The policy constraints that I offer as evidence of the general tendency towards reductionism in the treatment of inclusive education in fact restate the antecedents for collective indifference. First is the repeatedly stated problem of collapsing inclusive education into a concern with special educational needs. This understanding rests upon bestowed understandings and professional expertise about childhood disorders, defects and syndromes. As we have observed, disability and defectiveness is predominantly linked with individual pathology. The policy challenge thenceforth pivots on diagnosis, classification, appropriate placement and treatment. The policy discussion narrows to a set of fiscal and political calculations revolving around the following questions: How much will it cost? How many of these children are there? Are we establishing a funding precedent? Where do we find new money or what will be the impact of identifying old money to reallocate? What is the political risk of not funding particular disabilities and disorders (show us the numbers and the postcodes)? Can we convince Treasury that we are in control and capable of managing growth?

Disabled children's difficulty in accessing classrooms, and then participating and succeeding in learning is consequently said to reflect the nature and severity of their individual defects. Disability and disablement are not properly theorized as a social issue in which the structure of educational provision is the root problem.[10] Of course there are many who take a broader view in education jurisdictions globally. They struggle to provide alternative approaches to reforming educational structures, cultures and policies.[11]

The bureaucratic discourse[12] that focuses on the diagnosis of disability as a lever for delivering resources to individual students conceals reductive thinking on a number of fronts. First, it establishes very limited notions of identity. People are 'anatomized', reduced to the anatomical features of what is described as their syndrome or disorder.[13] Identity is always a complex amalgam, an often-messy matrix of human and social pathology. Dominant bureaucratic and medical explanations of disability conceal social dysfunction and disorder. The foundational assumptions of the knowledge are buried deeply below attractive and distractive explanations of individual student defectiveness. The language of inclusive education is used to deflect from the deployment of the traditional medical model of disability. This was John Maynard Keynes's critique of the traditional economic wisdom that he challenged in such elegant and prophetic prose, that it is worthy of careful reconsideration:

> The celebrated optimism of traditional economic theory, which has led to economists being looked upon as Candides, who, having left this world for the cultivation of their gardens, teach that all is for the best in the best of all possible worlds provided we will let well enough alone ... It may well be that the classical theory represents the way in which we should like our Economy to behave. But to assume that it does so is to assume our difficulties away.[14]

For the educator, critique can be an immensely practical activity. Reductive thinking is both destructive and costly. Opportunities are missed and people are discarded. However, I do not blame classroom teachers, as they have been encouraged to acquire limited and particular knowledge about disability and disablement and are constantly persuaded to defer and refer to experts. If we live and are schooled in artificial enclaves our knowledge of difference is predictably limited. Our anxieties and difficulties with difference are correspondingly abundant. In this climate 'mixaphobia'[15] is highly contagious. As Jules Henry postulates, we are educated for social stupidity.[16]

Tom Billington, a practising psychologist in England, describes something of the entanglement of policy and pathology when he reflects upon the growth in the recognition of childhood disorders such as autism, Asperger's Syndrome and ADHD. He argues that in recent years there has been a profound change in how we think about the meaning of children's behaviour and a growing inclination to equate it with symptoms of evolving disorders:

> It is a change, which I see in my work as an educational psychologist. The change in the patterns of pathologisation (but not necessarily the processes) is evidenced by the structural changes in school placement currently being tentatively proposed by different Local Authorities (for example, units/schools). There seem to be an increasing number of children whom I am called to assess who have already been diagnosed (or who soon will be) as having one particular form of specific disorder/pathology. Such categories act as reference points. I hesitate to call them fixed reference points, for it seems likely that psychology will be able to discover an unlimited supply of new 'disorders' which will supersede these current categories. It is not the individual category which is fixed, despite its appearance, but the stream of pathologisation.[17]

The disabled child[18] and the evolving and complex relationships between them (the 'abnormal') and what people insist on calling special and regular education, direct us to serious fault lines in an ever-changing body of scientific authority. I remember one of the Education Queensland senior management team briefing meetings, always intensely nerve-wracking as position, constituencies and power manoeuvred and collided across the table, shortly after my secondment to the Ministry. The agenda was broad. Before we dispersed the Director General asked if there were any other items anyone wanted to raise. One of my colleagues related a story heard on the radio about research 'in some university somewhere or other that showed that if a pregnant woman exposed her foetus to classical music, say Mozart or Beethoven' (perhaps it would be advisable to steer away from Mahler and Stravinsky?), 'it increased the chances of the child being born gifted'. The Director General deferred to me and said, 'You're the professor, what do you think?' I told the group that I was unfamiliar with the research and had not seen any of the data. I guess I revealed my scepticism by declaring that I would be fascinated to see the results a similar study might reveal in say Nashville, Tennessee or maybe Tamworth in Australia where country and western music is the preferred musical genre. All of this may indeed be redundant. We live in an age where we need not rely on the melodic lilt of Dvorjak or Dolly Parton in the nursery to boost the infant's IQ when the alternative is a smart drug to enhance cognition. Are we stumbling towards a *Brave new world*, an imagined utopia, where we can select and craft the kind of children we desire?

Biopolitics comes to school

The story from the Ministry is trite, but it does reveal people's fascination, sometimes obsession, with controlling and shaping life itself. Indeed, Nikolas Rose's continuing analysis of the biopolitics of the twenty-first century concerns just that; the production of modes of thinking allied to new scientific knowledge and technology, together with the conditions of political economy to optimize life and remove it from the control of the body.[19] His work complements and enhances the analysis of systems of thought that give rise to the oppressions that are the concern of those working in the field of disability studies. Martha Nussbaum underlines the urgent need for such analysis by observing that with the increasing publication of the scholarship of disabled people about their social situation, '...it is possible to take the measure of the isolation and marginalisation imposed upon them, and the extent of their routine humiliations'.[20] I will therefore refer closely to Nikolas Rose as the elaboration of his argument helps to frame questions about exclusion and is particularly pertinent to the global expansion of behaviour disorders and the reactions to these disorders when manifest or discovered in schools.[21]

In *The birth of the clinic*[22] Michel Foucault, Rose tells us, offers an important methodological lesson:

> ...the epistemological, ontological, and technical reshaping of medical perception at the start of the nineteenth century came about through the interconnections of changes along a series of dimensions, some of which seem, at first sight, rather distant from medicine.[23]

The confluence of changes in the education and organization of the medical profession, different forms of maintaining records in hospitals that in turn produced new health statistics, the development and growing sophistication of pathology and dissection of deceased patients and changes in laws and practices for attending to the ill, infirm and defective; all of these served to fix the clinical gaze firmly upon the body.[24]

Rose pursues the trajectory of medicine beyond the first publication of *The birth of the clinic* in the mid 1960s to present a different 'medical assemblage' to that of the nineteenth-century or mid-twentieth-century clinic. The reach of medical jurisdiction extended into 'the management of chronic illness and death, the administration of reproduction, the assessment and government of "risk", and the maintenance and optimization of the healthy body'.[25] Medicine has been reshaped by technology and changing disciplinary collaborations. The specialization of the profession has led to a redistribution and fragmentation of diagnosis and treatment. There has been a corresponding reconstruction of people in advanced Western countries as carriers, shapers and consumers of a health identity. The relationships between people and new ensembles of medical knowledge and practices are more complex and blurred.

Michel Foucault[26] and Sander Gilman,[27] followed by Nikolas Rose in his book entitled *Governing the soul*,[28] trace the rise of the 'psy-sciences' as physicians, followed by psychiatrists and psychologists, developed their anchoring beliefs about and descriptions of degeneracy,[29] normality and abnormality and in so doing they identify the processes of establishing authority for new medical explanations for social issues. The diagnosis of the maladies of the mind shifted from the doctor. Diagnostic authority spread to other fields. The more pervasive the knowledge and authority of the constitution of normality and the more precise we make our calibration and cartography of deviations from those norms, then the greater is our disciplinary power and ability to assert governance over complex populations.[30] For Foucault this was the production of governmentality – a system of rationality that enabled the government of complex populations.

This is pertinent to our consideration of how we classify schoolchildren and summons the following questions: By what means do we build a standard knowledge of behavioural normality and abnormality? How do we communicate and embed this standard knowledge as the common sense across large populations?

Of course, the answers to these questions are books in and of themselves. Let me attempt, however, to provide a summary of Rose's framework for the analysis of biomedical power to suggest another explanation for the significant growth in behavioural disorders and the numbers of children and young people that have been swept into the processes of diagnosis and treatment.[31] There is no doubt that there has been yet another collision of forces and events that have produced a new medicine of the mind which imbricates knowledge and policies in education. We see this in the adoption of brain science,[32] the authority of DSM IV-TR,[33] and what Fleck refers to as the 'thought collectives' that surround them.[34]

Nikolas Rose and the biopolitics of the twenty-first century

In *The politics of life itself*,[35] Nikolas Rose sets out five interlocking avenues of interrogation to trace the continuing transformation of medicine. The themes he applies are: *molecular biopolitics*; *technologies of optimization*; *subjectification*; *experts of life itself*; and *bioeconomics*. His analysis of biomedicine is useful to us with respect to the subject of and means for inquiry. Acknowledging my depletion of his detailed analysis and the limitations of my knowledge of this field, I will summarize these lines of interrogation and the picture they give us of the new workings of medical knowledge and authority. The illustration of Rose's interrogation of changes in medicine should encourage us to both broaden and deepen our critique of the uses of special education needs as a means for organizing children and schools. His analysis shows how a system of rationality takes shape, establishes itself as expert authority and is insinuated as the common sense.

Molecularization

The molecularization of medicine refers to the shift from seeing the body at the 'molar' level where we think of it as an intricate interconnection of tissues, limbs, joints, organs, bones, cartilages, hormones, blood flows and other fluids. Our view commences from the anterior to the interior of the body. This was the clinical gaze across the nineteenth and first half of the twentieth centuries as charted by Foucault.

Technological advances into the field of visualizing the body have transformed it. There came a revolution in the technology of visualization instigated through what Fleck refers to as a profound change of a 'style of thought'.[36] Reminiscent of Kuhn's *paradigmatic shift*,[37] a *style of thought* connotes particular formations of thought, distinct ways of seeing, practising and recognizable expressions of terms, concepts, references, assertions and relations.

The molecule became the new unit of analysis and new machines, concepts and ways of thinking were generated that rendered previous ways of knowing the body incomplete. Digital technologies produced new visualizations linked to anatomizing, decomposing, manipulating, amplifying and reproducing vitality (life) at the molecular level. We enter the world of the biomedical laboratory and are now able to see and also to manipulate the body in profoundly new ways. As Rose states:

> The molecular elements may be mobilized, controlled, and accorded properties and combined into processes that previously did not exist. At this level, that is to say, life itself has become open to politics.[38]

The Economist reports the inevitability that life forms will be 'routinely designed on a laptop'.[39] In a follow-up briefing entitled *Genesis redux*, the impact of the announcement by Craig Venter, Hamilton Smith and their laboratory colleagues in the 20 May issue of *Science* of the artificial creation of a living creature is assessed.

> ...It demonstrates more forcefully than anything else to date that life's essence is information. Henceforth that information has been passed

from one living thing to another. Now it does not have to be. Non-living matter can be brought to life with no need for lightning, a vital essence or a god. And this new power will allow the large-scale manipulation of living organisms. Hitherto, genetic modification has been the work of apprentices and journeymen. This new step is, in the true and original sense of the word, a masterpiece.[40]

The Human Genome Programme alters our understanding of the body. Instead of visualizing it in terms of deep probing down through tissue and cartilage to bone, we call on informatics and computational models developed across the disciplines of biology, physics, mathematics and engineering to model DNA sequences. We are witnessing the re-engineering of vitality:

> Contemporary medical technologies do not seek merely to cure diseases once they have manifested themselves, but to control the vital processes of the body and mind.[41]

Technologies of optimization

The second strand of Rose's analysis, the technologies of optimization of vitality (life), do not simply refer to advances in instruments and methods. Instead, he is talking about a different way of thinking about life and its manipulation. The progressive transfer of fluid and tissue from body to body to combat disease and death and to reduce stigmata proves the malleability of the body. Many children with achondroplasia have submitted to surgical stretching, while children with Down's syndrome have undergone cosmetic surgery to *normalize* facial features as well as to improve function.

Reproductive technologies reveal a new 'style of thought' where decisions about the constituents of a worthwhile life become a matter for calculation. In other words, what human features do we sponsor and what abnormalities are to be consigned to history. While these decisions are seen to be intensely personal, they have profound political implications. Life imitates art, echoing scenes from a Wilde novel of the 1890s; cosmetic surgery and hormone therapy allow us to optimize youth throughout the life span, the ordained sequences of the body are made negotiable.

The molecurization of the brain has also encouraged the optimization of behaviour through the engineering of our moods and intellectual capacity through greater surveillance and chemical regulation.[42] Behaviour and the brain are isolated to particular cells as sites for intervention to alter and improve the person. We will return to this point later as it is contingent on confidence in screening for and detection of the deviation from the norm. Schools, I will argue, have become fertile fields for the discovery of abnormalities.

Subjectification

The third strand in the analysis of biopolitics concerns **subjectification**. Here, Rose examines the rise of a new politics of health and medicine. Over time, advanced industrial societies have taken measures to improve the health of the citizenry first through surveillance of the quality of the water supply, the provision of sewers, protection of food quality, and then through developing and disseminating norms of health and hygiene. These norms were taken into the community through philanthropic groups, medical authorities, schools and local government.

In a lecture delivered at the State University of Rio de Janeiro in October 1974, Michel Foucault detailed the development of 'social medicine' or the medicalization of the citizenry by transporting us back to Germany in 1746 when the *Medicizinischepolizei* (medical police) originated. This force was interested in more than birth and mortality statistics. The medical police observed disease and illness by collecting information from doctors and infirmaries and collating and recording their findings at state level. They were instrumental in the standardization of the teaching and the qualifications of doctors.[43]

With the passage of time the standardization of medical education and practice and the mass dissemination of health knowledge globally, the populations of advanced Western societies were transformed into health consumers. Individuals and health groups were capable of making choices about their state of health and demanded rights in decision-making, attention to their needs or those of their family or health group, and inevitably to compensation.

People formed a new medical subjectivity where they sought to actively influence their vitality. Rabinow offers the term biosociality to describe this changed set of relations around medicine.[44] Individuals and groups form around genetic identities. We have witnessed the rise in the latter part of the twentieth century and the first decade of this century of the way in which projects and campaigns are developed around genetic identities. People intervene directly to support particular genetic research projects around particular diseases or genetic identities. Within this lie what Rose and Novas refer to as the question of biological citizenship that summons questions of race, disability, sterilization, euthanasia and death camps.[45]

Biomedicine forged profiles of genetic aspiration and hope to shape human futures. This, Rose refers to as ethopolitics – 'the politics of how we should conduct ourselves appropriately in relation to ourselves, and in our responsibilities for the future, forms the milieu within which novel forms of authority are taking shape'.[46]

Experts of life itself

The fourth area for interrogating biopolitics concerns the development of new '*experts of life itself*'.[47] The government of bio-subjectivities (or identities) is achieved through a complicated entanglement of relationships between work in laboratories, the imperatives of pharmaceutical companies, the regulatory frameworks of ethics research boards, drug licensing bodies and bioethics commissions. Doctors enjoyed a privileged position as arbiters of medical knowledge and its enforcement that reaches across civil society. The social relations of medicine have changed.

People invest in themselves, and their families, as an ongoing medical project. They seek authority, expertise, advice and treatment beyond the doctor's clinic. We enlist and defer to hybrid unions of *traditional medicine* and complementary medicines. Therapists representing disparate authority reach into all areas of our somatic selves. We congregate around medical conditions and identities in self-help, advocacy groups and charities to help individuals and fund further research. An expanding group of experts exert *pastoral power*[48] providing speech therapy, occupational therapy, art therapy, music therapy, physiotherapy, aromatherapy and psychotherapy. Dieticians and nutritionists, personal trainers and life coaches, sex counsellors, mental health counsellors, marriage counsellors, educational counsellors, genetic counsellors and fertility and reproduction counsellors augment their services. Bound by professional ethics, the language of informed consent and choice frames the relationship. This blurs reality. The process is not indifferent or disinterested.

Those being counselled receive new languages with which to consider alternative futures as set out for them. They can embrace the intervention in their plight or accept the perils that await them through inaction. Social responsibility lodges itself into the collective psyche. Only the irresponsible woman would not visualize the foetus or intervene if the foetus is the carrier of abnormalities (unacceptable differences). While one is fully cognizant of the profound difficulties that surround these issues, we must also concede that herein we steadily cross into the realms of eugenics.

In the university and industrial laboratory, the hospital board room and the doctor's clinic, due diligence is believed to maintain ethical standards. Bioethics insinuates itself in popular culture where we see the protagonists in television medical shows battling with ethics boards and hospital management. Driven by an amalgam of wanting to do the right thing and the mitigation of risk and litigation, these fora determine the field of ethical governance. Rose redirects our attention, however, to what does not come into the ethical discussion. Why is the failure to treat the legions of children who die each day for want of, often very inexpensive, medical intervention not registering as a question of ethics? How ethical is it to condone the world 'looking away' as Jeffrey Sachs[49] puts it? The façade or the limitations of bioethics is all the more flawed, when we turn away to fix our gaze on the embryos of the privileged. Collective indifference secures its footing.

Powerful 'thought collectives', as Fleck observes, form around biomedicine.

> From the stem cell experts to the molecular gerontologists, from neuro-scientists to the technologists of cloning, new specialists of the soma have emerged, each with their own apparatus of associations, meetings, jour-nals, esoteric languages, star performers and myths. Each of these is sur-rounded by, augmented by, a flock of popularisers, science writers and journalists. While often disowned by the researchers themselves, they play a key translational and meditational role in forming the associations – made up of politicians, lay people, patient groups, research councils, and venture capitalists and investors – on which such expertise depends.[50]

Bioeconomics

Rose's last theme for the analysis of biopolitics concerns the *capitalization of vitality*. His argument is not simply a linear critique that suggests that because the outlay of venture capital is so vast and the gestation of research results and shareholder dividends so delayed, the biotech com-panies, including the pharmaceutical giants, distort results consistent with their own fiscal interest. Rather he suggests greater subtlety:

> Where funds are required to generate truth in biomedicine, and where the allocation of such funds depends inescapably upon a calculation of financial return, commercial investment shapes the very direction, organisation, problem space, and solution effects of biomedicine and the basic biology that supports it.[51]

Reading Gary Greenberg's[52] account of the dispute between David Wong, the developer of Prozac, who announced in *Life Sciences* that he had pro-duced the first SSRI (selective serotonin reuptake inhibitor), and Arvid Carlsson who had in fact developed zimelidine five years earlier in his Par-kinson's disease research laboratory, we are offered insight into the com-mercial machinations of biomedical research. The rise of one drug and the disappearance of the other, argues Greenberg, reflects the level of commit-ment of the different pharmaceutical companies, Astra (Zelmid) and Eli Lilly (Prozac), to offset the investigation and amelioration of side-effects with their judgement of the potential market. As Greenberg wryly puts it:

> The company's executives just didn't think there was enough market for an antidepressant to make it worth the shareholders' while. Or to put it another way, they didn't think there were enough depressed people out there.

To judge from the industry's willingness to spend huge amounts of money to minimize their drugs' association with violence and suicide and other, less dramatic side effects, that's not a problem anymore.[53]

Biocapital shapes relationships, sets political priorities, traverses national borders, builds a discourse of urgency and benevolence, and defines the parameters of important knowledge and the next big question. Universities, governments and supra-national organizations such as OECD fall into step as they direct funds and join public/private consortia to reflect biomedical research priorities.

Notwithstanding the protection provided by the regulatory frameworks of biotech ethics, there are ethical questions arising from bioeconomics. We are now venturing across the boundaries of vitality – human and non-human – to eradicate disease, prolong life or enhance the gene pool. The advanced capitalist countries of the West continue to test pharmaceuticals for adverse side-effects in the disadvantaged communities of the developing world. These are pharmaceuticals to be purchased and applied by privileged medical consumers; they are not necessarily for the use of the trial countries. There is a reversal of the trend where outdated, flawed or dangerous pharmaceutical products are distributed across the developing world.

The anatomization of the disruptive child: a liberating science for learning?

In a bid to affirm the educational potential of a 'biopsychosocial' perspective on Attention Deficit/Hyperactivity Disorder, Paul Cooper fuses a limited interrogation of the arguments of those 'educationalists who deride the ADHD concept' with a restatement of the 'biopsycho' (i.e. the medical/psychiatric) position.[54] In the shadow of Nikolas Rose's analysis of the politics of biomedicine and its attendant systems of rationality, Cooper's paper is problematic. He argues for a more searching analysis of ADHD through the application of the biopsychosocial understanding of behaviour disorders. However, in this paper he fails to scrutinize his own assumptions, as he encourages others to do, and falls short of an analysis of the social. Thereby, he attenuates the impact of what might be a reasonable claim. 'Critics of ADHD', he argues, have sought either to deny ADHD or to build an antimony and choice 'between biomedical and environmental explanations for learning difficulties because they are incompatible'.[55]

As a counter-position he provides the profile of the disorder, its prevalence, co-morbidity and risk factors, causes and critical reactions. Understanding the aetiology of ADHD, conduct disorders and oppositional defiance disorder will help some 'suspicious British educationists and educational psychologists' and teachers in schools, he counsels, to reform approaches to school organization and teaching. Understanding the

aetiology of ADHD reveals the need to employ a range of cognitive interventions for more inclusive educational experience for these 'most vulnerable students'.

At face value, this position is commendable. Calls for educational
reform as a key action item on the inclusive education agenda are welcome.
However, Cooper does not subject the interface between biomedicine and
schooling to a level of analysis that we find in the work of others. Laurence
and McCallum, Tait, Danforth and Graham are indicative.[56] Despite widespread confidence in the promise of brain science for explaining and
improving learning and behaviour,[57] the neurobiologist (and brother of
Nikolas Rose) Steven Rose writes of the difficulties that neuroscience,
because of its many and often divided constituents, summons if expected
to produce a Grand Unified Theory.[58] Steven Rose does provide us with a
biopsychosocial analysis of ADHD. He traces the disorder's various explanations from the discovery of the child described by George Still in the
Lancet in 1902 as 'passionate, deviant, spiteful, and lacking in inhibitory
volition', through to the American Psychiatric Association's development
of standardized behavioural characteristics for Minimal Brain Damage.
The failure to isolate evidence of damage in the brain of affected children
prompted a rebranding; first Minimal Brain Dysfunction, followed by
Attention Deficit Disorder and then came Attention Deficit Hyperactivity
Disorder.[59]

Like many scientists and psychiatrists, both Steven and Nikolas Rose
challenge the veracity of explanations of the disorder as the specific location of brain dysfunction has shifted from one section to another to accommodate changing conjecture and anatomical evidence.[60] Forming a
diagnosis based on a checklist of abnormal behaviours is also scrutinized.
Questions are asked of the relational and contextual nature of the behaviours ascribed as indicators of the disorder and of deriving a statistical
notion of normality.

Guidance for the detection of ADHD and other forms of behaviour disorder and mental illness is provided in the pages of the *Diagnostic and statistical manual of mental disorders* (DSM) IV – TR.[61] Kutchins and Kirk
offer a detailed and critical analysis of the way in which the American Psychiatric Association have constructed their manual of mental illness and
behaviour disorders that catalogues an ever-increasing array of standardized disorders to guide practitioners' assessments. The *Diagnostic and statistical manual of mental disorders* (DSM), now in its fourth edition (DSM
IV) and with the fifth edition due in 2012, they argue: '. . . provides a tem-
plate for new knowledge, shaping what scientific questions get asked – and
which ones get ignored'.[62] Rather than being testimony to the advances of
scientific knowledge, each edition of DSM tells a different story:

> The story told . . . is not the conventional one of science triumphing
> over the mysteries of nature. Rather, we trace how the psychiatric

profession struggles with various political constituencies to create categories of mental disorder and to garner support for their official acceptance.[63]

For Kutchins and Kirk:

> ...professional biases can sweep seemingly normal behaviour into categories of mental illness,... definitions of mental illness often mask gender and racial bias ... the interpretation of scientific data is often distorted to serve the purposes of powerful professional groups.[64]

Social conventions, moral judgement and prejudice are blurred as definitions of normality are struck. It was not that long ago that DSM registered homosexuality as a form of mental illness, and Greenberg reflects on the struggle of feminists to strike out pre-menstrual dysphoric disorder (PMDD) as a mental illness.

> The idea that PMDD is a psychiatric illness must have looked good to someone. My money is on Eli Lilly, which wanted to squeeze a few more dollars out of Prozac, or Sarafem, as the company had relabelled it for treatment of PMDD. But despite (or perhaps because of) its corporate sponsorship, the diagnosis ran into stiff opposition from feminists who objected to the way that it pathologized what they considered to be a normal variant of human behaviour. PMDD has turned out to be a bust. It still languishes in the back of the book and may even disappear completely when the DSM-V comes out in 2012.[65]

The echoes of arcane speculation about women, reproduction and hysteria are audible in the noise of modern diagnosis.[66] As Kutchins and Kirk suggest, successive editions of DSM may best be regarded as a series of political settlements within a divided profession as it adjudicates on the behaviour of others.[67]

In contrast, Greenberg describes the DSM as 'an unparalleled literary achievement'.

> It renders the varieties of our psychospiritual suffering without any comment on where it comes from, what it means, or what ought to be done about it. It reads as if the authors were standing on Mars observing our discontents through a telescope.[68]

The DSM's authors, says Greenberg, are not disinterested observers. Intense struggles to transform what DSM IV describes as 'diagnoses in need of further study' (e.g. minor depressive disorder) into a four- or five-digit code disorder are fought out between successive editions. DSM is:

…indispensable to the business of therapy. Not only does it provide a taxonomy of mental disorders, which in turn gives us therapists a private language in which to talk to one another and a way to feel like we're part of a guild; it also assigns to each species of anguish a five-digit code. Written on a bill, that magic number unlocks the insurance treasuries, guaranteeing that because we therapists are treating a disease rather than, say, just sitting around talking to people about what matters to them, we will get paid for our trouble.[69]

Concluding these reflections on the influence that DSM IV exerts on the 'climate of opinion',[70] it is worth noting that some psychiatrists now sub-scribe to a notion that where a diagnosis cannot be struck in accordance with the conditions set out by the manual, then the patient or client may be said to be suffering from a shadow syndrome that is still in need of pro-fessional scrutiny and appropriate treatment.

Steven Rose also interrogates the *ex juvantibus* logic that is applied to identify causation. It was claimed by experts in the field of childhood beha-viour disorders that methylphenidate (Ritalin) which ordinarily has similar stimulant effects to amphetamines 'paradoxically' represses children with ADHD.[71] Hence if a child had ADHD, prescribing Ritalin would confirm or reject the diagnosis through the reaction of the child.

…before long it became apparent that the drug affected 'normal' and 'ADHD' children similarly; there was in fact no paradox. So the neu-rological argument shifted. It was proposed that by enhancing dopamine neurotransmission, methylphenidate 'improved communica-tion' between frontal cortex and midbrain/limbic system. This, it was hypothesised, put the 'higher' brain region in control of the 'lower', more impulsive brain systems, and hence diminished the excesses of the hyperactive child. It has to be said that there is no serious evidence to support this elaborate conjecture, but, as Prozac made 'normal' people 'better than well', so it was argued, Ritalin might enhance school performance even in 'normal' children. For the important thing is that the drug seemed to work.[72]

Finally, we are encouraged to consider the political economy of schooling as a driver of disruption. Herein we invite questions about the impact of changes in the labour market on school attendance, of high-stakes testing in shaping specific forms of curriculum and pedagogy that marginalize par-ticular student cohorts, on class sizes and on the systematic disengagement of reluctant students. The school effectiveness dream *à la* David Reynolds of 'high reliability organisations' and the 'fail-safe school', reinforced by the Blair government's Delivery Unit and more recently by the obsession with performance targets, confuses teachers and school administrators over the difference between education and standards on the one hand, and targets, tests and scores on the other. This approach to education policy creates the *at risk student*. Here we must ask, who or what is at risk? High-reliability schools cannot tolerate low-reliability pupils.[73]

The confluence of corporate interest with the influence of media in producing particular pathologies of behaviour or medical identities presses parents and teachers to submit children to diagnosis. CHADD (Children and Adults with Attention Deficit/Hyperactivity Disorder) is worthy of our attention in this discussion. CHADD is a community organization with some 12,000 members in 194 local affiliates (chapters, branches and satellites) in forty-one states across the USA, Puerto Rico, the Virgin Islands and the District of Columbia. CHADD's revenue was $4,569,950 according to its 2008–2009 Annual Report.[74] In the 2008–2009 Budget Report we see two interesting entries. First, Federal Government grants amounting to 21.9 per cent of the budget and, second, it reports that 35.9 per cent of its revenue came from pharmaceutical sources ($1,587,126). CHADD lobbied for the passage of the US Senate resolution recognizing 18 September, 2008 as ADHD Awareness Day.

The organization provides professional development support for teachers, having published a workbook with a 'new curriculum'. Two hundred and ninety-seven teachers are certificated by CHADD and it has trained more than 3,551 families. It has a national on-line resource centre and hosts culturally sensitive activities to reach out to the African American communities in Atlanta, Georgia and Maryland. It has also had special events for the Jewish community. The 20th annual conference in 2008 attracted nearly 1,200 delegates from around the world. In addition, there are regional conferences and rolling workshops and seminars. It has strong media connections. The attendance was described as reflecting the economic crisis. *Attention* is the organization's magazine that enjoys wide circulation. It provides scholarships and research support, and its Board includes legislators and senior medical officers. This is an influential organization.

Thought collectives, as described by Fleck, emerge and set the parameters for knowledge and discourse. The field of behaviour disorders is a noteworthy exemplar. There are numerous academic journals, research institutes, paid lobbyists, touring experts and media popularizers to have established ADHD and its siblings; conduct disorder and oppositional defiance disorder, as the proper concern of caring and vigilant parents, and also teachers, community nurses and school counsellors.

Understanding this phenomenon demands that we apply a comprehensive analysis so that we consider not only medical explanation, but also apply scrutiny to widely variant diagnosis rates in different geographic locations. Are we observing the absence of medical resources and knowledge or are we stumbling into much more complex relationships between the social and the pathological? The point is not to disprove science, for science regularly achieves that in and of itself. The point is to reveal the systems of thought that infuse it and how they impact on children and schools to generate particular patterns of inclusion and exclusion.

An intelligent discussion of emotions

A discussion of the biopolitics of schooling would be incomplete without a consideration of the discovery of emotional intelligence as a constituent of health and well-being. Kathryn Ecclestone and Dennis Hayes observe a dangerous rise of therapeutic education.[75] Popular culture celebrates what Frank Furedi describes as the cultivation of vulnerability and the quest for an understanding of the inner self as a panacea for the problems of everyday life.[76] Publishers line up to commission the printing of the autobiographic confessionals of celebrities who chronicle their abuse, addictions and/or adulterous journeys into self-understanding. An admixture of entertainment and voyeurism, this *literary* genre augments the raking over of human misery in radio talk shows and reality television to satiate our avaricious appetite for deprivation, tragedy and emotional triumph. Daytime television has transformed human frailty into a spectator sport. The journey from paying to view mentally ill people incarcerated in Bethlem Asylum (Bedlam) to the new coliseums of misery and suffering is not that far.[77]

In a parallel vein, Daniel Goleman's[78] blueprint for cultivating emotional intelligence has insinuated itself across public and private life. His best-selling book, its sequels, DVDs, audiophiles, podcasts and exercise notebooks have struck the framework for school pastoral curriculum, for job selection criteria, and for the arbitration of disputes in the workplace.

Having established a hyper concern for emotional well-being and ambiguous notions of happiness and mental wellness into the zeitgeist, there exists what Frank Furedi refers to as a therapeutic culture. No longer is therapy a set of interactions between the therapists and their client. In short, 'It ceases to be a clinical technique and becomes an instrument for the management of subjectivity.'[79] Eccleston and Hayes have demonstrated how the cultivation of emotional vulnerability and the emotions curriculum in schools has become an integral aspect of both surveillance and regulation in schools and of producing the emotionally intelligent worker for the therapeutic workplace. It stands as further evidence of the individuation of educational and social issues and therefore a reductive turn in thinking about education.

John Furlong has devised a more robust framework for dealing with emotions and schooling. Adapting Sennett and Cobb's study of the damage delivered by the social relations of production in their book entitled *The hidden injuries of class*, Furlong describes the 'hidden injuries of schooling'.[80] Raewyn Connell's proposition in *Gender and power* that the academy suffers from two forms of occupational blindness is his starting point.[81] Here Connell refers to '...the inability of sociologists to recognise the complexities of the person and the unwillingness of psychologists to recognise the dimension of social power'.[82]

Bringing psychology and sociology to an examination of the so-called disaffected pupil, he then sets about building what he calls a 'sociology of emotion' to help us to understand the complicated matrices of subjective experiences of disaffected students in schooling. Students are valued and devalued as they experience three sets of educational structures: first, the production of ability; second, the production of values; and third, the production of occupational identity.

Curriculum, pedagogy, assessment, grouping and streaming, SEN categorization, rules, the organization of the timetable and extra-curricular activities, the physical arrangement of classrooms and the selection of notices, mottoes, adornments, and uniforms (the list is indicative rather than exhaustive) intertwine to produce a school ethos which complements or clashes with the students and their home background. Students soon learn their place through a series of positive and negative experiences as they come to realize their academic identity, the appropriateness of the values they bring with them to school and ultimately their occupational identity. This work resonates and builds on Ken Polk's discussion of the *new marginal youth*.[83] Understanding of the composition of the gravity that pulls students to the centre or the margins of schooling, that includes or excludes, is not served by reductive thinking. Its detection and rejection is high on the agenda for the inclusive educator. Australian researchers such as Julie McLeod and Lyn Yates[84] and Stephen Ball, Meg Maguire and Sheila MacRae in England provide insight into the complexity of youth identities.[85]

A critique of emotional and behaviour disorders reveals the inherent reductionism of notions of special education needs policy and the need for school reform. Two further questions assist that critique. The first question is tragically straightforward. How do we explain the now thoroughly documented historic over-representation, and in some instances the under-representation, of ethnic minorities in different countries in special educational provision? Here, I refer specifically to the collusion between regular and special education in the reproduction of racial segregation in education. Sally Tomlinson's study of Caribbean boys in England in 1979 moved this from being seen as a statistical anomaly to its recognition as a social practice.[86]

In the USA, a number of researchers including Tom Parrish at the Centre for Special Education Finance,[87] Gary Orfield at the UCLA Civil Rights Project,[88] Oswald, Coutinho and Best whose fieldwork was supported by the US Department of Education,[89] and Ferri and Connor have reconsidered race and special education.[90] As I have mentioned, Tomlinson's earlier findings of disproportional referral rates of Caribbean boys were replicated by Gillborn,[91] and by Gillborn and Mirza in England.[92] Tomlinson has also revisited her work on racism in education and noted the systemic over-representation of Caribbean boys in some special educational needs categories (EBD) since her pioneering studies.[93] This line of research may be extended to consider First Nations students in Canada,

Indigenous students in Australia and Maori and Pacifica students in New Zealand as further indicators of the entrenched racial patterns of educational exclusion.

Of course, the blurring of the lines between special educational need and social control[94] are not simply intersections between minority ethnicity and schooling. Consider the significant changes over the past fifteen years in our understanding of and responses to disruption in schools or disruptive behaviour. The transformation of the naughty or disruptive, or even the maladjusted, pupil to the disordered child is almost complete and signifies a remarkable phenomenon in scientific and sociological terms.[95] In many respects, changes in researching, talking and writing about young people who disrupt, disengage from or who are turned away from schools plots points in a complicated story about economy, schools and psychological hegemony over the last twenty years.

The operation was successful but sadly the patient died

My second general question that points to reductive thinking is directed at the rates of diagnoses of behaviour disorders and the outcomes of interventions. The question is best pursued through a series of subsidiary questions: Why are we witnessing the recent exponential growth in the identification of particular categories of special education needs? Do changes in the type, volume and rate of diagnoses of schoolchildren tell us something about the growth of specific deficiencies in the twenty-first century child? Are we witnessing the resilience of traditional special education as it persuades the community that inclusive education is achieved through an acceleration of the diagnosis and treatment of more children than has been achieved hitherto? Are changing patterns of diagnoses suggestive of more pressure being exerted by schools to identify greater numbers of special educational needs students to offset the deleterious impact of hard to teach students on inspection and accountability targets? Are we observing the improvement of diagnostic techniques and a greater reach of overdue expertise? Why are there regional irregularities in diagnosis within and between countries? Does this reflect the uneven supply and availability of trained diagnosticians? Is the variance a reflection of diagnostic predisposition fuelled by the expansion and respectability of childhood medical identities in the community? Does the assignation of children to categories of special educational need secure better educational, vocational and social opportunities and destinations?

While I am not in possession of sufficient data, at this point in time, to supply definitive answers to the list of questions myself, it nevertheless remains important to register such lists of questions for collective investigation and response.

In Chapter 5, we noted the review of special educational services in Toronto, Canada by Bennett and Wynne. They reported that by 2003,

Ontario registered as one of the states or provinces of North America with the highest incidence of students with acute special needs. Like other jurisdictions, the growth of referrals was matched by significant leaps in the level of funding for students with special needs. The increase between the 2003–04 and 2004–05 year was 1 per cent, but it grew by a further 6.8 per cent in 2005–06.[96] Sheila Riddell, in an examination of the classification of students at the educational margins in Scotland, reminds us not only of the problem of gender disparity in categorizing students with 'special educational needs' or 'additional support needs', but of the intersection of special education and class, especially in areas of behavioural and emotional disorders.[97]

Findings from research conducted by Linda Graham and her colleagues in New South Wales are disconcerting.[98] The authors refer to David McRae's findings that between 1994 and 1995 while students identified with mild intellectual disabilities rose by 4.8 per cent and those with moderate disabilities rose by 8.1 per cent, students classified as having behaviour disorders rose by 33.4 per cent.[99] Linda Graham, Naomi Sweller and Penny Van Bergen report an acceleration of these trends.

> Between 1997 and 2007, the percentage of students with a disability classification more than doubled in NSW government schools; rising from 2.7 to 6.7% of total enrolments. While enrolments in special schools did decline in the mid 1980s, this trend abruptly reversed just a decade later. As students with physical, hearing, vision and mild intellectual impairment moved out, larger numbers of students classified with moderate intellectual impairment and behaviour disorders moved in, leading to an overall increase in the student population enrolled in special schools.[100]

They also note that the number of separate support classes in regular schools increased and that the

> ...largest increase in any segregated setting was found in the enrolment of students in secondary school support classes under the category of behaviour disorder (a percentage increase in the order of 585%).[101]

This was accompanied by significant increases in the number of students in primary and secondary schools being classified as emotionally disturbed. The researchers pursue their data to identify the greater vulnerability of boys to segregation than girls with the same impairment in the areas of behaviour disorders (BD), emotional disturbance (ED) and speech language impairment (SLI). The New South Wales data, though more transparent than that from other Australian states and territories, does not report adequately on the intersection of Aboriginality and ethnicity and special educational needs. What is most alarming and signals a need for further investigation by Graham and her colleagues is what Wald and Losen[102] call the *school-to-prison pipeline* that is set in the early years of schooling for the growing ranks of the behaviour disordered and emotionally disturbed students.[103]

The investigation of links between the marginalization of young people at school, exclusion, special education and incarceration are not new. In this respect, the work of criminologists and education researchers such as Ken Polk, Tony Knight, Bob Semmens, Garry Coventry and Art Pearl is instructive.[104] In 1987, Ben Bodna was investigating the transmission of people with intellectual impairments from segregated schooling to the criminal justice system.[105] What Graham, Sweller and Van Bergen have achieved is the mapping of the evolving technologies of surveillance and control and the way in which it would seem that large numbers of young people are diverted from the regular classroom to support classes and special schools to take the school-to-prison pipeline. The outcomes of diagnosis, placement and treatment remain extremely problematic and have not registered as a cause for concern.

Policy disconnection

In what seemed like an attempt to write an episode of the iconic British television series *Yes Minister*, the Department of Premier and Cabinet (Queensland) hit upon the idea of establishing a red tape reduction initiative to scale down administrative excess. A very reasonable idea as bureaucratic wastage equates with a depletion of services where they are needed. If the outcome is the deployment of resources where need exists, then the initiative is inspired. Sadly, an elaborate procedure was devised to coordinate the work across each department to identify unnecessary 'red-tape', dismantle it and report across government. Department red-tape committees became very busy, themselves shaping Kafka's bureaucratic nightmare.

Bureaucracy is labyrinthine, hard to manage and wilful. Internecine struggles rage around the formulation and ordering of priorities, personal ambition and position and political leverage. Across many jurisdictions, the notion of the separation of the civil service and government has receded, departmental heads often acting as the executive officer to their Minister. Large departments have the capacity to become quite fragmented as you drill down through their structures organized around silos of responsibility and specific projects. Education departments are complex organizations, cumbersome and history-laden. We know that education is a site of intense struggle over what to teach, how to teach and what kind of fiscal and administrative arrangements will deliver the settled goals (if a settlement is reached). In short, there is a tendency towards fragmentation and contradiction within education jurisdictions, though it is refreshing to read Ben Levin's account of leading the Education Ministry in the Canadian province of Manitoba. He provides alternative insights into the complexity of governing education and prioritizing reform and securing greater levels of policy coherence and alignment.[106]

The administrative structures that are required to drive the educational dream across large geographic regions add further complexity. The picture is not yet complete as I must now bring schools into the picture and you will appreciate the idiosyncratic nature of the school organization. Gillian Fulcher's analysis of policy-making, which we discussed earlier, reminds us that policy is made at all levels.[107] The latitude for interpretation, and therefore for distortion and fragmentation, is broad. In other words, the policy scriptwriters may create lucid, clear and well-presented glossy policy brochures. These publications and memoranda are often replete with obligatory photographs that sample students of all ethnic hues, conspicuous disabilities and choreographed gender balances, to chop up the text. Setting out the principles that inform the new policy direction, the values it hopes to establish in practice, the aims and intended outcomes and prescriptive steps for implementation, the policy brochures and memorandum aim to avoid ambiguity. As people across the education organization come to the document, they bring their own views and aspirations and will fuse the policy text with their own predispositions as they pursue their part of the implementation cycle. It then becomes possible for all manner of distortions to be described as being faithful to the letter and spirit of the policy agenda.

I could never have imagined a segregated special school announcing itself as a centre for inclusion. Yet this is precisely what has happened. A number of special schools were involved in the New Basics project in Queensland, an initiative to reform the content, organization and teaching of curriculum. It also developed rich assessment tasks and aimed to change the organization and culture of the project schools. Having reformed their curriculum and teaching, consistent with the new basics research, the special schools then self-declared as inclusive schools. For me this was a staggering display of interpretive latitude if not self-serving deception. Segregation is segregation.

I do not intend to labour the point. When working in Education Queensland I suggested that inclusion is everybody's business. It is not just the concern of those who work in the inclusive education directorate. Those engaged in curriculum and assessment reform need to consider the varying impacts of reform proposals on all students. Those working in operations and budget portfolios likewise need to consider the impact of their proposals on all students. Are some students favoured? Are others further marginalized? How might we direct our sphere of work to ameliorate exclusion?

England is an interesting case for consideration. Under the Blair New Labour government whose priorities were 'education, education, education', there was an impossible amalgam of inclusive education rhetoric with the practice of high-stakes testing, ritualistic inspection and the public spectacle of national league tables where the affluent were celebrated and the disadvantaged vilified. Failing schools, mostly in disadvantaged areas, were put in special measures and head teachers and their teachers are derided for failing to meet targets. The stocks may have been dismantled in the village square, but naming and shaming remains a cultural predisposition in English public life.

While there was genuine effort and resources were committed to examining social exclusion and its antecedents to commence Third Way reparations, a lack of policy alignment in education in England meant that inclusive education remains elusive. Let me quickly suggest why. Supporting the neo-liberal ethos of competitive individualism in the shape of a testing culture and sponsoring residual tracks for the growing second- and third-tier students is not a blueprint for inclusive education.

In 1978, Her Majesty's Inspectors in England published a report into Behaviour Units.[108] At that time they listed a number of concerns arising from their visits to 239 units across England. The major concerns, and they had many, can be summarized as follows. The procedures for transferring students to units were more developed and smoother than the procedures for reintegrating students into their regular school. Administrative procedures varied markedly across the units. The curriculum was generally very narrow, concentrating on social skills (45 per cent), remedial work (16 per cent) and both roles (30 per cent). As a result students fell further behind. The existence of the units removed pressure from schools to think about the antecedents to student referrals attributable to school factors. Off-site centres beget their own need. The more that exist, then more students are identified for referral and exclusion from school. Racial disproportionality was evident in referrals. The units were extremely costly when adjudicated in terms of their stated aim, the reintegration of students to successful educational pathways.

Denis Mongon asks the obvious question: 'cui bono?' (to whose benefit?)

> Since units appear to be, on the whole, of little benefit to those young people who attend them it is difficult to conclude anything other than that, in a reversal of practice, they are established for the benefit of people who do not attend them rather than for those who do.[109]

Many other researchers in Britain, the USA and Australia have reported on the problems associated with this type of provision.[110] More than three decades on, England has developed a panoply of alternative provisions for the difficult to place student. This includes Pupil Referral Units that are an updated rendition of behaviour units. In September 2007, data published by the Department for Children, Schools and Families showed that there were 448 PRUs with a headcount of 15,160 pupils.[111] By May 2009 the number of PRUs had grown to 456 with a headcount of 15,370.[112] These data are inconsistent with the findings of Brian Lamb who wrote later that year in his report on SEN and Parental Confidence to the Secretary of State that: '...the high numbers of pupils with SEN in pupil referral units (PRUs), 18,964 out of a total PRU population of 25,288 or 75%.'[113] He therefore recommended that: '...the requirements on SEN policies are extended to pupil referral units'.[114]

Clearly there is a need to be vigilant when reviewing government published data on schools and students. While it is said that segregated school provision and special school pupil headcounts are holding steady, the question is how are we achieving segregation under a smokescreen of inclusive education policy. Are PRUs the segregated provision for the fastest growing group of ascertained students: the so-called Emotionally and Behaviourally Disturbed (EBD)? If so, then how do we maintain a discourse of inclusive education?

In the English context it would be also interesting to consider the role of Academies in the segmentation and regulation of the total school population. The Labour government academies scheme which sought to bring private sponsorship and management to the campus to boost educational funding and outcomes echoes Margaret Thatcher and Kenneth Baker's earlier attempts to boost private interest in, and ownership of, public education through the City Technology Colleges. As Francis Beckett reports, David Blunkett announced that the government would commit £60 million to kick off the project.[115] The expectation was that each academy could be established at a cost of £12 million. The academies were to be flagships boasting state-of-the-art buildings and facilities to support excellence in teaching and learning. The private investor would contribute £2 million with the government providing the remaining start-up costs. The government would be responsible for annual running costs of the school that would be managed by a board at the behest of the private investor. The school would be freed from the usual intrusions of bureaucracy, which might more precisely be understood as Local Authority control, in its operations. Beckett reports that the average start-up cost for the first twelve academies was closer to £23 million and that the *Times Educational Supplement* revealed in 2004 that half of the academies had not received the full £2 million from the private investor. He adds that one must surmise from the significant disparity between the expenditure on children at academies and Local Authority schools (£21,000 versus less than £14,000), that 'the government not only wanted academies to be good: it wanted other schools to be worse than academies'.[116]

The DfES 'Statistical First Release' for January 2009 showed that the number of academies has grown from three in 2003 with an enrolment of 2,720 pupils to 133 academies enrolling 121,700 in 2009. The increase in academies between 2008 and 2009 was from eighty-three to 133. This acceleration of academies was pursued despite a government commissioned PricewaterhouseCoopers review that highlighted serious shortcomings in their operation, a failure to provide innovative teaching and learning initiatives and an inevitable deepening of the class divide through a two-tiered system. The Cameron and Clegg Conservative Liberal Democratic government, through its Education Secretary is pledging unprecedented levels of opting out and support for academies in an increasingly deregulated schools sector. Originally academies were championed as a means for providing better chances for disadvantaged pupils, a superior education would deliver them from social deprivation. Academies, it would seem, will not in themselves bridge the gap between privilege and disadvantage.

Education jurisdictions around the world, according to the European Agency for Development in Special Needs Education in 2009, are engaged in 'reviewing and changing their policies and legislation for inclusive education, based either upon knowledge and experiences from on-going pilot projects, or by introducing new financing strategies for special needs education (SNE), or by implementing new policies/laws regarding quality systems and monitoring for education'.[117] The concentration on the special needs agenda as the vehicle for reform has led to its disconnection from inclusive education as substantive education reform.

Policy resources

Education has long been considered to be an important investment in the future. Colonial governments in the Australian penal colonies progressively introduced compulsory non-secular elementary schooling in the second part of the eighteenth century as a means for the improvement of the population. Better that a God-fearing, if unsophisticated, imported teaching force take responsibility for shaping the characters of the convicts' children than leave them to be schooled by their parents. A curriculum staple of drilling in catechism, obedience, manners and rudimentary skills in reading, writing and number was delivered before delivering the children into the developing labour market. Schooling served the formation and regulation of human capital.

Wilkinson and Pickett note the benefits of educational performance.

> ...everybody agrees about the importance of education. It's good for society, which needs the contributions and economic productivity – not to mention the tax – of a skilled workforce, and it's good for individuals. People with more education earn more, are more satisfied with their work and leisure time, are less likely to be unemployed, more likely to be healthy, less likely to be criminals...[118]

The success of children at school is directly influenced by family background. The level of family income and the level of education achieved by the parents are directly related to educational attainment of their offspring. As Wilkinson and Pickett put it:

> Children do better if their parents have higher incomes and more education themselves, and they do better if they come from homes where they have a place to study, where there are reference books and newspapers, and where education is valued.[119]

Richard Teese and John Polesel are amongst a number of researchers who argue that school exerts its role in the production of academic success and failure. Curriculum is not benign. It is experienced differentially by different groups of students and those from disadvantaged backgrounds in particular will experience the negative force of the 'exercise of institutional power'.[120] The intersection of social characteristics such as poverty, geographic isolation, disability and Aboriginality intensify the difficulty of educational attainment at school.

The Canadian researcher, Doug Willms,[121] together with Andy Hargreaves and Dennis Shirley[122] and Wilkinson and Pickett argue that more unequal societies show greater disparities in school attainment. A stimulating and supportive social environment inside and outside the home is a key to preparation for learning in the early years. Countries with a developed welfare state reflect better performances in school in their students. Redistributive policies in education, such as greater levels of support for candidates from disadvantaged backgrounds for undertaking degree and higher degree studies, are vital for improving intergenerational mobility according to the findings of Blanden, Gregg and Machin who plot its recent decline in Britain.[123]

Counting backwards, Ben Levin puts the level of expenditure on education into sharp relief.

> The $40 billion spent in Canada on schools is a lot of money, but to put it into perspective it is less than the $47 billion Canadians spent on new cars and trucks in the same year. To put it another way, Canada spends in total about $7,500 per student per year for our schools. This amounts to about eight dollars per student per hour, based on 900 hours of school time per year – about what one would pay a babysitter?[124]

A good education is expensive as has been recognized by countries like Singapore. Deferring again to Ben Levin, there are four questions around school funding in every jurisdiction. How much money is enough? Who pays? What does the money buy? How is the money distributed?[125]

To these we can add further questions. How much does educational failure and exclusion cost? And how does the multiplier and opportunity cost come into our equation? Failure, disaffection and exclusion are costly.

The costs inevitably return through the health sector, the juvenile justice and policing systems. There are lateral and more productive ways for thinking about the economics of education.[126]

Schools in the state of Victoria were shaken by the recommendations of the 1984 Collin's Report, *Integration in Victorian education*. Declaring that all children can learn and be taught, it recommended that all students be enrolled in their neighbourhood school. Characteristically, the response of teachers' unions in that state was instrumental and conservative. Integration represented an attack on teachers' working conditions. There was a sense that the floodgates had been opened for unmanageable students to distract teachers from the normal children. Pressure was applied and the Director General, after what must have been a long backroom discussion over syntax and semantics, inserted a caveat that he hoped would appease teachers and not distress too many parents. Thenceforth children with *disabilities, impairments and problems in schooling* could enrol in their local school, but their admission would be delayed until the resources to support their education were in place.

An administrative sleight of hand, this policy manoeuvre stood as a monument to discrimination and closed thinking. Arguments about resources have always been at the centre of debates about inclusive education.[127] Attempting to supplement the resources available to disadvantaged and disabled students demands distributive justice. In particular, disabled students are seen to be an additional burden on the school and on those whose right of access is taken for granted. Many may argue that this is costly, but this is not followed by an analysis of the cost of exclusion or indeed the cost of systems where the duplication of provision is encouraged so as to warehouse disabled and difficult children in separate centres (in-school or separate campuses).

Most models for disbursing funds to support disabled students in regular classrooms have developed diagnostic schedules for identifying the nature and the 'level' of disability. The determination of the level of disability pinpoints the entitlement of additional funding that will follow the student to the school. This process was referred to as 'ascertainment' in Queensland. Let me describe the system that was applied when I was working in that state. This is not done to suggest that it was worse than other places, it was not. I simply want to unravel the logic and the perverse effects of fiscal policy. There were six levels of disability, one being the lowest level of disability and six the highest. A guidance officer would assess the student's level of disability. If the child's assessment rated level 5 or 6 the school would be eligible for additional funding.

The gravity of the funding model was to produce a diagnosis of more severe levels of disablement otherwise there was little point in assessing a child. As has been recorded by Parrish in the USA and Marsh in England, the demand for and completion of assessments together with total expenditure on support for disabled students grew exponentially. In Queensland the Minister was under pressure from the state Treasurer to take control of the ascertainment budget. It may seem ironical but I supported that call, but for different reasons. It had always been conspicuous that there was little coordination in the ascertainment process so that the diagnoses varied between districts depending on who administered the ascertainment assessment. Moreover, because the budget was applied to individual children, most often in the form of an inclusion aide, the demand for more aides grew and inclusion focused on ensuring that there was an adult with the child and did not think about how the school could develop as an inclusive campus with programmes that recognized the value of difference and used this as an opportunity to develop innovative curriculum and pedagogy. It is important to acknowledge that this was what some schools did, but they were the outliers. There seemed to be no overall movement towards an increasing capacity of schools to become more inclusive or to draw benefit from the diversity of its student cohort. Resources were an inadequate measure of inclusion.

Further questions we might add to Ben Levin's list might include inquiries into the benefits derived by building community capital in and around schools. How do we mine parents' knowledge, hopes, energy and skills to transform schools? How do we build critical partnerships with higher education, local industry, community agencies and organizations to extend the curriculum around local questions of community well-being and sustainability? Of course, you will recognize this line of thinking. It is not new. Moreover, there is evidence of the productive and educational value of this kind of resource gathering. A new accounting rationality is needed that is not based on short-term expediences, but values investment in education reform for the long haul.

This chapter has been concerned with the production of forms of thinking and practices that reinforce social division and strengthen injustice and exclusion. The apparent sophistication and refinement of categories of special educational needs builds and is sustained by the community zeitgeist. The medicalization of failure and disengagement from school is more pervasive and powerful. It refracts questions about school and poverty. Education policy provides a window through which to observe larger political and social relations. Education policy embraces and advances beliefs and values as the tools with which to construct the future. The growth of biomedicine as a complicated entanglement of sometimes competing, sometimes coalescing epistemologies and disciplines, and political and economic relations is offering the knowledge and technology to fashion ourselves as the people we want to be. The fear of the other is now manifesting in medical identities. The reduction of social problems to defective individual pathology has a stronger footing in new forms of neuroscience. Traditional special education and exclusion is privileged under these conditions.

In many countries, education policy, in its expression of inclusive education, has tended towards reductionism. This is revealed by a continuing belief that inclusion is achieved through special education needs policy frameworks. As I have suggested, exclusion is ubiquitous. Accordingly, change requires a comprehensive education reform programme. In the absence of this approach we continue to see the lack of alignment, the perverse effects of funding and a failure to move beyond superficial accounts for school failure, disruption and disengagement. The naughty child, the fidgety child, the disengaged child has been refashioned as the maladjusted, the troubled, the disordered and the genetically compromised. This is an incomplete understanding that feeds social stasis, the medicalization of oppression and segregation. In policy terms we have seen transitions from regular and special schooling to integration and then to inclusive education. In reality we are in some respects back where we started as the patterns of separation are built through new geographies and structures of collective indifference.

In his recent writing, Stephen Ball has registered dissatisfaction with 'the discourse of endings'.[128] This is a way of segmenting history to describe the ending of one age and the beginnings of another. Alternatively, he argues that a proper grasp of education policy is achieved when we understand what has changed and what has stayed the same – 'dissolution and conservation'.[129] So it is for inclusive education. We have seen changes, some of which are very positive, and we have seen the resilience of old forms of exclusion, albeit in the new explanatory frameworks.

We now confront the multiple challenges provided by this consideration of inclusive education. We move from foundations of exclusion, and inclusion, to futures for inclusive education. Given the ubiquity and antiquity of exclusion and the flaws in inclusive education policy and practice the challenges are grand. Once again I will eschew the temptation to join the school leadership and improvement research genre by offering a blueprint for reform. Again, Stephen Ball offers wise counsel:

> Book conclusions are modernist conventions which typically represent knowledge in a particularly authoritative way, and I see what I have started here as a set of starting points and methodological possibilities rather than as conclusive.[130]

This book has set out to be deliberately argumentative. It has contested the movement of inclusive education from the margins of education research to its entrenchment in respectability. Gains partner losses. Critique is an easy task when compared with reform and reconstruction. In Chapter 8 I will avoid the blueprint approach, this will not be a Fourth Way.[131] I will, however, set out strong principles for change and an indicative agenda to guide our collaboration to assist in the identification and dismantling of exclusion and for building stronger communities that shape more adventurous, innovative and inclusive approaches to teaching and learning.

8 Considering other possibilities – the irregular school

Yan Ba was reminded of a journey he had made a few years earlier with a geologist friend. They had traveled to the remote mountainous regions where the source of the Yangtze River is located. They had followed the winding and increasingly narrow stream to a point where it was no more than a trickle of water.

His friend had put down his foot and said: 'Now I am stopping the mighty Yangtze in its tracks.'

Henning Mankell, *The man from Beijing*

I began this discussion of exclusion by observing that its resilience may be attributed both to its antiquity and to its ubiquity. These characteristics have dulled our responses to the injustices exclusion visits upon individuals and communities. We have learned or are advised to look away. As Daniel Dorling, a professor of human geography at the University of Sheffield, writes:

Although few say they agree with injustice, nevertheless we live in an unjust world. In the world's richest countries injustice is caused less and less by having too few resources to share around fairly and it is increasingly maintained by widespread adherence to the beliefs that actually propagate it. These beliefs are often presented as natural and long-standing, but in fact they are mostly modern creations. What appeared fair and normal yesterday will often be seen as unjust tomorrow. Changing what is injustice today means telling some people, usually those in positions of power, that what they consider to be fair is in fact in many ways unjust.[1]

Securing competitive advantage for our children through school choice, either as a straight financial transaction to a so-called private school, or by moving house, or despatching our children to live with a friend or relative 'in the zone', is in many affluent countries accepted as the proper duty of a responsible and caring parent.[2] Our children's grip on a future of privilege cannot be left to chance. To this end, some people agitate to have the disabled child removed from their own child's classroom for fear of that different child *retarding* their child's progress. We rob our children of their time for play and condemn them to cram for tests that distract them from deeper learning born of a mistake or a time-thirsty problem. There is financial interest in writing elaborate and foolishly predictive report cards on the uniform-clad three or four year old for anxious parents. Millions of pounds are pumped into an industry that inspects and rates schools, and doing so divides communities. Teachers are not entrusted to innovate or build creative learning spaces. National curriculum syllabi avoid truthful accounts of the world we live in. Australian children do not learn about the suffering of the people of Doomadgee in the Gulf of Carpentaria. Schooling equips children for individual advancement as community falls away. Too many of our children live out their school lives under the 'spectre of uselessness'.

We seek explanation for children's failure, disengagement, distraction, anger and defiance in their genetic and medical profiles. Even when the evidence of the intersections of poverty and school failure, Aboriginality and school failure, minority ethnicity and language differences and failure are overwhelming we confer titles of defectiveness on these children. That this process of special educational assignation can lead to their separation and increasingly to unemployment or incarceration does not unsettle us enough to reconsider the work of the unsatisfactory alliance of the regular and special school.

This is the neo-liberal dream of competitive individualism that guides our educational consciousness and sensibilities. It is the dream that provides simultaneous and uneven succour for privilege and disadvantage. And, we have been gullible enough to believe that if only our country could claw its way up the international PISA and TIMSS league table, then the children of the poor, disabled and immigrant children, who even if they are scoring marginally better on a test and have unlocked the mysteries of phonics, will be delivered from poverty.

How did we become so gullible? How did we lose regard for community? Why do we not see and *'fess up'* to our complicity in the creation of surplus populations – the unwanted? It is worse, we help to extend the waste as we work to separate and sort children into their allotted tracks, into the streams that assign them to unequal destinations.

Writers in the field of inclusive education such as Keith Ballard and Len Barton liken inclusive education to a journey, a struggle continually 'reducing barriers to participation and learning as we go'.[3] In this respect the future for inclusive education will be a continuation of its past – a struggle against exclusion and oppression. It remains a political struggle to affirm the rights of all to access, participation and success in education. The journey must take us back to the sources of exclusion. By exposing the fragility of the sources of exclusion, we may be able to put our feet down and stem the flow. The foundational questions are intensely political. In plain speak, they can be summarized with elegant simplicity.[4] Who's in? Who's out? How come? Then follows the subsidiary, perhaps more difficult, question that presses us to consider logistics and tactics; what are we going to do about it?

In New Zealand, the Inclusive Education Action Group (IEAG) unites academics, disability rights activists, parents, Ministry of Education workers and teachers to advocate for more inclusive schools and communities. In September 2009, the IEAG convened a conference under the banner of 'Making Inclusive Education Happen'. I was one of a number of invited speakers. Delighted to be able to participate, it was also a daunting prospect – these people, many of whom had grown impatient with theory and analysis, were looking for an agenda for change. I was reminded of a tale Mel Ainscow tells about the eminent professor who is invited by a local school head-teacher to visit the school. The professor is impressed by what he sees: the mutual industry of happy teachers and children, the sense of educational purpose, the bright and colourful surroundings and the evidence of scholarship. He cannot help but betray his uneasiness about what he has seen. 'What do you think?' asks the head-teacher fishing for affirmation. 'Well, it's a marvellous display of fine practice', he retorts, a frown etched deeply into his forehead. 'But', he adds, looking beyond the head-teacher into the middle-distance where ideas form and fall away, 'will it work in theory?'

I have often sat through conference addresses and workshops in which metaphorical steps are confidently painted on the floor for people to follow when they return home after the oration. Retracing the steps will, they are promised, ameliorate their troubles. Acknowledgement of the difficulties of contextual specificity ought to be mandatory. However, it should not deter readers from learning from divergent contexts. For that reason I wanted to avoid delivering a well-rehearsed critique and then telling the conference delegates that their homework was to fix it! I settled upon elaborating the principles and policy critique followed by offering 'an agenda that may make inclusive education happen a little more frequently'. I hoped it proved to be a useful heuristic device for others as they thought about action in their own schools and communities.

This chapter intends to continue to provoke thinking about exclusion and inclusion in education by setting out four organizing propositions followed by a series of tasks. Needless to say, this work is not complete. It invites readers to engage in a number of tasks, there are many others, pursuant to a more inclusive education. Since policy is made at all levels, an agenda needs to reach across and engage all policy sites and constituencies. I will then simply describe exemplars of irregular schooling as beacons of hope. These are drawn from my own encounters and observations.

Checking our foundations

Following are four broad propositions for approaching inclusive education in the future. The list is not ordered according to priority or urgency. The propositions instead serve as prompts for debate, application or rejection in the struggle to dismantle established and evolving forms of exclusion in education. I will present the propositions in two forms. First, there is a table that reflects my thinking behind them. Second, I provide a statement of each of the propositions accompanied by an explanation. The propositions take a modernist turn. The aspirations are ambitious. I do this deliberately for if we set low aspirations, we may just succeed. Thereafter follows an agenda of tasks where I attempt to carry the propositions, though the headings are different, through to activism (see Table 8.1).

In 'Mapping critical education', Michael Apple, Wayne Au and Luis Armando Gandin conclude with a warning against the corrosive character of cynicism and a call to action:

> A famous political theorist and activist once reminded us that people make their own history, but not under conditions of their own choosing. We may not be able to control all of the conditions of our work but, above all, let us continue to make our own history.[5]

Stating and explaining the four propositions

Proposition #1: Re-framing the field

Inclusive education declares its commitment to identifying and dismantling educational exclusion.

The discourse of inclusive education has been absorbed into and has, in turn, itself refashioned the spin of education jurisdictions, traditional special education departments in universities and the mainstream of educational research. Inclusive education has been popularized and adopted as a global organizing motif. Indeed, while *Education for all* as championed by UNESCO has received endorsement, the terms of this education for all remains deliberately ambiguous. Inclusive education has become what Edward Said describes as a travelling theory.[6] And, as he pointed out in relation to other travelling theories, in their movement across time and space they lose their original insurrectionary force. They are tamed and domesticated.[7]

In the many renditions of inclusive education, strong indicators reveal an inauthentic engagement with the aspirations for social reconstruction that were at the heart of the original inclusive education project. During the

Table 8.1 Framing four propositions

Proposition	Themes	Elements
Re-framing the field	• Establishing inclusion as a political project concerned with the examination of identity, difference, privilege, disadvantage and oppression; • Exposing the blockages within neo-liberal (competition state) formations of education; • Engaging the constituents; • New research partnerships.	• A new focus (not 'looking away'); • Segregation versus community; • Human value, interdependence and utility; • An apprenticeship in democracy; • Recognition, presentation and redistribution; • Transparent assumptions. • Collective responsibility; • Encouraging debate and accepting the need to confront and explore difficult and uncomfortable questions.
Re-righting language	• Rights, interests and needs; • Who speaks for whom? • Deflective vocabularies: regular and special education? • Deconstruction with purpose; • Acknowledging oppression and exclusion; • Recognizing transformations and conservations (following Stephen Ball and Nikolas Rose); • Detecting co-option and the unacceptable compromise.	• Apprenticeship in democracy (following the work of Art Pearl and Tony Knight); • Recognition, presentation and redistribution; • Confronting linguistic evasion – debunking notions of 'choice', 'continuum of placement options' based on disenfranchisement and absence of real choices; • Building knowledge of anti-discrimination legislation and conventions.
Re-searching for inclusion	• Framing a values framework for researching exclusion and inclusion; • Decoupling inclusive education research from special education research; • Forming trans-disciplinary and trans-identity research alliances to reflect the intersections of oppression; • Reconsidering the nature of validity and reliability in research.	• A reminder of the inextricable link between ideology and research and the implications of this for pursuing rigour; • Acknowledging the importance of voice and insider leadership and perspective; • Understanding the social relations and oppressive tendencies of research (following Mike Oliver); • Broadening rather than closing our questions.
Re-visioning education	• Interrogating the neo-liberal education template; • Education for democratic citizenship; • Curriculum, pedagogy and assessment for authentic learning; • Inclusion as an educational aspiration and strategy; • Educating teachers for community; • Engaging teachers and community in policy development.	• Building curriculum from transparent principles and ethical values; • Establishing policy flows that enlist the constituents in development, implementation and review; • Building assessment literacy to distinguish between standards, tests, performance targets, compliance regimes and achievement tables for international comparison.

dying embers of the last century and the beginning of this one, education jurisdictions around the world mandated for compulsory courses of special education in teacher education programmes because they believed that by doing so they would promote inclusive education in schools. Faculties of education hurried proposals through their universities' course-accreditation committees. Degrees in the impossible union of 'inclusive and special education' were hatched. Traditional special educators inserted chapters on inclusive education in their special education handbooks,[8] adjusted their language as they reworked the lecture notes, but retained their embedded assumptions about individual defectiveness and special educational needs. Student teachers have been treated to a Grey's Anatomy approach to inclusive education where they are instructed in the pathology of human differences and 'defects'. Such responses represent a form of incremental liberalism. This form of teacher preparation is dangerous as it consorts with conservative forces to maintain oppressive social relations. In some quarters, inclusive education has become a Trojan horse, a justification for maintaining the structures, processes and values of regular and special education alike. While inclusive education sometimes describes genuine attempts to challenge injustices in education, it can also be deployed to sustain these injustices. Under the rallying cry of inclusion, changing patterns of special education unfold and impose more subtle forms of segregation in the regular school.

Inclusive education needs to be decoupled from special education. In this way it may be restored as a genuine platform for addressing oppression and disadvantage across a range of constituencies. Inclusive education should exercise impatience and reject tokenism. The real and extensive suffering from which the demand for inclusive education is born does not afford a slow gestation for reform. A reframing of the field is required to disentangle itself from the neo-liberal education imagination and the values of competitive individualism. In this respect it must direct the interrogative spotlight towards the structures, policies and practices of schooling[9] that create surplus populations of difficult to manage students. Inclusive education needs to be forthright about its values, principles for action and intentions. It values community, the recognition and representation of difference, and fosters interdependence across constituencies to enlist schooling as an agent for an education in democracy and social change.

In short, inclusive education is an icon on the education screen, that, when opened, reveals a complicated theory of and agenda for educational reconstruction. Inclusion is a precondition, as Bernstein contends,[10] for democratic education. As such, notions of it representing the amalgamation of regular and special education is a blockage to productive reform. A subset of critical education, inclusive education asks questions about the power relations of schooling, bears witness to injustice and seeks an educational settlement that will provide the knowledge, skills and dispositions necessary for a better world.

Proposition #2: Re-righting language

Inclusive education recognizes language as an instrument of power and seeks to restore and embed a vocabulary of rights and justice in education.

Throughout this book I have reflected upon the opportunistic uses of imprecise language. Language not only describes the world, it orders and recreates it. Correspondingly, language can frame and mobilize change. Hence we need to talk about our words as instruments of power. Thinking about language should not be dismissed as an academic indulgence, or as the fixation of political correctness. The stakes are high and we need to exercise care.

In many instances the application of the term 'inclusive education' is imprecise and misleading. I have encountered schools with an inclusion room. This is often a room where difficult, disruptive and disabled students are gathered so that we can say they remain part of the mainstream school. When William Glasser's Reality Therapy dominated the field of school discipline these rooms were time-out rooms. In Queensland I encountered schools that called their isolation rooms 'responsible thinking rooms'. Our euphemisms continue to insult the intelligence of young people.

Support classes have replaced Arthur Hauser's invention of the so-called opportunity grades of the early to mid-twentieth-century school.[11] These enclaves do not strengthen community; they reinforce arbitrary social divisions and carve out surplus populations. Prospects for the future whither, as care collides with marginalization. Statements like 'catering for parental choice' and 'a range of placement options' are updated renditions of traditional special education's lexicon of 'least restrictive environment', 'most appropriate setting' and 'cascade models of services' that distract from the structure and politics of choice. Within this discourse segregation is achieved by stealth. Inclusive education pivots on questions of justice and rights. 'Who speaks for whom?'; 'With what authority?'; and 'To what ends?', become our guiding foundation questions.

At a recent meeting where, with colleagues, we presented our initial thinking for a research proposal to academics in Edinburgh, I was advised against using the word segregation. It is emotive, inflammatory and unsettling. Settling on softer words builds more comfortable conversations and eases pressure for change. We lose the friction and force for change. I am, however, willing to enter into discussions about the accuracy of my language. The point here is that the term inclusive education may be deployed to conceal different views that are not complementary and need to be explored openly and respectfully.

Deconstructing language assists us to isolate assumptions and intentions, to challenge authority and open the possibility of counter intelligences. This is achieved when the voices of marginalized people are countenanced. To restate Martha Nussbaum's important observation, '...the measure of the isolation and marginalisation imposed upon them, and the extent of their routine humiliations'[12] is authenticated by reference to disabled people. In this respect, disability studies, critical race theory, feminist research, queer studies, post-colonial studies disrupt the foundations of the canons. Representing voices rather than inscribing them advances discord and offers overdue tests to the commonsense. As a challenge to the dominance of the Western (Northern) sociological canon Raewyn Connell, in her work on Southern Theory, quotes Mamadou Diawara thus:

> As social scientists, we have to leave the campus and talk to the people face-to-face. This is perhaps even more imperative for African social scientists. For they will only find listeners in their own countries if they adapt to their language. On the other hand, it is only through contact with local knowledge that they can acquire the insights which are today of prime importance for the questions of developmental politics.[13]

Re-righting the language of inclusive education calls for vigilance against reductionism. Inclusive education presupposes a hierarchy of questions. First are the questions about the power relations articulated through the structures, processes and culture of schooling. After the question about who benefits from the current arrangements come the vexatious questions of reorganization and resources. To commence with resources assumes that the child seeking inclusion is an outsider and a potential burden and thereby privileges the status quo and exclusion. The practice of assigning children to categories and levels of disability and considering their entitlements according to category attenuates thinking about more important issues such as rights and justice. Martha Nussbaum reflects on this:

> Still, it would be progress if we could acknowledge that there is really no such thing as 'the normal child': instead, there are <u>children</u>, with varying capabilities and varying impediments, all of whom need individualized attention as their capabilities are developed.[14]

Within this frame of reference, the special school and the regular school are equally problematic and distractive notions. Thinking and talking beyond such a bifurcation is necessary. The question of place has not been resolved. Segregation, alternative and timetable signify place and politics.[15] We need to be able to embrace a very different notion of learning space that makes education flexible enough to respond to the context of communities and students. As the high-street coffee shop becomes the learning space for the twenty-first century university student, so too do we need to re-think school architecture. Care needs to be exercised that this does not become the justification for new forms of segregation.

Proposition #3: Re-searching for inclusion

Inclusive education employs a comprehensive array of research methodologies and tools in search of the complex structure and properties of exclusion and for ways to overcome its deleterious impacts.

> I think if we see, and I want to see research as an activity that is going to produce useful and meaningful social change, then one of the first things that we do is we state our ideological position up front in that research rather than somehow try to pretend that we don't have an ideological position. Saying that I don't have an ideological position is, in fact, an ideological position. Even Marx knew that and even two hundred years later it's bizarre that most people don't recognize that.[16]

In this extract from an interview with Mike Oliver, he acknowledges a widely held belief that ideology is at work whether we care to acknowledge it or not. Traditional special educators, such as James Kaufmann[17] have argued that the fundamental flaw of inclusive education is that it is ideologically motivated, and therefore unscientific and incapable of being considered as substantive research. Terry Eagleton points out that attempts to dismiss the validity or authority of research on a charge of ideology is a dangerous path to tread: 'In pulling the rug out from beneath one's intellectual antagonist, one is always in danger of pulling it out from beneath oneself.'[18] The charge registers the lack of reflexivity of the accuser. This proposition insists that we acknowledge our commitment to the challenge of identifying and understanding the destructive workings of power, privilege, disadvantage and exclusion in education and renew a determination for redress. As critical scholars, inclusive education researchers embrace rigour by enlisting a range of research methodologies to achieve depth, detect nuance and stumble across surprises that push the inquiry in new directions.[19]

Emphasizing the search in research, this proposition underlines the explorative nature of inclusive education inquiries. Inclusive education research is genuinely eclectic and finds footing in a commitment to the challenge of not replicating oppression in the relations of research.[20] As disability organizations say, 'Nothing about us without us.' Inclusive education research embraces scepticism and attempts to resist cynicism. It draws energy from a belief in the possibility and importance of change.

Understanding the complexity and dynamism of exclusion is the central challenge. The intricacies of the structure and processes of schooling combined with the intersections of disadvantage and exclusion across idio-syncratic jurisdictions force a broad and ambitious research agenda. Organizations such as UNESCO and the OECD exert a gravity that draws jurisdictions in disparate countries to converge around invented measures of performance and values enshrined by PISA and TIMSS. The influence of this on policy-making in education jurisdictions globally should not be underestimated. Such activity registers a value of worth and worthlessness. What can be measured is now the educational main-game; the rest is a dis-traction. The research explores the global and local, the social and per-sonal. We are a part of our research and can never be apart from it.

Proposition #4: Re-visioning education

Inclusive education provides an alternative vision for education as a demo-cratic apprenticeship to build sustainable communities.

Schools attach different values to students. This has always been so. For many students the experience of schooling is successful, if punctuated by periods of repetition, disengagement and boredom. Others, and the numbers are increasing, are directed into an elaborated process of classifi-cation and re-assignment. Different jurisdictions manage these processes in different ways, but they converge on producing a multi-tiered system of schooling. Martha Nussbaum reflects upon the perverse effects of the Indi-viduals with Disabilities Education Act (1990) in the USA:

> …the financial incentives created by IDEA give school districts reasons to rush towards classifying children as learning disabled, in order to qualify for federal funding. Such classifications may not always help the child: they can be stigmatizing in their own right, and they do not always point to a useful course of treatment. Moreover, they tend to be unfair to the children who have problems in school but who cannot be plausibly classified as learning disabled. One feels that all children should be helped to reach their cognitive potential; but the system pro-motes some children over others in a way that is more than a little arbitrary. In practice, this defect has been somewhat mitigated by the looseness of the classificatory system, as school districts seek to include as many children as possible in the funding eligible pool.[21]

Many of the affluent countries of the world are witnessing changing pat-terns of special and regular schooling. While enrolment levels have remained fairly constant over time, the types of children attending special schools are changing. Regular and special schools have agreed new franch-ising and operating agreements, creating satellites in and around the regular school. Pupil referral units (PRUs), support classrooms, behaviour centres, alternative programmes and managed moves all serve to govern those pupils who challenge the institutional equilibrium of schools. These students present a risk to the performance of schools. Ironically they are described as being 'at risk'.

The many attempts to fabricate inclusive education by grafting special education onto the regular school have produced little more than a bifurcated system of sponsored and marginal pupils. When assessed against student destinations, it is possible to observe students being locked out.[22] Described as being in their best interests and as saving them from the harshness of the regular school, these arrangements compromise the democratic enterprise. There seems to be little justification for allowing schools to be harsh places for those students tagged as different. This is not a preparation for a peaceful and sustainable world where interdependence, mutuality and community will prevail. New times require new thinking. The invention of schooling is in need of radical intervention. The neo-liberal experiment has failed.

In their work on school reform entitled *The fourth way*, Andy Hargreaves and Dennis Shirley call for a bold change agenda for education responsive to the 'vulnerable New World of the 21st century'.

> At a time of global economic meltdown, increasing dependence on oil, and accelerating climate change, we need bold new solutions, not stale old slogans. Cutbacks do not equip us to be competitive in the future. The unregulated markets that got us into our current financial mess and pushed market-driven solutions into the public sector are not going to get us out of it. Educational standardization has dumbed down our curriculum and burdened our schools with bigger government and overbearing bureaucracy, and has not enabled us to adapt flexibly to the future.[23]

This characterization of the impact of market-driven neo-liberal thinking on schooling is apposite. Talk about an educational crisis is commonplace. Nussbaum refers to the 'silent crisis' in education where the humanities are being systematically dismantled as a distraction from the knowledge and skills required to build economic advantage in favour of the hard sciences. Distracted by economic meltdown and 'material coverings' we have failed, argues Nussbaum in her defence of the humanities in education, to recognize and confront the cancer that depletes our soul.[24] Soul is not used or rejected as a religious concept. Rather, she refers to:

> ...the faculties of thought and imagination that make us human and make our relationships rich human relationships, rather than relationships of mere use and manipulation. When we meet in society, if we have not learned to see both self and other in that way, imagining in one another inner faculties of thought and emotion, democracy is bound to fail, because democracy is built upon respect and concern,

and these in turn are built upon the ability to see other people as human beings, not simply as objects.[25]

Too often education is at risk, as John Dewey counselled, of being reduced to the 'activity of well-planned machines'.[26] Nussbaum navigates the limits of the neo-liberal economic imagination. Educating people to build economic prosperity must be acknowledged as a means, for living in a prosperous and despotic state, is a truncated view of the civic role of education. Economic interest '...requires us to draw on the humanities and arts, in order to promote a climate of responsible and watchful stewardship and a culture of creative innovation'.[27]

An education in and for democracy cannot be assumed as intrinsic to schooling. Democratic schooling assumes educational reconstruction. According to Tony Knight and Art Pearl, school should prepare students to become effective problem solvers within a democratic culture.[28] Curriculum and pedagogy become the front-line for reform. Some Australian jurisdictions have attempted this, most notably Queensland in its New Basics Project,[29] followed by Tasmania's Essential Learnings. The New Basics Project, developed as a school reform trial for years 1–9:

> was undertaken by Education Queensland to prepare our students for the future. It dealt with new student identities, new economies and workplaces, new technologies, diverse communities and complex cultures.
>
> The New Basics aimed to improve the learning outcomes of our students. Community members, teachers and students worked together to ensure that the richness and relevance of students' academic and social growth was enhanced.[30]

The New Basics addressed the challenges of those calling for a return to the basics on the one hand, and those challenging schools to educate students for the future. This was not simply a new way of organizing curriculum content. Enlisting the evidence from the Queensland School Reform Longitudinal Study,[31] it pursued a more fundamental reform of teaching, learning and the organization of schools through four domains: ensuring that learning was intellectually demanding; ensuring greater connection between the curriculum, pedagogy and the world of the student; providing a caring and supportive environment; and recognizing diversity. A systematic approach to professional development was produced to provide teachers with time for their own reflection and learning. Critical friends who would engage with the school to interrogate and support the implementation of the reform were enlisted and attached to the trial schools. Comprehensive support that revolved around the core areas of authentic teaching and learning in the classroom – curriculum content organizers, productive pedagogy and rich tasks were provided. The core elements of the New Basics project is represented in the following table (Table 8.2).

Table 8.2 The New Basics research project

New basics	Productive pedagogies	Rich tasks
What is taught	How it is taught	How kids show it

The New Basics curriculum content and learning areas were arranged in four clusters of practices consistent with the world into which students would graduate. The clusters had an organizing question to guide the work:

Despite the fact that the evaluation of the New Basics research pilot reported improvement in teacher commitment and knowledge of pedagogy and assessment, improvements in the quality of student work and results, and a reversal of student drift in the middle years of schooling, Education Queensland joined a regressive move in 2003 for 'consistency of national curriculum outcomes' and national testing prescriptions. The school curriculum returned to its traditional discipline or Key Learning Areas base and turned away from opportunities for reforms consistent with the goals and practices of inclusive education. As Pearl and Knight argue, choices we make in the education of young people have profound implications.

> An education that does not examine the range of plausible explanations for and solutions to important problems can only exacerbate those problems.[32]

Re-visioning education speaks to all facets of how we school our young people. 'Our' is used purposely to signal collective engagement. Bearing in mind the warnings of Basil Bernstein and Alain Touraine, that absorption cannot be mistaken for inclusion, new education arrangements demand recognition and representation of those who have languished in an absent presence. Moreover, an education, as Touraine teaches us, in recognizing and understanding the relations of cultural domination is a precursor for building communities of difference.[33] Without such an education we violate

Table 8.3 The New Basics curriculum organisers

Life pathways and social futures	Multiliteracies and communications media	Active citizenship	Environments and technologies
Who am I and where am I going?	How do I make sense of and communicate with the world?	What are my rights and responsibilities in communities, cultures and economies?	How do I describe, analyse and shape the world around me?

people. People schooled for the economy are incapable of crossing 'the boundaries of inequality with mutual respect'.[34] Our language, devoid of critical perspective and introspection, adopts the phrases and *death sentences* that Don Watson derides.[35] We require a schooling in a new language that eschews charity and benevolence; a language that does not heap oppression on oppression. Sennett explains this in his call for respect:

> This social-work jargon (e.g. 'deprivation syndromes' and 'low-esteem anxieties') can certainly be demeaning, treating the poor like damaged goods, or can descend into ludicrous psychobabble ... people of a higher class who had the power to violate the poor, as my mother wrote; if they had dedicated their lives to the poor, charity itself has the power to wound; pity can beget contempt; compassion can be intimately linked to inequality.[36]

Education is replete with specific and segmented clinical and benevolent discourses that in effect form a general 'discourse of derision'.[37] The language of special educational needs is not a language that values people, nor does it equip us for social intelligence.

I recently asked Kevin McDonald, a sociologist, to speak with an inclusive education class on cultural perspectives on inclusion, exclusion and education. The ploy was transparent. I wanted the students to engage with someone outside of the education discipline so that they might encounter alternative questions and observe someone working with different sets of assumptions and conceptual tools. He spoke of the formation of global social movements. His descriptions of the Silhouettes action (El Siluetazo) in Argentina in the early 1980s were striking. At the time estimates ranged from 20,000 to 30,000 people 'disappearing'. The ruling junta hosted 200–300 camps for detestation, torture and execution.

El Siluetazo[38] aimed to create an event that would contest the disappearances, attract media attention and thereby challenge the military regime. Artists involved as many people as possible to produce 30,000 silhouettes

Figure 8.1 Creating the silhouettes, creating community.

to be placed around the city to bear silent witness and bring people back to the forefront of public consciousness. Though, as Kevin described, the artists wanted uniformity, ordinary people embraced and shaped the project so that the silhouettes became idiosyncratic representing their missing family and loved ones.

The Silhouettes appeared throughout the city, standing (not prostrate) 'looking at those who had not seen them'.

Figure 8.2 Silent witnesses.

This was the presence of absence.[39]

Figure 8.3 A presence for the missing.

Reforming education as an inclusive enterprise is a manifold and complex task that reaches into the deep structures of education and schooling to produce different policies, practices and cultures. A democratic education implies the necessity of redistribution, recognition and representation. There are many who have been dispersed from education into the shadow-lands of schooling whom we must repatriate. Their silhouettes should haunt us. Let me sketch an agenda as a prompt to our collective thinking, debate and practice. I will enlist the People's Front to remind us of the urgency of the need for reform and action.

What do we want? When do we want it?

> **Life of Brian Script**
>
> *Scene 23: The people's front engage in frantic discourse*
>
> REG: Right. Now, uh, item four: attainment of world supremacy within the next five years. Uh, Francis, you've been doing some work on this.
>
> FRANCIS: Yeah. Thank you, Reg. Well, quite frankly, siblings, I think five years is optimistic, unless we can smash the Roman Empire within the next twelve months.
>
> REG: Twelve months?
>
> FRANCIS: Yeah, twelve months. And, let's face it. As empires go, this is the big one, so we've got to get up off our arses and stop just talking about it!
>
> COMMANDOS: Hear! Hear!
>
> LORETTA: I agree. It's action that counts, not words, and we need action now.
>
> COMMANDOS: Hear! Hear!
>
> REG: You're right. We could sit around here all day talking, passing resolutions, making clever speeches. It's not going to shift one Roman soldier!
>
> FRANCIS: So, let's just stop gabbing on about it. It's completely pointless and it's getting us nowhere!
>
> COMMANDOS: Right!
>
> LORETTA: I agree. This is a complete waste of time.
>
> JUDITH: They've arrested Brian!
>
> REG: What?
>
> COMMANDOS: What?
>
> JUDITH: They've dragged him off! They're going to crucify him!
>
> REG: Right! This calls for immediate discussion!
>
> COMMANDO #1: Yeah.
>
> JUDITH: What?!
>
> COMMANDO #2: Immediate.
>
> COMMANDO #1: Right.
>
> LORETTA: New motion?
>
> REG: Completely new motion, eh, that, ah – that there be, ah, immediate action–
>
> FRANCIS: Ah, once the vote has been taken.
>
> REG: Well, obviously once the vote's been taken. You can't act another resolution till you've voted on it...
>
> REG: Oh, sorry, Loretta. Ahh, oh, read that back, would you?
>
> (Extract from *The Life of Brian*)[40]

Table 8.4 An agenda for collective action

Task	Elements	Actions
The restorative task	• Trust, authentic community dialogue. • From adversaries to partners? Legislating for rights, practising anti-discrimination. • Respecting voice, learning to listen. • New forums resembling the communities we strive for. • A framework for pursuing democratic educational policies, programmes and practices.	• Finding new meaning for inclusive education by recasting language and structures. • Establish a respectful communications strategy. • Develop a framework for democratic decision-making including flexible consultation processes. • New approach to striking fora: from neutral ground to common ground. • Authenticity of meetings and tasks. • Privileging and respecting the voices of the marginalized and the disadvantaged.
The analytic task	• Critical analysis of how we arrived at this point. • Analysis of exclusion and sharing the data. • Critique of artificial professional boundaries. • Whose knowledge counts? • Interrogation of our approach to resource modelling and the assumptions that feed the perverse effects of policy-making. • Review of structures and protocols in public education – bringing the public into education. • What is the nature and extent of inequality?	• Establish representative and collaborative research partnerships. • Preparation of preliminary position papers to structure review and reform. • Explain and pursue cultural reviews. • Learn to work across jurisdictions, service providers and community constituences.
The policy task	• A common understanding of inclusive and democratic education and implications for all levels of the policy cycles. • Alignment and consistency within and across policy jurisdictions. • Interrogate the practices of schools as they manoeuvre to seek advantage from testing, inspection and league table performances.	• Build a common understanding of inclusive education that pivots on the interrogation of exclusion and thinks beyond Special Educational Needs. • Build democratic practice into the policy cycle. • Communicate differences between standards and tests. • Reconsider the value of league tables.

Table 8.4 Continued

Task	Elements	Actions
	• Building knowledge of the risk this presents to students and communities. • Leadership in curriculum, pedagogy and assessment. • Agreed values and examine implications for practice. • Recognition and elimination of perverse policy effects. • Bringing other knowledge to the table. • Examine the costs of providing an education for the future in unequal societies.	• Disband expensive bodies such as OfSTED (England) that diverts resources from the education of children. Engage a critical friend scheme to assist schools and jurisdictions with review and improvement procedures. • Build policy partnerships that revalue teachers, parents and students. • Renegotiate education budgets and reconsider the notion of resource and allocation for school capacity building. • Meet the challenge of redistribution (to disadvantaged and marginalized students, rather than to the captains of capital). • Build a shared understanding of social investment, opportunity cost, welfare and well-being.
The education task	• Establish educational values and goals to be embedded in curriculum, pedagogy, assessment and school organization. • Establish authentic learning communities. • Instate intellectual leadership as a function of the critical educator. • Consider the curriculum, pedagogic and assessment requirements for a democratic education that builds civic engagement and critical understanding. • Teacher education for democratic education. • Classrooms for innovative learning for all. • Understanding the balance between 'delivery' and 'measurement'. • Education for living in and changing the world.	• Encouraging professional and community dialogue about the purpose and form of an inclusive education – an apprenticeship in democracy. • Building teacher knowledge, confidence and intellectual leadership. • Reinstating difference and diversity in schools – recognizing the silhouettes. • Reduce the reliance on special educational needs as comprehensive education reform accelerates. • Build a culture of on-going professional development. • Establish for educational conversations and decision-making that embrace rather than exclude the community. • Reinstate risk and the mistake as a fundamental element of innovation and learning.

continued

Table 8.4 Continued

Task	Elements	Actions
The values task	• Establish the kind of community we want our schools to model. Communities that recognize, represent, authorize and learn from difference. • Build an understanding of institutional violence and cultural domination and its articulation through the rituals and practices of schooling: curriculum, pedagogy, assessment and physical arrangement of schools.	• Get to know the community. • Build a school/class framework of values for living, learning and working together that honours difference, understands prejudice and enlists young people in acquiring the knowledge skills and disposition to expunge prejudice.

Of course, Loretta, Judith, Reg and Francis are members of the fictitious People's Front and we could never imagine in real life, government, the Academy or even community organizations being so paralysed by protocol, bureaucracy and convention. The educational exclusion empire is a large agenda item, and 'as empires go, this is the big one'. The urgency cannot be understated as this book has attempted to reveal the presence, the pervasiveness, the depth and the commonplace of exclusion. We are complicit. There is a choice. What follows is a suggestion of the terms of engagement and the spheres of action.

The above agenda is no more than an extended prompt for establishing a culture of thought-full activism in and through education. Setting out the agenda in tabular form is no more than an organizing device. Tables are flat and do not make clear the interrelationships between and circularity of the agenda items. In other words, the theatres of action are far messier than depicted in the calm of the table. I will briefly set out the tasks with a brief explanation for each.

The restorative task

Priorities

As is the case elsewhere, inclusive education in the Australian state of Queensland has been an area of contest between the interested parties. Negotiations between schools, the state Ministry, the Queensland Teachers' Union, teachers and parents are often heated and sometimes spill onto the pages of *The Courier Mail* (the daily Queensland-wide newspaper) or into Human Rights and Equal Opportunities Commission hearings. Trust is an early casualty in these matters. It seemed to me that fora needed to be established where people could put their issues on the table and pursue respectful discussions. To that end, I invited some people I had known from Queensland Parents of People with a Disability (QPPD), an advocacy organization set up in the early 1980s, to join me for lunch in Education House. To my surprise they told me that this was the first time that they had been there, it was their first invitation to discuss mutual interests. This seemed to be such a lost opportunity. Who is better able to talk about the needs and aspirations of disabled children than the children themselves and their parents?

Following this I suggested to the Queensland Minister, Anna Bligh, that she form a Ministerial Advisory Committee on Inclusive Education that brought together representatives from the Queensland Teachers' Union, the Catholic Education Office, QPPD, Education Queensland, the Independent Schools sector, the Queensland Council of Parents and Citizens Association, the primary and secondary principals' associations, the Association of Special Education Administrators in Queensland. The Ministerial Advisory Committee was invited to engage with key issues pertaining to establishing more inclusive education across Queensland and make a series of recommendations to the Minister. Professor John Elkins was invited to Chair the Advisory Committee.

Although I hold mixed feelings about the outcomes of this work, it was an important restorative step. The aim was to bring all parties to the table, to provide a respectful forum for the direct representation of voices across the system and build policy for the future rather than simply respond to crises.

Principles

There are some important principles that guide this important restorative work. First is ensuring the direct representation of all parties, especially those who hitherto have been marginalized and silenced. Second is an adherence to democratic processes, building a relevant agenda that is treated seriously and with urgency. Third, is the attempt to build the confidence of less powerful agents at the table. Fourth, is to ensure that time is dedicated to clarifying the meanings and objectives of inclusive education and to establishing a language that transcends the language of special needs. Related to this point was the less than subtle attempts that were made to establish inclusive education as a matter of general education reform incorporating curriculum, pedagogy, assessment and school organization. It was never intended to be a forum for reorganizing the work of special education for disabled students.

I have used this example to describe principles and process. Similar things were happening in Queensland with the 'Partners For Success' work on indigenous education. It is important to note that while I have described a state-wide initiative at the senior levels of the bureaucracy, the restorative process is also important for advancement at the school and classroom level. The same principles apply and the processes may be developed according to local practices, or with local sensitivities to change practices. Key elements are broad and representative engagement, enfranchisement of the hitherto excluded or marginalized, democratic processes, the building of respect, trust and a partnership in the educational enterprise.

None of this happens spontaneously. Brokers are required to bring people to the new fora and to build knowledge through shared communications. Teacher cadres can be mobilized. Investment of time and resources is required, but the potential returns are considerable.

The analytic task

Priorities

I am not inferring that education jurisdictions around the world, teachers' professional associations, assessment and qualifications authorities, or local schools have not been analytic in discharging their duties. They have. Each invests heavily in securing a snapshot of performance that details student enrolment, student profiles and projections, workforce and teacher qualifications data, academic achievement, school statistics for internal review, and for projections for resource requirements and budget prioritizing bids. Different portfolio areas within the education bureaucracy build and review their own data in the expedition of their projects and presenting resource claims. This analytic work is mirrored in schools and classrooms.

The immediate priority for the analytic task is not a call for the establishment of research as a key element of the education worker's portfolio; it is instead a call for its reorientation. Hence, I would be particularly interested in scrutinizing diagnostic and classification patterns and seeing what trends and questions arise before distributing SEN resources to satiate the rising levels of need. A different set of questions could be brought to the table to ask what changing patterns of behaviour classification might signify. Are we looking at individual deficits? Are we looking at problems in the relationships with or the performance of schools? Are we looking at indicators of poverty and privilege? How might we respond in ways that build schools' capacities for embracing difference? Can we build an amalgam of an individual needs model of resources delivery where there are particular requirements for maintaining access and participation with a school reform and capacity-building programme? What alternative analytic skills might we bring to the table? If we want to avoid the perverse effects of an SEN-dominated allocation model, who should be at the research table to make a difference?

How can we build research partnerships that recognize and build the intellectual leadership of the teaching workforce? How do we support people marginalized in and through education to build their data for consideration and response? How do we build value into research tenders and open critique for general response? The questions here are indicative rather than exhaustive, and they lead directly, or are entwined with, the policy task.

Principles

It is important to build analysis that broadens our understanding of exclusion across education systems and in particular demographic profiles. From this point it would be possible to build a research orientation towards the amelioration of exclusion, disengagement and failure. Research ought to be built around a principle of changing the architecture of schooling, and here I am not referring simply to the built environment, pursuant to inclusion. More effort should be put into interrogating how schools might innovate to keep students in school and rely less on outside facilities and placements.

The policy task

Priorities

Policy-making needs to proceed from clearer understandings of exclusion across the portfolio, sectors of government and community agencies. Inclusive education needs to be redefined so that it is decoupled from Special Educational Needs and is part of the motivation for general education reform.

The policy frame needs to engage in serious ways with the articulation of educational failure, disadvantage and poverty. This varies across jurisdictions, but remains a challenge for all.

Policy-makers should shift their view that enhanced performance on tests of functional literacy and mathematics constitutes the measure of achievement for schooling. Here lessons are required to improve assessment literacy so that we can discern differences between tests, standards and assessment for learning.

The professionalization of the teaching force in areas of pedagogy, assessment, curriculum and school reform is a matter of urgency. The difference between performance targets, accountability frameworks and organizational learning is a priority for incorporation in policy reform. In this way valuable resources could be diverted from wasteful inspection measures and put into educational programmes, professional development for teachers and communities and into building networks of learning support to encourage innovation and organizational development.

Principles

The principles of coherence and alignment are critical. There needs to be scans to ensure that different policy initiatives are not compromising each other. And if they are, policy energy should be committed to alignment for educational achievement and inclusion.

All of this does not assume that jurisdictions should start their work from scratch. There exists an impressive international research repository that can be accessed to assist local analyses. Position papers should be distributed to build knowledge and discussion within and across jurisdictions.

Teachers, parents and students should be enlisted in the policy processes. Knowing that policy is made at all levels, policy writers need to develop implementation frameworks that are inclusive and allow for reciprocal engagements over meaning and language, aims and outcomes.

The education task

Priorities

Inclusive education needs to be incorporated as a goal and strategy in the overall reform agenda for education. The measure of education needs to be broadened to reinstate value for socially connected learning, for innovation, for creativity, for critical understanding, for mutuality in learning processes, for connected and thematic teaching and learning, for ongoing assessment and compiling portfolios in preference to high-stakes testing.

Teachers require greater incentive and encouragement to learn throughout their career and be instated as educational leaders in their communities (schools, professional associations and the neighbourhood). Consistency should be applied to the improvement of pedagogy and assessment and teachers should be dissuaded through a recasting of educational priorities from suspending teaching and learning to drill children for tests.

Inclusive education should be seen to be everybody's business in the school. Educating communities about exclusion is critical. Reconnecting equity to education at large to avoid reducing it to functional literacy is required. Improving scores on a reading test do not guarantee equity. Critical Literacy is a more sustaining goal.

Building an understanding of education and schooling as a democratic apprenticeship will necessitate schools rethinking approaches to curriculum planning, pedagogy and decision-making.

Principles

In summary, this is straightforward. I return to the work of Mike Rose, Basil Bernstein, Alain Touraine, Michael Apple and James Beane, and Art Pearl and Tony Knight.[41] Schooling ought to provide an education in democracy. This works at a number of levels. First, the provision of mass compulsory education is itself a democratic initiative. However, the form, content, processes and cultures of that schooling may subvert the democratic intent. I have detailed this at length through the exclusions documented in this book. To be able to critically engage with their world students need requisite knowledge, skills and dispositions. The emphasis here falls on critical understanding and therefore presupposes a curriculum of engagement with the world. Inclusion is obviously a feature of the democratic classroom and that has curriculum, pedagogy, assessment and organizational implications as schools go about reform.

I have assumed a principled stance that departs from the neo-liberal education imagination. Competitive individualism produces a culture that accepts the inevitability and the justifications for injustice and elitism. This is the kind of education that condemns us to continue to endure the major problems of our time: sectarian division, environmental degradation, widening gaps between the affluent and the poor, racism, xenophobia, disablism, sexism and homophobia.

The values task

Priorities

Although the agenda items that precede this represent particular values, I have listed this as a separate agenda item. I use value in two ways. First is to reemphasize the importance of the task of reinstating value to those who have not been valued by or in schools. Schools are often described as a community hub. As such they can represent communities divided by privilege and poverty, competition and personal ambition, racism and prejudice, and neglect. Communities represent and reproduce the collective indifference of which I have been speaking. There is an opportunity to build communities that recognize and represent others who have been shunned, to build rich learning communities of difference.

Second, I list values as an agenda item to stress the necessity for schools to be unequivocal about their values and to integrate those values into curriculum, pedagogy, assessment and organization. The values need to be represented in and articulated through the culture of the school.

Principles

Democratic education and organization presupposes the value of recognition, representation, respect, trust, collaboration, the peaceful resolution of conflict, the presence and recognition of all, informed and participatory decision-making, and the list goes on. In short, I am proposing the school ought to model and be a building block for social improvement. It does not accept inequality and injustice as natural or as a social good.

Reasons to be cheerful (with thanks to Ian Dury)

There is every reason to feel hopeful. We stumble across research and practice that does make a difference. Years ago I met with Chris Sarra, an Indigenous Australian educator, when he was the principal of the Cherbourg Community School. Chris had moved to the school with his wife, another teacher, Grace to take up the challenge of revivifying a dissolute school and community. Adopting the organizing mantra: Strong and Smart, they went about working with and through the community to recapturing a strong and vibrant Aboriginal culture that infused all aspects of the education programme. Theirs was a belief that the children could and would succeed and that the history of underachievement, disengagement, absenteeism, profound alienation and self-doubt was a legacy of a racist education. The Cherbourg Aboriginal children were exhorted to find strength through an alternative vision of Aboriginal identity to that of the racist stereotypes. They were also pressed to understand the need to be smart in order to meet the challenge of the world outside of the school. Chris wanted support to make a film about the school. Publicizing success is an important tactic in building self-confidence and belief. The school turned the numbers on truancy and academic performance. This was achieved by calculated risk and innovation. The audacity to build a culturally specific and rich curriculum, strong pedagogy and authentic assessment. Chris rejected the lowering of expectations and calling it Indigenous education. There is now a vibrant Strong and Smart network across Australia and the Strong and Smart Institute provides leadership for an inclusive education for Aboriginal, Torres Strait Island and all Australian students.

The Royal Children's Hospital in the southern Australian city of Melbourne has long held a commitment to maintain lessons for children whose schooling is disrupted by illness. Transferring from the beachside suburb of Mt. Eliza the school officially opened in its Parkville hospital site in 1969. Like hospital schools across many jurisdictions, the school fell under the administrative authority of the Division of Special Services in the Victorian Department of Education. It was a special school to be staffed by special teachers. This only makes sense as an administrative rationale for dealing with peripheral educational facilities.

The school was closed in 2008 to make way for the Royal Children's Hospital Education Institute. The RCH Education Institute founders, Glenda Strong and Julie Green, exemplify the radical shift in thinking about education and organization imagined by the task agenda. The focus shifted from compensatory education and from children as patients. There was a determination to keep children connected to learning and to schools through long-term and short-term illnesses. Technology was the building block in the architecture of the new school where the student could contact a teacher, somewhere else in the state, in real time. In this way they re-enter their classrooms to participate in the unfolding lessons. Investment was made in the technology and in building the skills of the teaching workforce to engage in this reconnection with and inclusion in learning.

The RCH Education Institute has seriously assumed that learning is a part of its own development. Working with academics like Lyn Yates and Julianne Moss at the University of Melbourne, large research grant funds have been secured to build thirty-nine case studies of young people in hospital to mine their perceptions and incorporate this new intelligence in building inclusive education programmes that keep young people connected through difficult situations, promote health and increase well-being. The RCH Education Institute is also a point of engagement for multidisciplinary health and education teams to build a culture of learning that reaches across all dimensions of the hospital's activity. The RCH Education Institute was a surprise to me as I imagined it to be anchored to and weighed down by the special education model.

These two examples could be augmented by inspiring vignettes from around the world of real schools operating under extreme difficulties. Mithu Alur, an Indian researcher, teacher and mother of a very successful young disabled activist Malini Chib, has an astonishing story to tell about the way in which women in India working with social outcasts in extreme poverty in Mumbai have built their school and established the pride and confidence for mothers and fathers to bring their children back into the world.[42] Developing international partnerships with her colleagues Michael Bach and Vianne Timmons in Canada, Mithu reminds us of the global and local mutuality of the inclusion project. The projects which now span the Indian sub-continent have resulted in the provision of education to children who otherwise would remain outside of school. This work has also commenced the slow and often painful work of changing attitudes towards disabled children and modelling curriculum and pedagogy that demonstrates the educability of all children. Mithu Alur has also strived to connect researchers and educators from around the world to this work, so that the lessons from the projects may be useful to others and to build collective responsibility for sustaining the work.

Readers will be able to add many more stories and examples of inclusive practice that highlight a determination to confront injustice, reduce widening gaps between the affluent and impoverished, change approaches to teaching and learning and build school reform agenda built on principles of democracy and inclusion.

When do we want it? Who does it? Are we capable? On the recording of his concert in London in 2009, Leonard Cohen announces that it is a long time since he stood on a stage in London. 'Fourteen, fifteen years ago. I was sixty; just a kid with a crazy dream.' It is never too early or too late.

I commenced this chapter with reference to Daniel Dorling. Let me call him back to reflect on the depth of inequality in affluent societies:

> ...a seventh of children being labelled today the equivalent of delinquents, a sixth of households excluded from social norms, a fifth of people finding it difficult or very difficult to get by in these times of prejudice; a quarter not having essentials, when there is enough for all; a third now living in families where someone is suffering from mental ill health. The fraction that ends this series of statistics concerns people's ability to choose alternative ways of living and how limited those choices are: *half are disenfranchised*. In the USA almost half of

those old enough to vote either choose not to vote or are barred from voting.[43]

Apathy has risen, contends Dorling, and we are distracted by trying to make a living and by the never-ending quest of consumerism. He further argues that while we were outraged by the disenfranchisement of women and we fought to secure their vote, we now are enveloped by a sense of uselessness. This is the pall of collective indifference.

We want an acknowledgement of exclusion and a determination to dismantle it now, but we know that the task condemns or privileges us to a life of vigilance. All must share in this and this will create difficulty, struggle, tension and new productive relationships. Are we capable? Not alone, we're not.

Notes

1 Approaching accents

1 Sharpe, E. and Rowles, J. H. (2007) *How to do accents*. London, Oberon Books.
2 George Pelecanos, based in Washington, DC, writes American crime fiction and is celebrated as a scriptwriter for the television series, *The Wire*.
3 Public education is a recurrent and important concept in this book. The term is used differentially between countries. For example, in England it refers to privately funded schooling. In Australia it refers to the school systems that are funded by the state and territory governments. Australia has seen a flight from the public system to the misnamed private system of schooling. I say misnamed, because a significant component of the funding for this sector, by Act of parliament, comes from the federal government. The growing drift of pupils from public schools to private schools represents a shift of funding from the state governments to the federal government. Seeing accelerating demand, churches and property developers provide a lower-cost private education for the aspiring lower-middle- and working-class parents wanting to move their children out of the state sector. There has emerged an often heated dinner table conversation about responsible parenting and school choice. In England the variation on this theme is that more affluent parents not able or wanting to pay fees for independent (we struggle for precision) schools will move houses to be in a zone of a high-performing school. It is timely to note that private and public are blurring in public administration (see Ball, S. J. (2003) *Class strategies and the education market: The middle classes and social advantage*. London, Routledge/Falmer; Ball, S. (2007) *Education plc: Understanding private sector participation in public sector education*. London, Routledge; Crump, S. and Slee, R. (2005) Robbing public to pay private? 2 cases of refinancing education infrastructure in Australia. *Journal of Education Policy*, 20(2), 243–258.
4 Watson, D. (2003) *Death sentence: The decay of public language*. Milsons Point, Random House Australia, p. 1.
5 Pearl, A. and Knight, T. (2010) Rejoinder to D. Brent Edwards Jr. and his interpretation of our position on democratic education and social justice. *The Urban Review*.
6 See Oliver, M. (1992) Changing the social relations of research production?, *Disability Handicap and Society*, 7(2), 101–114; Oliver, M. (2009) *Understanding disability: From theory to practice* (2nd Edition). Basingstoke, Palgrave Macmillan; also Allan, J. (2005) Inclusion as an ethical project. In S. Tremain (Ed.) *Foucault and the government of disability*. Ann Arbor, The University of Michigan Press, 281–297 for a counterpoint.
7 Kureishi, H. (2008) *Something to tell you*. London, Faber and Faber Limited.

8 Cowley, S. (2001) *Getting the buggers to behave*. London, Continuum; Cowley, S. (2004) *Getting the buggers to write*. London, Continuum; Farmery, C. (2005) *Getting the buggers into science*. London, Continuum; McCormack, I. and Healey, J. (2008) *Getting the buggers in tune*. London, Continuum; Ollerton, M. (2006) *Getting the buggers to add up*. London, Continuum. This is not a complete listing of this series of texts. It is indicative. There are many other examples of these kinds of 'tips for teachers' texts. It.

9 Cowley, S. (2003) *The guerrilla guide to teaching*. London, Continuum.

10 See Apple, M. W. (2006) *Educating the 'right' way: Markets, standards, god, and inequality* (2nd edition). New York, Routledge. Ball, S. J. (1994) *Education reform: A critical and post-structural approach*. Buckingham, Open University Press; Ball, S. J. (2007) *Education plc: Understanding private sector participation in public sector education*. London, Routledge; Ball, S. J. (2008) *The education debate*. Bristol, Policy Press.

11 Machin, S. and Vignoles, A. (2005) *What's the good of education? The economics of education in the UK*. Princeton, Princeton University Press.

12 Rose, M. (1995) *Possible lives: the promise of public education in America*. Boston, Houghton Mifflin Co.

13 Watson, D. (2004) *Watson's dictionary of weasel words, contemporary cliches, cant and management jargon*. Milsons Point, NSW, Knopf.

14 Here I am alluding to *Newspeak*, the state-invented language to control public thought in his novel, *Nineteen eighty-four*.

15 In fact Watson suggests as much in passing comments on new education jargon. He registers his suspicion of applying the word studies to subject titles in curriculum prospectuses and of the uses and abuses of 'deconstruction'. (See Watson, D. (2003) *Death sentence: The decay of public language*. Milsons Point, NSW, Random House, Australia.)

16 Slee, R. (1993) The politics of integration: New sites for old practices? *Disability, Handicap and Society*, 8(4), 351–360.

17 See Sacks, P. (1999) *Standardized minds: The high price of America's testing culture and what we can do to change it*. Cambridge, Mass., Perseus Books; Stobart, G. (2008) *Testing times: the uses and abuses of assessment*. London, Routledge; Johnson, D. D. and Johnson, B. (2006) *High stakes: Poverty, testing, and failure in American schools* (2nd edition). Lanham, Rowman and Littlefield Publishers.

18 Stobart, G. (2008) *Testing times: The uses and abuses of assessment*. London, Routledge, p. 29.

19 Wilby, P. (2007) Ken Boston: Big brother is testing you. *The Guardian*, Tuesday 25 September. www.guardian.co.uk/education/2007/sep/25/highereducation. schools – retrieved July 12th 18.45.

20 See Slee, R., Weiner, G. and Tomlinson, S. (1998) *School effectiveness for whom? Challenges to the school effectiveness and school improvement movements*. London, Falmer; Hargreaves, A. (2008) *The persistence of presentism and the struggle for lasting improvement*. London, Institute of Education, University of London; Ball, S. J. (2008) *The education debate*. Bristol, Policy Press.

21 See Luke, A. (2003) After the marketplace: Evidence, social science and educational research. *The Australian Educational Researcher*, 30(2), 87–107; Ball, S. J. (1994) *Education reform: A critical and post-structural approach*. Buckingham, Open University Press.

22 Penketh, C. (2010) A clumsy encounter: The dyspraxic ideal meets drawing from observation as an official discriminatory discourse. London, Goldsmiths, unpublished PhD thesis.

23 See Brown, M. (1998) The tyranny of the international horse race. In R. Slee, G. Weiner and S. Tomlinson (Eds) *School effectiveness for whom?* London,

Falmer Press; Black, P. J. (2002) *Working inside the black box: Assessment for learning in the classroom*. London, King's College London, Department of Education and Professional Studies; Lingard, B. and Ozga, J. (2007) *The Routledge Falmer reader in education policy and politics*. London, Routledge.

24 See op. cit. Apple (2006); also Apple, M. W. (2000) *Official knowledge: Democratic education in a conservative age* (2nd edition). New York, Routledge.

25 Kozol, J. (2000) Foreword. In D. Meier, J. Cohen and J. Rogers (Eds) *Will standards save public education?* Boston, Beacon Press, p. xiii.

26 *Civic Imagination* is borrowed from the previously cited Mike Rose (1995) *Possible Lives* research.

27 Garner, H. (2008) *The spare room*. London, Canongate Books, p. 171.

28 Ball, S. (1994) *Education reform: A critical and post-structural approach*. Buckingham, Open University Press.

29 PISA refers to the OECD Programme for International Student Assessment of 15 year olds that is led by the Australian Council for Educational Research (ACER). PISA is implemented triennially and in 2006 involved students from fifty-seven countries. TIMSS refers to the Trends in International Mathematics and Science Study that is governed by the International Association for Evaluation and Educational Achievement. Commencing in 1995 to track the achievement of students in mathematics and science at grade 4 and grade 8, the study reported in 2007 on fifty-eight countries and educational jurisdictions that participated in TIMSS in grade 4, grade 8 or both levels.

30 When I wrote the first draft of this chapter the call to terminate the contract with the US-based company Educational Testing Service and to seek compensation for students and schools was issued following the debacle of the delay in the posting of national test results, the emergence of numerous complaints from script markers and escalating student appeals (supported by their head-teachers) echoed across England. Subsequently the test was dropped at the Year X level, and months later the Secretary of State for Education has suggested that the tests may not be supported in the future.

31 See Apple, M. W. (2006) *Educating the 'right' way: Markets, standards, god, and inequality* (2nd edition). New York, Routledge; Whitty, G. (2002) *Making sense of education policy: Studies in the sociology and politics of education*. London, Paul Chapman Publishers.

32 Op. cit. Stobart (2008), p. 134.

33 Gipps, C. V. and Murphy, P. (1994) *A fair test?: Assessment, achievement and equity*. Buckingham, Open University Press; Black, P. J. (1998) *Testing: Friend or foe? Theory and practice of assessment and testing*. London, Falmer Press.

34 Op. cit. Stobart (2008), p. 116.

35 Gillborn, D. and Youdell, D. (2000) *Rationing education: Policy, practice, reform, and equity*. Buckingham, Open University Press.

36 Michael Gove speech to Conservative Party Conference, 1 September, 2007.

37 William, D. (2001) Reliability, validity and all that jazz. *Education*, 29(3), 3–13.

38 Op. cit. Stobart (2008), p. 143. See also Black, P. J. (2003) *Assessment for learning: Putting it into practice*. Maidenhead, Open University Press; William, D., Lee, C., Harrison, C. and Black, P. (2004) Teachers developing assessment for learning impact on student achievement. *Assessment in Education: Principles, Policy and Practice*, 11(1), 49–66; and Newmann, F. M. (1996) *Authentic achievement: Restructuring schools for intellectual quality*. San Francisco, Jossey-Bass.

39 Johnson, D. D. and Johnson, B. (2006) *High stakes: Poverty, testing, and failure in American schools* (2nd edition). Lanham, Rowman and Littlefield Publishers.

40 Luke, A. (2003) After the marketplace: Evidence, social science and educational research. *The Australian Educational Researcher*, 30(2), 87–107.
41 Queensland Department of Education (2001) *New basics: Curriculum organisers* (Brisbane, Education Queensland).
42 Queensland Department of Education (2001) *The Queensland school reform longitudinal study*. Brisbane, The State of Queensland (Department of Education).
43 Rose, J., Department for Children, Schools and Families (2009) *The independent review of the primary curriculum: Final report*. London, Department for Children, Schools and Families.
44 Alexander, R. J. (2009) *Towards a new primary curriculum*. Cambridge, Cambridge Primary Review, University of Cambridge Faculty of Education.
45 Ball, S. (2008) *The education debate*. Bristol, Policy Press.
46 Fairclough, N. (2000) *New labour, new language?* London, Routledge.
47 Ball, S. (2007) Education plc: *Understanding private sector participation in public sector education*. London, Routledge, p. 2.
48 See, for example, the Minister of State for School Standards, David Miliband's address to The Education Network Conference in London on 11 February 2004.
49 Tony Blair in Barber, M. (2007) *Instruction to deliver: Tony Blair, public services and the challenge of achieving targets*. London, Politico's, p. 23.
50 See Wilkinson, R. G. and Pickett, K. (2009) *The spirit level: Why more equal societies almost always do better*. London, Allen Lane. Also Sibieta, L., Chowdry, H. and Muriel, A. (2008) *Level playing field? The implications of school funding*. London, CfBT Education Trust.
51 Op. cit. Ball (2007) and Slee, R., Weiner, G. and Tomlinson, S. (1998) *School effectiveness for whom? Challenges to the school effectiveness and school improvement movements*. London, Falmer Press.
52 Watson, D. (2003) *Death sentence: The decay of public language*. Milsons Point, Random House Australia.
53 Op. cit. Fairclough.
54 Op. cit. Barber (2007) p. 36.
55 www.standards.dfes.gov.uk/phonics/programmes/ referred to on the DCSF 'Standards Site' on Friday, 22 August, 2008 at 11.30am.
56 www.ioe.ac.uk/schools/ecpe/readingrecovery/pp./index_Preventing%20lit%20 failure%20leaflet.pdf referred to on Friday, 22 August, 2008 at 11.35 am. See also Clay, M. M. (1994) *Reading recovery: A guidebook for teachers in training*. Portsmouth, Heinemann.
57 www.education.vic.gov.au/studentlearning/teachingresources/english/literacy/ strategies/4txtparttsl4.htm referred to on Friday, 22 August, 2008 at 12.05pm. See also Freebody, P., Muspratt, S. and Dwyer, B. (2001) *Difference, silence, and textual practice: Studies in critical literacy*. Cresskill, NJ, Hampton Press.
58 Polk, K. (1984) The new marginal youth. *Crime and Delinquency*, 30: 462–480. McDonald, K. (1999) *Struggles for subjectivity: Identity, action, and youth experience*. Cambridge, Cambridge University Press; Thomson, P. (2002) *Schooling the rustbelt kids: Making the difference in changing times*. Stoke-on-Trent, Trentham Books.
59 Reid, K. (1999) *Truancy and schools*. London, Routledge.
60 Ball, S. (2008) *The education debate*. Bristol, Policy Press, p. 176.
61 BBC Report, http://news.bbc.co.uk/1/hi/education/4232643.stm Friday, 22 August, 2008 at 12.35 pm.
62 Parsons, C. and Ebrary, I. (1999) *Education, exclusion, and citizenship*. London, Routledge; Parsons, C. (2009) *Strategic alternatives to exclusion from school*. Stoke on Trent, Trentham Books.

63 Slee, R. (1994) *Changing theories and practices of discipline*. London, Falmer Press.

64 Ibid. Slee (1994); Rose, S. (2005) *The 21st century brain: Explaining, mending and manipulating the mind*. London, Vintage; Laurence, J. and McCallum, D. (2009) *Inside the child's head. Histories of childhood behavioural disorders*. Rotterdam, Sense Publishers.

65 Graham, L. J. and Slee, R. (2008) An illusory interiority: Interrogating the discourse/s of inclusion. *Educational Philosophy and Theory*, 40(2), 277–293; Graham, L. J. and Sweller, N. (in press) The inclusion lottery: Who's in and who's out? Tracking inclusion and exclusion in New South Wales government schools. *International Journal of Inclusive Education*.

66 Cooper, P. (2008) Like alligators bobbing for poodles? A critical discussion of education, ADHD and the biopsychosocial perspective. *Journal of Philosophy in Education*, 42(3–4), 457–474.

67 Daniels, H. (2006) The dangers of corruption in special needs education. *British Journal of Special Education*, 33(1), 4–10; Tait, G. (2010) *Philosophy, behaviour disorders and the school*. Rotterdam, Sense Publishers.

68 Canute was the son of Sweyn Forkbeard, King of Denmark and it is believed that he was born between 980AD and 990AD. A fearsome Viking warrior and powerful ruler throughout Scandinavia and parts of Britain he died in Shaftesbury in Dorset in the year 1035. My reference to him concerns the legendary tale of how he demonstrated the fallibility of man in the face of God by having his throne set at the water's edge on the beach so that he could stem the tide. 'Let all men know how empty and worthless is the power of kings. For there is none worthy of the name but God, whom heaven, earth and sea obey'.

69 Hargreaves, A. and Shirley, D. (2009) *The fourth way: The inspiring future for educational change*. Thousand Oaks, Calif., Corwin Press, pp. 36–37.

70 Ibid., p. 36.

71 Deveson, A. (1991) *Tell me I'm here*. Ringwood, Penguin Books, p. 2.

72 Kauffman, J. M. and Hallahan, D. P. (2005) *The illusion of full inclusion: A comprehensive critique of a current special education bandwagon* (2nd Edition). Austin, Pro-Ed; Kavale, K. A. and Mostert, M. P. (2004) *The positive side of special education: Minimizing its fads, fancies, and follies* (Lanham, Scarecrow Education; Kauffman, J. and Sasso, G. (2006) Toward ending cultural and cognitive relativism in special education. *Exceptionality*, 14(2), 65–90; Farrell, M. (2006) *Celebrating the special school*. London, Routledge.

73 Brantlinger, E. (1997) Using ideology: Cases of non-recognition of the politics of research and practice in special education. *Review of Educational Research*, 67(4), 425–459; Allan, J. and Slee, R. (2008) *Doing inclusive education research*. Rotterdam, Sense Publishers; Brantlinger, E. A. (Ed.) (2006) *Who benefits from special education?: Remediating (fixing) other people's children*. Mahwah, NJ, Erlbaum Associates.

74 Bourdieu, P. (1998) *Practical reason: On the theory of action*. Stanford, Calif., Stanford University Press, pp. 8–9.

75 Mount, F. (2004) *Mind the gap: The new class divide in Britain*. London, Short Books.

76 Ibid., p. 10.

77 Ibid., p. 11.

78 Op. cit. (Wilkinson and Pickett).

79 Mussolini's fascists in Rome imprisoned Antonio Gramsci (1891–1937) under the provisions of a series of Exceptional Laws on 8 November, 1926. Whilst incarcerated he wrote more than thirty prison notebooks and 3,000 pp. of history and analysis during his imprisonment. His contributions to social and political theory are many, but here I simply refer to his notion that capitalism

had achieved its resilience through *cultural hegemony*. Simply put, the perspectives of the bourgeoisie had been established as natural or as the *common sense* and formed a proletarian false consciousness. Social and cultural institutions such as schools and universities, art and literature became instruments for the development and sustaining of this dominant perspective.

80 Department for Education and Skills (2003) *Every child matters: Summary*. Nottingham, DfES Publications.

81 One of the most moving scenes in the play is where Galileo's student visits him after he has recanted his scientific proclamations and suggests to him that he was being strategic in backing down so that he could continue the scientific project. Hence, Andrea's statement is offered to reassure his mentor and retain pride, about taking a lateral course of action in the face of obstacles. Brecht, B. (1963) *The life of Galileo*. London, Methuen.

82 Kutchins, H. and Kirk, S. A. (1997) *Making us crazy: DSM – The psychiatric bible and the creation of mental disorders*. New York, Free Press.

83 Norwich, B. (2008) *Dilemmas of difference, inclusion and disability: International perspectives and future directions*. London, Routledge.

84 Pearl, A. and Knight, T. (1998) *The democratic classroom: Theory to inform practice*. Cresskill, NJ, Hampton Press; Gutman, A. (1999) *Democratic education*. Princeton, NJ, Princeton University Press; Allan, J. (Ed.) (2003) *Inclusion, participation and democracy: What is the purpose?* Dordrecht, Kluwer Academic.

85 Hall, S. and Jacques, M. (1989) *New times: The changing face of politics in the 1990s*. London, Lawrence and Wishart in association with 'Marxism Today'. Hall and Jacques's book with the title *New times* was a signal to the traditional left that their analysis was lagging, that it had failed to recognize that Conservatism was the new force of radicalism, albeit a radical right agenda, and that left, adhering to old analytic frames was incapable of recognizing the forces at work in 'new times'. This is a powerful metaphor that Allan Luke adopted in attempting to shift the education agenda in Queensland and I will retain for this discussion.

86 As cited in Thomas, G. and Loxley, A. (2007) *Deconstructing special education and constructing inclusion* (2nd Edition). Maidenhead, Open University Press, p. 10. See also Rizvi, F. and Lingard, B. (2009) *Globalizing education policy*. London, Routledge.

87 Allan, J. (2005) Inclusion as an ethical project. In S. Tremain (Ed.) *Foucault and the government of disability*. Ann Arbor, The University of Michigan Press, p. 293.

88 Bronfenbrenner, U. (2005) *Making human beings human: Bioecological perspectives on human development*. Thousand Oaks, Sage.

89 Here I refer to Mike Rose's (1995) declaration that public education is America's boldest democratic experiment.

90 Bernstein, B. (1996) *Pedagogy, symbolic control and identity: Theory, research, critique*. London, Taylor & Francis, p. 6.

91 Ball, S. (2007) *Education plc: Understanding private sector participation in public sector education*. London, Routledge, p. 184.

92 Op. cit. Norwich (2008).

93 UNESCO (2000) *World education report 2000: The right to education: Towards education for all throughout life*. Paris, UNESCO.

2 The worlds we live in

1 Sachs, J. (2005) *The end of poverty: How we can make it happen in our lifetime*. Harmondsworth, Penguin, p. 1.

2 Ibid., p. 1.
3 Chen, S. and Ravallion, M. (2008) *The developing world is poorer than we thought, but no less successful in the fight against poverty*. Report for World Bank. Washington, DC, p. 3.
4 Ibid., p. 1.
5 Fraser, A. and Emmett, B. (2005) *Paying the price: Why rich countries must invest now in a war on poverty*. Oxford, Oxfam International, p. 11.
6 Emmett, B., Green, D. and Wateraid (2006) *In the public interest: Health, education, and water and sanitation for all*. Oxford, Oxfam International, p. 73.
7 Jones, P. W. (2006) *Education, poverty and the World Bank*. Rotterdam, Sense Publishers, p. 165.
8 Ibid., Jones p. 23.
9 Ibid., Jones (2006), p. 23.
10 See Jones (2006). 'Rogernomics' refers to the conservative economic agenda of the New Zealand government led by the charismatic fourth Labour Prime Minister David Lange. Lange appointed Roger Douglas as his Minister of Finance in 1984, a position he occupied until the end of 1988. Rogernomics was an adaptation of 'Reaganomics', a term used to describe the monetarist policies of President Ronald Reagan in the USA. Like Reagan in the USA and Thatcher in the UK, Lange's ardent Finance Minister – Roger Owen Douglas – pursued a programme of deregulation and the dismantling of the public sector. The backlash to this economic course was heightened when Douglas proposed a flat tax scheme and resulted in David Lange dismissing him from the Finance Office and cabinet.
11 Moyo, D. (2009) *Dead aid: Why aid is not working and how there is another way for Africa*. London, Penguin Books, pp. 38–39.
12 Lewis, S. (2005) *Race against time*. Toronto, House of Anansi Press.
13 Ibid., pp. 4–5.
14 Ibid., p. 5.
15 Emmett, B., Green, D., Lawson, M., Calaguas, B., Aikman, S., Kamal-Yanni, M. and Smyth, I. (2006) *In the public interest: Health, education, and water and sanitation for all*. Oxford, Oxfam International.
16 Ball, S. J. and Youdell, D. (2008) *Hidden privatisation in public education*. Report for Institute of Education, University of London.
17 Op. cit., Lewis (2005), pp. 5–6.
18 Beyers, C. and Hay, J. (2007) Can inclusive education in South(ern) Africa survive the HIV and AIDS pandemic? *International Journal of Inclusive Education*, 11(4), 387–399.
19 Op. cit., Lewis (2005), p. 12.
20 Ibid., p. 17.
21 Ibid., p. 23.
22 Ibid., p. 22.
23 Op. cit. Moyo (2009), p. 144.
24 Riddell, R. (2008) *Does foreign aid really work?* Oxford, Oxford University Press.
25 Connell, R. (1994) Education and poverty. *Harvard Educational Review*, 64(2), 125–149.
26 Ahwan, L. (2002) 50 sew lips together in hunger strike, detainees claim. *The Age*, 27 June. www.theage.com.au/articles/2002/06/27/1023864626046.html viewed on 12 July, 2010 at 20.29.
27 Baudrillard, J. and Redhead, S. (2008) *The Jean Baudrillard reader*. Edinburgh, Edinburgh University Press.
28 Op. cit., Sachs (2006).
29 Sen, A. (2003) Humanity, security and educational gaps. Keynote Presentation

at the 15th Conference of the Commonwealth Ministers of Education. Access, inclusion and achievement: closing the gaps. Edinburgh.

30 UNICEF (2007) Child poverty in perspective: An overview of child well-being in rich countries. A comprehensive assessment of the lives and well-being of children and adolescents in the economically advanced nations. Report Card 7. Report for Innocenti Research Centre. Florence, UNICEF.

31 Ibid., p. 3.

32 Rainwater, L. and Smeeding, T. M. (2003) *Poor kids in a rich country. America's children in comparative perspective.* New York, Russell Sage Foundation, p. 31.

33 Fabian Society (2006) Narrowing the gap: The final report of the Fabian commission on life chances and child poverty. London, Fabian Society, p. 115.

34 Ibid., p. 119.

35 Ibid., p. 140.

36 Ibid., p. 141.

37 Ibid., p. 119.

38 Ibid., p. 136.

39 Toynbee, P. and Walker, D. N. (2008) *Unjust rewards: Exposing greed and inequality in Britain today.* London, Granta, pp. 43–44.

40 Ibid., pp. 82–83.

41 Op. cit. Fabian Society (2006), p. 118.

42 Op. cit. Toynbee and Walker (2007), p. 44.

43 Op. cit. Wilkinson and Pickett (2009).

44 Kozol, J. (1991) *Savage inequalities: Children in America's schools.* New York, Crown Publishers and Kozol, J. and Ebrary, I. (2005) *The shame of the nation: The restoration of apartheid schooling in America.* New York, Crown Publishers.

45 Op. cit. Kozol (1991), p. 7.

46 Op. cit. Jones (2006), p. 3.

47 Op. cit. Kozol (1991), p. 4.

48 Op. cit. Kozol and Ebrary (2005), p. 19.

49 Ibid., pp. 20–22.

50 Ibid., p. 20.

51 www.cityofsydney.nsw.gov.au/community/HomelessnessServices/InformationKitForVolunteers/Module1/OverviewOfHomelessness.asp (10.38 pm, 4/3/2010).

52 Layton, J. (2000) *Homelessness: The making and unmaking of a crisis.* Toronto, Penguin.

53 Greater Toronto Area Task Force (Ontario) and Golden, A. (1996) *Greater Toronto: Taking responsibility for homelessness: an action plan for Toronto.* Toronto, Queen's Printer.

54 U.S. Department of Housing and Urban Development (2008) *The third annual homeless assessment report to congress.* Report for the Office of Community Planning and Development, Washington, D.C.

55 Ibid., p. 2.

56 Op. cit. Connell (1994).

57 Ibid., p. 130.

58 See Oliver, M. (1996) *Understanding disability: From theory to practice.* Basingstoke, Macmillan; Barnes, C., Oliver, M. and Barton, L. (2002) *Disability studies today.* Cambridge, Polity Press in association with Blackwell Publishers.

59 Op. cit. Wilkinson and Pickett (2009).

60 Bhopal, K. and Myers, M. (2008) *Insiders, outsiders and others: Gypsies and identity.* Hatfield, University of Hertfordshire Press.

61 Reynolds, H. (1999) *Why weren't we told? A personal search for the truth about our history.* Ringwood, Viking; Sarra, C. and Australian College of

Educators. (2003) *Young and black and deadly: Strategies for improving outcomes for indigenous students*. Deakin West, ACT, Australian College of Educators.

62 Op. cit. Wilkinson and Pickett (2009), p. 4.
63 Sibley, D. (1995) *Geographies of exclusion: Society and difference in the west*. London, Routledge.
64 Giddens, A. (1998) *The third way: The renewal of social democracy*. Cambridge, Polity Press.
65 Harvey, D. (1996) *Justice, nature, and the geography of difference*. Oxford, Blackwell Publishers.
66 Op. cit. Wilkinson and Pickett (2009).
67 Mirza, H. S. (2009) *Race, gender and educational desire: Why black women succeed and fail*. London, Routledge; Reiss, M. J., Depalma, R. E. and Atkinson, E. (Eds) (2007) *Marginality and difference in education and beyond*. Stoke on Trent, Trentham Books; Youdell, D. (2006c) 'Diversity, inequality and a post-structural politics for education, *Discourse*, 27(1), 33–42.
68 Slee (1996) Disabled People and Poverty. In C. Christensen and F. Rizvi (Eds) (1996) *Disability and dilemmas of education and justice*. Buckingham, Open University Press.
69 Bauman, Z. (1997) *Postmodernity and its discontents*. Cambridge, Polity.
70 Op. cit. Wilkinson and Pickett (2009), p. 190.
71 Op. cit. Kozol (1991), p. 5.
72 Matthews, J. (2008) Schooling and settlement: Refugee education in Australia. *International Studies in Sociology of Education*, 18(1), 31–45.
73 Op. cit. Rizvi and Lingard (2009).
74 Op. cit. Bauman (1997), p. 22.
75 Allan, J. (2005) Inclusion as an ethical project. In S. Tremain (Ed.) *Foucault and the government of disability*. Ann Arbor, The University of Michigan Press, p. 293.
76 Oliver, M. (1990) *The politics of disablement*. London, Macmillan.
77 Wright Mills, C. (1959) *The sociological imagination*. New York, Oxford University Press.

3 Unravelling collective indifference

1 Sachs, J. (2005) *The end of poverty: How we can make it happen in our lifetime*. Harmondsworth, Penguin.
2 Rizvi, F. and Lingard, B. (2009) *Globalizing education policy*. London, Routledge.
3 Taylor, C. (2004) *Modern social imaginaries*. Durham, Duke University Press.
4 Knight, T. (1985) An apprenticeship in democracy. *The Australian Teacher*, 11(1), 5–7; Pearl, A. and Knight, T. (1998) *The democratic classroom: Theory to inform practice*. Cresskill, NJ, Hampton Press.
5 'First of all, there are the conditions for an effective democracy. I am not going to derive these from high-order principles; I am just going to announce them. The first condition is that people must feel they have a stake in society.' Bernstein, B. (1996) *Pedagogy, symbolic control and identity: Theory, research, critique*. London, Taylor & Francis, pp. 6 and 7.
6 Touraine, A. (2000) *Can we live together? Equality and difference*. Cambridge, Polity Press, p. 195.
7 Sen, A. (1999) *Development as freedom*. New York, Knopf, p. 3.
8 Cigman, R. (Ed.) (2007) *Included or excluded? The challenge of the mainstream for some SEN children*. London, Routledge; Farrell, M. (2006) *Celebrating the special school*. London, Routledge.

9 www.edgazette.govt.nz/Articles/Article.aspx?ArticleId=7901 (From Values to Action. An interview with Professor Tony Booth. *Education Gazette*, New Zealand Ministry of Education. Retrieved on 8/03/2010 at 2.28 am).

10 Op. cit. Farrell (2006).

11 Zizek, S. (2008) *In defense of lost causes*. London, Verso.

12 Ibid., p. 7.

13 Op. cit. Farrell (2006), pp. 1–2.

14 Graham, L.J. and Sweller, N. (in press) The inclusion lottery: Who's in and who's out? Tracking inclusion and exclusion in New South Wales government schools. *International Journal of Inclusive Education*.

15 American Psychiatric Association (2000) *Diagnostic and statistical manual of mental disorders: DSM-IV-TR* (4th Edition). Washington, DC, American Psychiatric Association.

16 Kutchins, H. and Kirk, S. A. (1997) *Making us crazy. DSM: The psychiatric bible and the creation of mental disorders*. New York, Free Press.

17 Daniels, H. (2006) The dangers of corruption in special needs education. *British Journal of Special Education*, 33(1), 4–10.

18 Op. cit. Farrell (2006), pp. 16 and 17.

19 Baroness Mary Warnock famously chaired the Committee of Enquiry into the education of handicapped children and young people, publishing its report, *Special Educational Needs*, in 1978. The report had profound and positive impacts on education in England and Wales and supported greater levels of integration of children with special educational needs in ordinary classrooms in their neighbourhood schools. In 2005 in a pamphlet written for The Philosophy Society of Great Britain's Impact series (Number 11) entitled, *Special Educational needs: A new look*, Baroness Warnock pronounced inclusive education to be 'the most disastrous legacy of the 1978 report' (p. 22).

20 Kauffman, J. M. and Hallahan, D. P. (2005) *The illusion of full inclusion: A comprehensive critique of a current special education bandwagon.* (2nd Edition). Austin, Tex., Pro-Ed.

21 Kauffman, J. and Sasso, G. (2006) Toward ending cultural and cognitive relativism in special education. *Exceptionality*, 14(2), 65–90.

22 Kavale, K. and Mostert, M. (2004) *The positive side of special education. Minimizing its fads, fancies and follies*. Lanham, Scarecrow Education.

23 Mostert, M. P., Kavale, K. A. and Kauffman, J. M. (2008) *Challenging the refusal of reasoning in special education*. Denver, Love Publishing.

24 Armstrong, D. (2003) *Experiences of special education: Re-evaluating policy and practice through life stories*. London, Routledge Falmer.

25 Op. cit. Zizek (2008), p. 7.

26 Barton, L. (2003) Inclusive education and teacher education: A basis for hope or a discourse of delusion. Professorial Lecture. London, Institute of Education, University of London.

27 Oliver, M. (1992) Changing the social relations of research production? *Disability Handicap and Society*, 7(2), 101–114.

28 Ballard, K. (2003) Including ourselves: Teaching, trust, identity and community. In J. Allan (Ed.) *Inclusion, participation and democracy: What is the purpose?* Dordrecht, Kluwer Academic Publishers, pp. 11–32 and Ballard, K. and McDonald, T. (1999) Disability, inclusion and exclusion: Some insider accounts and interpretations. In K. Ballard (Ed.) *Inclusive education. International voices on disability and justice*. London, Falmer Press, pp. 97–115.

29 Barton, L. (2005) *Special educational needs: An alternative look. A response to Warnock, M. 2005: Special educational needs – a new look*. Available online at: www.leeds.ac.uk/disability-studies/archiveuk/barton/Warnock.pdf (accessed 9 January 2010).

30 Armstrong, F. and Barton, L. (1999) *Disability, human rights and education: Cross-cultural perspectives*. Buckingham, Open University Press.

31 An allusion to the protagonist's anxiety about moving from the superficial to a more meaningful social interrogation in 'The Love Song of J. Alfred Prufrock'. T. S. Eliot (1917) *Prufrock and Other Observations*. London, Faber and Faber.

32 Bourdieu, P. and Passeron, J.-C. (1977) *Reproduction in education, society and culture*. London, Sage Publications.

33 Uditsky, B. (1993) From integration to inclusion: The canadian experience. In R. Slee (Ed.) *Is there a desk with my name on it?* London, Falmer Press; Rice, M. (1993) Integration: Another form of specialism. In R. Slee (Ed.) *Is there a desk with my name on it?* London, Falmer Press. Marks, G. (1993) Contetsts in decision-making at the school level. In R. Slee (Ed.) *Is there a desk with my name on it?* London, Falmer Press; Rogers, C. (2007) *Parenting and inclusive education: Discovering difference, experiencing difficulty*. Basingstoke, Palgrave Macmillan.

34 Bauman, Z. (2004) *Wasted lives: Modernity and its outcasts*. Oxford, Polity.

35 Ball, S. J. (1994) *Education reform: A critical and post-structural approach*. Buckingham, Open University Press; Gewirtz, S., Ball, S. J. and Bowe, R. (1995) *Markets, choice, and equity in education*. Buckingham, Open University Press.

36 Slee, R. (1998) High reliability organisations and liability students – the politics of recognition. In R. Slee, G. Weiner and S. Tomlinson (Eds) *School effectiveness for whom?* London, Falmer Press, pp. 101–114.

37 Individual Education Plans (IEP), which in some jurisdictions are mandated to demonstrate compliance with disability discrimination legislation, are plans drawn up by teachers in collaboration with relevant professional workers and parents to outline the educational objectives and teaching strategies for their child. The IEP will also contain statements of resource requirements and of the roles of various adults working with the child. For some, IEPs are seen as the guarantee of an inclusive education, for others it is seen as an instrument of the child's separation – an instrument of surveillance, control and exclusion.

38 Kearney, A. (2008) *Barriers to school inclusion: An investigation into the exclusion of disabled students from and within New Zealand schools*. Palmerston North, Massey University.

39 Florian, L. and Mclaughlin, M. J. (2008) *Disability classification in education: Issues and perspectives*. Thousand Oaks, CA, Corwin Press; Op. cit. Rogers (2007); Galloway, D., Armstrong, D. and Tomlinson, S. (1994) *The assessment of special educational needs: Whose problem?* Harlow, Longman; Slee, R. (1996) Clauses of conditionality. In L. Barton (Ed.) *Disability and society: Emerging issues and insights*. London, Longman.

40 Balshaw, M. H. and Farrell, P. (2002) *Teaching assistants: Practical strategies for effective classroom support*. London, David Fulton. Giangreco, M. (2003) Working with paraprofessionals. *Educational Leadership*, 61(2): 50–53. Bourke, P. E. (2009) Professional development and teaching assistants in inclusive education contexts: Where to from here? *International Journal of Inclusive Education*, 13(8): 817–827.

41 Biklen, D. (1985) *Achieving the complete school*. New York, Teachers College Press.

42 McDonald, K. (2006) *Global movements: Action and culture*. Oxford, Blackwell, p. viii.

43 Ibid., p. 13.

44 Op. cit. Rizvi and Lingard (2009), pp. 22 and 23.

45 Ibid., pp. 4–6.

46 Friedman, T. L. (2000) *The Lexus and the olive tree*. New York, Anchor Books.

47 Giddens, A. (1999) *Runaway world: How globalisation is reshaping our lives*. London, Profile.

48 Op. cit. McDonald (2006), p. 9.
49 Castells, M. (2000) *The rise of the network society*. Oxford, Blackwell.
50 Appadurai, A. (1996) *Modernity at large: Cultural dimensions of globalization*. Minneapolis, University of Minnesota Press.
51 Ibid., p. 17.
52 Law, J. and Urry, J. (2004) Enacting the social. *Economy and Society*, 33(3), 390–410.
53 Kenway, J. and Bullen, E. (2001) *Consuming children: Educational-entertainment advertising*. Buckingham, Open University Press.
54 McLeod, J. and Yates, L. (2006) *Making modern lives: Subjectivity, schooling, and social change*. Albany, NY, State University of New York Press; McLeod, J. and Allard, A. (2007) *Learning from the margins: Young women, social exclusion and education*. London, Routledge; Thomson, P. (2002) *Schooling the rustbelt kids: Making the difference in changing times*. Stoke-on-Trent, Trentham Books.
55 Sennett, R. (2006) *The culture of the new capitalism*. London, Yale University Press.
56 Ibid., p. 1.
57 Jessop, B. (2002) *The future of the capitalist state*. Oxford, Polity.
58 Op. cit. Sennett (2006), p. 2.
59 Ignatieff, M. (1986) *The needs of strangers*. New York, Penguin Books, p. 16.
60 Ibid., p. 18.
61 Giddens, A. (2000) *The third way and its critics*. Cambridge, Polity Press.
62 Sennett (1991), p. 126.
63 Op. cit. Sennett (2006), p. 3.
64 Op. cit. McDonald (2006), p. 86.
65 Op. cit. Sennett (2006), p. 181.
66 Ibid., pp. 86–99.
67 Op. cit. Bauman (2004), p. 39.
68 Ibid., p. 40.
69 Ibid., p. 40.
70 Bauman, Z. (1997) *Postmodernity and its discontents*. Cambridge, Polity, p. 22.
71 Ibid., p. 81.
72 Levitin, D. J. (2008) *The world in six songs: How the musical brain created human nature*. New York, Dutton, p. 2.
73 Allan, J. (2005) Disability arts and the performance of ideology. In S. L. Gabel (Ed.) *Disability studies in education. Readings in theory and method*. New York, Peter Lang, pp. 37–51; Allan, J. (2004) The aesthetics of disability as a productive ideology. In L. Ware (Ed.) *Ideology and the politics of (in)exclusion*. New York, Peter Lang, pp. 32–45; Titchkosky, T. (2003) *Disability, self, and society*, Toronto, University of Toronto Press; Johnston, K. (2009) New strategies for representing mental illness on Canadian stages. *International Journal of Inclusive Education*, 13(7), 755–766.
74 Oliver, M. (2009) *Understanding disability: From theory to practice* (2nd edn). Basingstoke, Palgrave Macmillan; Roman, L. G. (2009) Go figure! Public pedagogies, invisible impairments and the performative paradoxes of visibility as veracity. *International Journal of Inclusive Education*, 13(7), 677–698.
75 Hevey, D. (1992) *The creatures time forgot: Photography and disability imagery*. New York, Routledge; Bogdan, R. (1988) *Freak show: Presenting human oddities for amusement and profit*. Chicago, University of Chicago Press.
76 Barnartt, S. N. and Kabzems, V. (1992) Zimbabwean teachers' attitudes towards the integration of pupils with disabilities into regular classrooms. *International Journal of Disability, Development and Education*, 39(2), 135–146;

Berryman, J. D. (1988) Attitudes toward mainstreaming: Factorial validity for a lay population. *Educational and Psychological Measurement*, 48: 231–236; Hudson, A. and Clunies-Ross, G. (1984) A study of the integration of children with intellectual handicaps into regular schools. *Australian and New Zealand Journal of Developmental Disabilities*, 10: 165–177.

77 Center, Y. and Ward, J. (1987) Teachers' attitudes towards the integration of disabled children into the regular classroom. *The Exceptional Child*, 34(1), 41–56.

78 Center, Y., Ward, J., Parmenter, T. and Nash, R. (1985) Principals' attitudes to the integration of disabled children into regular classes. *The Exceptional Child*, 32: 149–161.

79 Center, Y. and Ward, J. (1989) Attitudes of school psychologists towards the integration (mainstreaming) of children with disabilities. *International Journal of Disability, Development and Education*, 36: 117–132.

80 Bochner, S. and Pieterse, M. (1989) Preschool directors' attitudes towards the integration of children with disabilities into regular preschools in New South Wales. *International Journal of Disability, Development and Education*, 36:133–150.

81 Underwood, K. (2008) *The construction of disability in our schools. Teacher and parent perspectives on the experience of labelled students.* Rotterdam, Sense Publishers.

82 Ibid.

83 Jordan, A. (2007) *Introduction to inclusive education.* Mississauga, Ontario, J. Wiley and Sons Canada.

84 Flyvbjerg, B. (2001) *Making social science matter: Why social inquiry fails and how it can succeed again*, Cambridge, Cambridge University Press.

85 Oliver, M. (2009) *Understanding disability: From theory to practice.* 2nd Edition. Basingstoke, Palgrave Macmillan.

86 Gould, S. J. (1981) *The mismeasure of man.* Harmondsworth, Penguin Books.

87 Lewis, J. (1989) Removing the grit: The development of special education in Victoria 1887–1947. Unpublished thesis (PhD) Submitted to the School of Education, La Trobe University, Melbourne,1989.

88 Duster, T. (2003) *Backdoor to eugenics* (2nd Edition). New York, Routledge; Stiker, H.-J. (1999) *A history of disability*. Ann Arbor, University of Michigan Press; Rose, N. (2007) *The politics of life itself: Biomedicine, power and subjectivity in the twenty-first century.* New Jersey, Princeton University Press.

89 Herrnstein, R. J. and Murray, C. A. (1994) *The bell curve: Intelligence and class structure in American life.* New York, Free Press.

90 www.guardian.co.uk/lifeandstyle/2009/jan/12/autism-screening-health.

91 Rose, H. (2001) Gendered genetics in Iceland. *New Genetics and Society*, 20: pp. 119–138.

92 Henry, J. (1971) *Essays on education.* Harmondsworth, Penguin.

93 Ward, R. (1958) *The Australian Legend.* Melbourne, Oxford University Press.

94 Fairclough, N. (2000), p. 10.

95 Op. cit. Ball (2007), p. 34.

4 Building a theory of inclusive education

1 One can find these already in various forms and states.

2 Hegel (1770–1831) was a German philosopher who was central, with Kant, to the development of German idealism. The problem I refer to is of establishing a starting point for a teleological representation of inclusive education.

3 The Hegelian dialectic serves some in this endeavour, others take a genealogical.

4 See Apple (2009).

5 By conditional forms of inclusive education I refer to earlier work where I considered the caveats and conditional language applied in government policy documents to the education of students with disabilities. Examples of this are 'least restrictive environment', 'most appropriate setting', and 'undue institutional hardship'. The list is indicative rather than exhaustive (see Slee, 1996).

6 Ellen Brantlinger (2006) refers to these texts in a chapter entitled 'The Big Glossies: How Textbooks Structure (Special) Education'.

7 Troyna, B. (1994) Blind faith? Empowerment and educational research. *International Studies in Sociology of Education*, 4(1), 3–24.

8 Here Gallie uses the examples of 'works of art', 'democracy' and 'Christian doctrine'. See Gallie, W. B. (1955–1956) Essentially contested concepts. *Proceedings of the Aristotelian Society*, 56, pp. 167–198.

9 Op. cit. (Troyna, 1994) pp. 3–4.

10 Rizvi, F. (1993) Critical introduction. In B. Troyna (Ed.) *Racism and education: Research perspectives*. Buckingham, Open University Press.

11 Op. cit. (Gallie), p. 169.

12 Said, E. W. (2000) Travelling theory reconsidered. In E. W. Said (Ed.) *Reflections on exile and other literary and cultural essays*. London, Granta Publications), 436–452.

13 Ibid., p. 426.

14 Slee, R. (2008) Beyond special and regular schooling? An inclusive education reform agenda. *International Studies in Sociology of Education*, 18(2), 104.

15 Op. cit. (Said, 2000), p. 436.

16 Ibid., p. 437.

17 Op. cit. (Slee, 2008), p. 104.

18 Allan, J. and Slee, R. (2008) *Doing inclusive education research*. Rotterdam, Sense Publishers.

19 Allan and Slee (2008), pp. 15–16.

20 Skidmore, D. (2004) *Inclusion: The dynamic of school development*. Buckingham, Open University Press.

21 Thomas, G. and Loxley, A. (2007) *Deconstructing special education and constructing inclusion* (2nd edn). Maidenhead, Open University Press, p. 3.

22 Typing the phrase 'inclusive education' into general search engines provides overwhelming results. Google returned 2,460,000 entries in 0.36 seconds, Yahoo Search 43,000,000 and search.com 1,040,010. Google Scholar refined the search to return 643,000 in 0.09 seconds.

23 Ford, Mongon and Whelan (1982); Barton and Tomlinson (1982); Booth (1987); Oliver (1990).

24 Including authors such as Michael Apple, Michael Young, Basil Bernstein, Geoff Whitty.

25 See Morris, J. (1989) *Able lives: Women's experience of paralysis*. London, Women's Press; Morris, J. (1991) *Pride against prejudice: A personal politics of disability*. London, Women's Press; also Thomas, C. (1999) *Female forms: Experiencing and understanding disability*. Buckinghamshire, Open University Press.

26 Tomlinson, S. (2000) Journeys in inclusive education. In P. Clough and J. Corbett (Eds) *Theories of inclusive education: A students' guide*. London, Paul Chapman Publishing, pp. 131–132.

27 Ibid., p. 132.

28 Barton, L. and Tomlinson, S. (1981) *Special education: Policy, practices and social issues*, London, Harper and Row.

29 Barton, L. and Tomlinson, S. (1984) *Special education and social interests*. London, Croom Helm.

30 Barton, L. (2003) *Inclusive education and teacher education: A basis for hope or a discourse of delusion*. London, Institute of Education, University of London.

31 Barton, L. (2005) Special Educational Needs: an alternative look. *A Response to Warnock M. 2005: Special Educational Needs – A New Look* www.leeds. ac.uk/disability-studies/archiveuk/barton/Warnock.pdf (retrieved November 18th, 2009 at 8.45 am).

32 See Committee of Enquiry into the Education of Handicapped (1978) Special educational needs: Report of the committee of enquiry into the education of handicapped children and young people. (Warnock Report). London, HMSO.

33 Oliver, M. (2009) *Understanding disability: From theory to practice*, (2nd edition), Basingstoke, Palgrave Macmillan, p. 42.

34 Ibid., p. 43.

35 Mills, C. W. (1959) *The sociological imagination*. New York, Oxford University Press, 1959.

36 Ryan, W. (1971) *Blaming the victim*. London, Orbach and Chambers.

37 Oliver, 1996, pp. 13–17.

38 Wolfensberger, W. (1972) *The principle of normalization in human services*. Toronto, National Institute on Mental Retardation.

39 Tomlinson (2000), p. 130.

40 See for the UK: Daniels, H. (2006) The dangers of corruption in special needs education. *British Journal of Special Education*, 33(1), 4–10; Galloway, D., Armstrong, D. and Tomlinson, S. (1994) *The assessment of special educational needs: Whose problem?* Harlow, Longman; Armstrong, D. (2003) *Experiences of special education: Re-evaluating policy and practice through life stories*. London, Routledge Falmer; Armstrong, D. (1995) *Power and partnership in education: Parents, children and special educational needs*. London, Routledge; for Australia see Graham, L. J. and Slee, R. (2008) An illusory interiority: Interrogating the discourse/s of inclusion. *Educational Philosophy and Theory*, 40(2), 277–293; and for New Zealand see Kearney, A. (2008) *Barriers to school inclusion: An investigation into the exclusion of disabled students from and within New Zealand schools*. Unpublished PhD thesis, Massey University, Palmerston North, New Zealand.

41 See Gillian Fulcher (1989) for a description for disability discourses.

42 See Ball, S. (1994) *Education reform: A critical and post-structural approach*. Buckingham, Open University Press; Ball, S. J. (2003) *Class strategies and the education market: The middle classes and social advantage*. London, Routledge/Falmer; Ball, S. J. and Youdell, D. (2008) *Hidden privatisation in public education*. Report for Institute of Education, University of London; Gillborn, D. and Youdell, D. (2000) *Rationing education: Policy, practice, reform, and equity*. Buckingham, Open University Press; Gewirtz, S., Ball, S. J. and Bowe, R. (1995) *Markets, choice and equity in education*. Open University Press; Slee, R. (1998) High reliability organisations and liability students – the politics of recognition. In R. Slee, G. Weiner and S. Tomlinson (Eds) *School effectiveness for whom?* London, Falmer Press, pp. 101–114.

43 See Skrtic, T. M. (1991) *Behind special education: A critical analysis of professional culture and school organization*. Denver, Col., Love Pub. Co.; op. cit. Tomlinson, 1982; Slee, R. (1998) High reliability organisations and liability students – the politics of recognition. In R. Slee, G. Weiner and S. Tomlinson (Eds.) *School effectiveness for whom?* London, Falmer Press, pp. 101–114; Graham, L. J. and Slee, R. (2008) An illusory interiority: Interrogating the discourse/s of inclusion. *Educational Philosophy and Theory*, 40(2), 277–293.

44 Foucault, M. (1965) *Madness and civilization*. New York, Pantheon Books.

45 Alur, M. (1998) *Invisible children: A study of policy, exclusion.* PhD, Institute of Education, University of London.

46 Franklin, B. M. (1994) *From 'Backwardness' to 'At-risk': Childhood learning difficulties and the contradictions of school reform.* Albany, State University of New York Press.

47 Danforth, S. (2009) *The incomplete child: An intellectual history of learning disabilities.* New York, Peter Lang.

48 Danforth (2009), pp. 1–2.

49 Ibid., p. 3.

50 See Franklin, B. M. (1994) *From 'Backwardness' to 'At-risk': Childhood learning difficulties and the contradictions of school reform.* Albany, State University of New York Press; Kanner, L. (1964) *A history of the care and study of the mentally retarded.* Springfield, Ill., Charles Thomas; Gould, S.J. (1981) *The mismeasure of man.* Harmondsworth, Penguin.

51 See Lewis, J. (1989) *Removing the grit: The development of special education in Victoria 1887–1947.* Thesis (PhD) submitted to the School of Education, La Trobe University and Lewis, J. (1983) *The development of remedial education in Victoria 1910–40.* Thesis (MEd) submitted to the Education Faculty (Urban Centre), La Trobe University.

52 Lewis (1989), p. 13.

53 Gould, S. J. (1981) *The mismeasure of man.* Harmondsworth, Penguin.

54 Gilman, S. L. (1988) *Disease and representation: Images of illness from madness to AIDS.* Ithaca, Cornell University Press.

55 Danforth (2009), p. 3.

56 John Fishborne, Stanley Porteus and Charles Pearson.

57 Slee, R. (1995) *Changing theories and practices of discipline.* London, Falmer Press, p. 65.

58 Kanner, L. (1964) *A history of the care and study of the mentally retarded,* Springfield, Ill., Charles Thomas.

59 Duster, T. (2003) *Backdoor to eugenics* (2nd edition). New York, Routledge.

60 Rose, N. (2007); Snyder, S. L. and Mitchell, D. T. (2006) *Cultural locations of disability.* Chicago, University of Chicago Press.

61 Stiker, H.-J. (1999) *A history of disability.* Ann Arbor, University of Michigan Press, p. 8.

62 Slee (1995)

63 Laurence, J. and McCallum, D. (2009) *Inside the child's head. Histories of childhood behavioural disorders.* Rotterdam, Sense Publishers; Tait, G. (2010) *Philosophy, behaviour disorders and the school.* Rotterdam, Sense Publishers. Graham, L. (Ed.) (2010) *(De) Constructing ADHD.* New York, Peter Lang Publishing. Harwood, V. (2006) *Diagnosing 'disorderly' children: A critique of behaviour disorder discourses.* London, Routledge.

64 Visiting two private schools in Western Sumatra and Java in Indonesia teachers and school counsellors spoke of the increasing recognition of children with ADHD in their schools.

65 Connell, 1993.

66 Ware, L. P. (2004) *Ideology and the politics of (in)exclusion.* New York, Peter Lang.

67 Dyson, A., Clark, C. and Millward, A. (1995) *Towards inclusive schools?* London, David Fulton Publishers.

68 Slee, R. (1998) High reliability organisations and liability students – the politics of recognition. In R. Slee, G. Weiner and S. Tomlinson (Eds) *School effectiveness for whom?* London, Falmer Press, pp. 101–114.

69 Oliver, M. (2000) Decoupling education policy from the economy in late capitalist societies: Some implications for special education. Keynote Address at

ISEC 2000, Manchester, July. www.leeds.ac.uk/disability-studies/archiveuk/Oliver/SENMAN1.pdf.

70 Brantlinger, E. (1997) Using ideology: Cases of non-recognition of the politics of research and practice in special education. *Review of Educational Research*, 67(4), 425–459.

71 Fuchs, D. and Fuchs, L. (1994) Inclusive schools movement and the radicalization of special education reform. *Exceptional Children*, 60(4), 294–309.

72 See Kauffman, J. M. and Hallahan, D. P. (1995) *The illusion of full inclusion: A comprehensive critique of a current special education bandwagon*. (Austin, Tex. Pro-Ed).

73 Brantlinger (1997), p. 427.

74 Skrtic, T. M. (1991) *Behind special education: A critical analysis of professional culture and school organization*. Denver, Love Publishing, p. 51.

75 Ibid., p. 428.

76 Morton, M. (2009) Silenced in the court: Meanings of research and difference in the US legal system. *Disability & Society*, 24(7): pp. 883–895. Minow, M. (1990) *Making all the difference: Inclusion, exclusion, and American law*. Ithaca, New York, Cornell University Press. Norwich, B. (2008) *Dilemmas of difference, inclusion and disability: International perspectives and future directions*. London, Routledge.

77 Slee, R. (1996) Clauses of conditionality. In L. Barton (Ed.) *Disability and society: Emerging issues and insights*. London, Longman.

78 See for examples: Linton, S. (1998) *Claiming disability: Knowledge and identity*. New York, New York University Press; Titchkosky, T. (2003) *Disability, self, and society*. Toronto, University of Toronto Press; Oliver, M. (2009) *Understanding disability: From theory to practice* (2nd edition). Basingstoke, Palgrave Macmillan.

79 Dunkin, M. (1996) Types of errors in synthesizing research in education. *Review of Educational Research*, 66(2), 87–97.

80 Ibid., p. 87.

81 Op. cit. (Brantlinger, 1997), p. 431.

82 Lather, P. (1986) Research as praxis? *Harvard Educational Review*, 65, 257–277; Guba, E. G. (1990) *The paradigm dialog*. Newbury Park, Calif., Sage Publications; Punch, K. (2009) *Introduction to research methods in education*. London, Sage.

83 Op. cit. Kauffmann and Hallahan.

84 Bourdieu, P. and Eagleton, T. (1994) Doxa and common life: An interview. In S. Zizek (Ed.) *Mapping ideology*. New York, Verso, p. 266.

85 Transcript of interview (Gillborn and Youdell), 2005.

86 Foucault, M. (1984) Truth and Method. In P. Rabinow (Ed.) *The Foucault reader* (1st edition). New York, Pantheon Books, p. 60.

87 Zizek, S. (1994) *Mapping ideology*, London; New York, Verso, p. 4.

88 Troyna, B. (1995) Beyond reasonable doubt? Researching 'race' in educational settings. *Oxford Review of Education*, 21(4), 395–408.

89 See Kauffman, J. and Sasso, G. (2006) Toward ending cultural and cognitive relativism in special education. *Exceptionality*, 14(2), 65–90; Gallagher, D. (2006) If not absolute objectivity, then what? A reply to Kauffman and Sasso. *Exceptionality*, 14(2), 91–107; Kauffman, J. and Sasso, G. (2006) Rejoinder: Certainty, doubt and the reduction of uncertainty. *Exceptionality*, 14(2), 109–120; Gallagher, D. (Ed.) (2004) *Challenging orthodoxy in special education: Dissenting voices*. Denver, Love Publishing. For a fuller discussion see Allan, J. (2008) *Rethinking inclusive education: The philosophers of difference in practice*. Dordrecht, Springer; Allan, J. and Slee, R. (2008) *Doing inclusive education research*. Rotterdam, Sense Publishers.

90 Committee of Enquiry into the Education of Handicapped Children and Young People Warnock, M. (1978) *Special educational needs: Report*, London, HMSO.
91 Warnock, M. (2005) *Special educational needs: A new look*. Keele, Philosophy of Education Society of Great Britain, p. 40.
92 Ibid., p. 49.
93 Ainscow, M. (2007) Towards a more inclusive education system: Where next for special schools? In R. Cigman (Ed.) *Included or excluded? The challenge of the mainstream for some SEN children*. London, Routledge.
94 See Cigman, R. (2007) *Included or excluded? The challenge of the mainstream for some SEN children*. London, Routledge; Farrell, M. (2008) *The special school's handbook: Key issues for all*. London, Routledge; Farrell, M. (2008) *Educating special children: An introduction to provision for pupils with disabilities and disorders*. London, Routledge.
95 Warnock, M. (2006) Foreword. In: M. Farrell (Ed.) *Celebrating the special school*. London, Routledge.
96 Farrell, M. (2006) *Celebrating the special school*. London, Routledge, pp. 1–2.
97 Ibid., p. 2.
98 Ibid., p. 16.
99 American Psychiatric Association (2000) *Diagnostic and statistical manual of mental disorders: DSM-IV-TR* (4th Edition). Washington, DC, American Psychiatric Association.
100 Slee/Graham.
101 Op. cit. (Farrell, 2006), p. 17.
102 Kauffman, J. M. and Hallahan, D. P. (1995) *The illusion of full inclusion: A comprehensive critique of a current special education bandwagon*. Austin, Pro-Ed.
103 Kavale, K. and Mostert, M. (2004) *The positive side of special education. Minimizing its fads, fancies and follies*. Lanham, Scarecrow Education.
104 Biklen, D. (1985) *Achieving the complete school: Strategies for effective mainstreaming*. New York, Teachers College Press; Cook, S. and Slee, R. (1999) Struggling with the fabric of disablement: Picking up the threads of the law and education. In M. Jones and L. Basser Marks (Eds) *Disability, divers-ability and legal change*. The Hague, Martinus Nijhoff. Op. cit., Brantlinger.
105 Barton, L. (2005) *Special educational needs: An alternative look. A response to Warnock, M. 2005: Special educational needs – a new look*. Available online at: www.leeds.ac.uk/disability-studies/archiveuk/barton/Warnock.pdf (accessed 9 January 2010).
106 Ibid., pp. 1 and 2.
107 Oliver, M. (1996) *Understanding disability: From theory to practice*, (1st Edition). Basingstoke, Macmillan, p. 9.
108 Oliver, M. (1992) Changing the social relations of research production? *Disability Handicap and Society*, 7(2), p. 110.
109 Ibid., p. 107.
110 Ibid., p. 101.
111 Ibid., p. 108.
112 Ibid., p. 101.
113 Ibid., p. 102.
114 Ibid., p. 105.
115 Edgerton, R. B. (1967) *The cloak of competence: Stigma in the lives of the mentally retarded*. Berkeley, University of California Press.
116 Marx, K. and Engels, F. (1965) *The German ideology*. London, Lawrence and Wishart.
117 Allan, J. (2005) Inclusion as an ethical project. In S. Tremain (Ed.) *Foucault*

and the government of disability. Ann Arbor, The University of Michigan Press), 281–297.

118 Ibid., p. 281.
119 Barton, L. (2005) Transcript of interview.
120 Op. cit. (Allan, 2005), p. 281. See also Allan, J. (2008) *Rethinking inclusive education: The philosophers of difference in practice.* Dordrecht, Springer, pp. 90–92.
121 Ibid. (Allan, 2008), p. 90.
122 Op. cit. (Allan, 2005), p. 281.
123 Corbett, J. and Slee, R. (2000) An international conversation on inclusive education. In F. Armstrong, D. Armstrong and L. Barton (Eds) *Inclusive education: Policy, contexts, and comparative perspectives.* London, David Fulton, p. 134.
124 Reynolds, D. and Farrell, S. (1996) *Worlds apart? A review of international surveys of educational achievement involving England.* Ofsted, London, HMSO.
125 Knight, T. (1985) An apprenticeship in democracy. *The Australian Teacher,* 11(1), 5–7; Pearl, A. and Knight, T. (1998) *The democratic classroom: Theory to inform practice,* Cresskill, NJ, Hampton Press; Pearl, A., Pryor, C. R. and Association of Teacher Educators. (2005) *Democratic practices in education: Implications for teacher education.* Lanham, Rowan and Littlefield Education.
126 Bernstein, B. (1996) *Pedagogy, symbolic control and identity: theory, research, critique.* London, Taylor & Francis.
127 Touraine, A. (2000) *Can we live together? Equality and difference.* Cambridge, Polity Press, p. 195.
128 Ibid., p. 270.

5 It's what governments do – policy inaction

1 See Tomlinson, C. A. (2003) *Fulfilling the promise of the differentiated classroom: Strategies and tools for responsive teaching.* Alexandria, VA, Association for Supervision and Curriculum Development; Tomlinson, C. A. and Association for Supervision and Curriculum Development (2008) *Differentiated instruction in action.* Alexandria, VA, Association for Supervision and Curriculum Development; Tomlinson, C. A., Wiggins, G. P., Marzano, R. J. and Association for Supervision and Curriculum Development. (2008) Connecting an exploration of research-based strategies. Alexandria, VA, ASCD.
2 See Newmann, F. M. (1996) *Authentic achievement: Restructuring schools for intellectual quality* (1st Edition). San Francisco, Jossey-Bass; Stobart, G. (2008) *Testing times: The uses and abuses of assessment.* London, Routledge; Wiliam, D. (2006). Assessment: learning communities can use it to engineer a bridge connecting teaching and learning. *Journal of Staff Development,* 27(1), 16–20.
3 Here I use the term 'Other' as it is deployed by postcolonial theorists such as Edward Said; see Said, E. W. (1979) *Orientalism* (1st Edition). New York, Vintage Books.
4 Graham, L.J. and Sweller, N. (in press) The inclusion lottery. Who's in and who's out? Inclusion in New South Wales government schools. *International Journal of Inclusive Education.*
5 Michele Moore paper presented at Inclusive Education Conference, Athens, Greece, Friday, 13 November.
6 Ainscow, M. (1999) *Understanding the development of inclusive schools.* London, Falmer Press, p. 2.
7 See Williams, R. (1989) *Resources of hope: Culture, democracy, socialism.* London, Verso.

8 Ball, S. (2008) *The education debate*. Bristol, Policy Press, p. 6.
9 Considine, M. (1994) *Public policy: A critical approach*. South Melbourne, Macmillan Education Australia.
10 Op. cit. (Ball, 2008), pp. 2 and 3. In his use of the term 'hyperactivism', Ball cites Dunleavy, P. and O'Leary, B. (1987) *Theories of the state: The politics of liberal democracy*. Houndmills, Macmillan Education.
11 Ibid. (Ball), p. 7.
12 Dye, T. R. (1972) *Understanding public policy*. Englewood Cliffs, NJ, Prentice-Hall.
13 Ball, S. J. (1990) *Politics and policy making in education: Explorations in policy sociology*. London, Routledge; Ball, S. (1994) *Education reform: A critical and post-structural approach*. Buckingham, Open University Press.
14 Easton, D. (1953) *The political system, an inquiry into the state of political science* (1st Edition). New York, Knopf.
15 Rizvi, F. and Lingard, B. (2009) *Globalizing education policy*. London, Routledge, p. 3.
16 Op. cit. Easton, pp. 129–130.
17 Op. cit. (Rizvi and Lingard), pp. 72 and 73.
18 For comprehensive accounts of these programmes see: Connell, R. (1993) *Schools and social justice*. Philadelphia, Temple University Press; White, V., Johnston, K. and Connell, R. (1991) *Running twice as hard: The disadvantaged schools program in Australia*. Geelong, Victoria, Deakin University: distributed by Deakin University Press; Connell, R., White, V. and Johnston, K. (1990) *Poverty, education and the disadvantaged schools program (DSP): Project overview and discussion of policy questions: General report on the project, submitted to the Department of Employment, Education and Training*. Sydney, School of Behavioural Sciences, Macquarie University.
19 See Fraser, N. (1997) *Justice interruptus: Critical reflections on the 'Postsocialist' Condition*. New York, Routledge; Fraser, N. (2009) *Scales of justice: Reimagining political space in a globalizing world*. New York, Columbia University Press.
20 Lingard, B. (1998) The disadvantaged schools programme: Caught between literacy and local management. *International Journal of Inclusive Education*, 2(1), 1–14.
21 Basil Fawlty is the main protagonist in a BBC television comedy series, Fawlty Towers.
22 Fairclough, N. (2000) *New labour, new language?* London, Routledge, p. 157. For an elaboration of this argument see Ball, S. (2007) *Education plc: Understanding private sector participation in public sector education*. London, Routledge, pp. 2 and 34.
23 *QSE 2010*, Education Queensland, Brisbane, 2000.
24 See http://education.qld.gov.au/strategic/accountability/destination/revision.html (retrieved 19 February 2010); also http://education.qld.gov.au/strategic/accountability/destination/dg-message.html (retrieved 19 February 2010); also Taylor, S. and Singh, P. (2005) The logic and practice in Queensland State Education 2010. *Journal of Education Policy*, 20(6), 725–740.
25 Luke, A. (2003) After the marketplace: Evidence, social science and educational research. *The Australian Educational Researcher*, 30(2), 87–107.
26 The State of Queensland (Department of Education) (2000) *Literate Futures: The teacher summary version*. Brisbane, Education Queensland, p. 3.
27 Newmann, F. M. (1996) *Authentic achievement: Restructuring schools for intellectual quality* (1st Edition). San Francisco, Jossey-Bass.
28 Dorling, D. (2010) *Injustice: Why social inequality persists*. Bristol, The Policy Press.

29 Ibid., see Chapter 2.
30 Ball, S. (2007) *Education plc: Understanding private sector participation in public sector education. London*, Routledge.
31 Kahn, S. and Minnich, E. K. (2005) *The fox in the henhouse: How privatization threatens democracy.* San Francisco, Berrett-Koehler, p. 132.
32 Ibid., p. 185.
33 Ibid., p. 191.
34 Sen, A. (2003) Humanity, security and educational gaps. Paper presented at the 15th Conference of the Commonwealth Ministers of Education. Access, inclusion and achievement: closing the gaps. 28 October, Edinburgh.
35 See Johnson, D. D. and Johnson, B. (2006) *High stakes: Poverty, testing, and failure in American schools* (2nd Edition). Lanham, Rowman and Littlefield Publishers; Teese, R. and Polesel, J. (2003) *Undemocratic schooling: Equity and quality in mass secondary education in Australia.* Carlton, Melbourne University Publishing; and Stobart, G. (2008) *Testing times: The uses and abuses of assessment.* London, Routledge.
36 See ibid. (Johnson and Johnson), p. xvii.
37 Ibid., p. xviii. This story has been logged elsewhere in the USA by a range of researchers and activists. See Kozol, J. (1991) *Savage inequalities: Children in America's schools.* New York, Crown Publishers; Brantlinger, E. A. (2003) *Dividing classes: How the middle class negotiates and rationalizes school advantage.* London, RoutledgeFalmer; Tyack, D. and Cuban, L. (1995) *Tinkering toward Utopia: A century of public school reform.* Cambridge, Mass., Harvard University Press.
38 Op. cit. Sennett (2006), p. 86.
39 Victorian Ministry of Education (1984) *Integration in Victorian Education. Report of the Ministerial Review of Educational Services for the Disabled. (Kevin Collins Chair).* Melbourne, Ministry of Education.
40 Committee of Enquiry into the Education of Handicapped Children and Young People and Warnock, M. (1978) *Special educational needs: Report of the committee of enquiry into the education of handicapped children and young people* (The Warnock Report). London, HM Stationery Office.
41 1975 Education for All Handicapped Children Act – PL 94–142 (EAHCA); 1990 Individuals with Disabilities Education Act (IDEA) amended in 1997 and 2004; see also Section 504 of the 1973 Vocational Rehabilitation Act and Title II Americans with Disabilities Act (ADA, 1990).
42 Bennett, S. and Wynne, K. (2006) *Special education transformation: The report of the co-chairs with the recommendations of the working table on special education*, Ottawa, Queen's Printer of Ontario.
43 Watson, D. (2002) *Recollections of a bleeding heart: A portrait of Paul Keating PM.* Milson's Point, NSW, Knopf.
44 See Deno, E. (1970) Special education as developmental capital. *Exceptional Children*, 37(3), 229–237.
45 Op. cit. Bennett and Wynne.
46 Fulcher, G. (1989a) *Disabling policies? A comparative approach to education policy and disability.* London, Falmer Press.
47 Fulcher, G. (1989b) Integrate and mainstream? Comparative issues in the politics of these policies. In L. Barton (Ed.) *Integration: Myth or reality.* Lewes, Falmer Press. 6–29. P. 9.
48 Rice, M. (1993) Integration: Another form of specialism. In R. Slee (Ed.) *Is there a desk with my name on it?* London, Falmer Press; Marks, G. (1993) Contests in decision-making at the school level. In R. Slee (Ed.) *Is there a desk with my name on it?* London, Falmer Press; Armstrong, D. (1995) *Power and partnership in education: Parents, children and special educational needs.*

London, Routledge; Tomlinson, S. (1982) *A sociology of special education.* London, Routledge and Kegan Paul; Tomlinson, S. (1985) The expansion of special education. *Oxford Review of Education,* 11(2), 157–165.

49 Thomas, G. and Loxley, A. (2007) *Deconstructing special education and constructing inclusion* (2nd Edition). Maidenhead, Open University Press.

50 Op. cit. Fulcher (1989b), p. 9.

51 Victoria Education Department (1983) *Ministerial Papers 1–4: 1. Decision making in Victorian education. 2. The school improvement plan. 3. The State Board of Education. 4. School councils. Ministerial Paper 5 (1985): Regional Boards of Education and Ministerial Paper 6 (1985): Curriculum development and planning in Victoria.* Melbourne: Education Department of Victoria.

52 Skrtic, T. M. (1991) *Behind special education: A critical analysis of professional culture and school organization.* Denver, Love Publishing; Skrtic, T. M. (1995) *Disability and democracy: Reconstructing (special) education for postmodernity.* New York, Teachers College Press.

53 Op. cit. Victorian Ministry of Education, 1984, p. 6.

54 Op. cit. Fulcher.

55 Op. cit. (Fulcher, 1989), p. 1.

56 Ibid., p. 2.

57 See Fulcher, G. (1988) Integration: Inclusion or exclusion? In R. Slee (Ed.) *Discipline and schools: A curriculum perspective.* Melbourne, Macmillan and also Fulcher (1989a) p. 190 and 1989b, p. 9.

58 See Foucault, M. (1979) *Discipline and punish: The birth of the prison.* Harmondsworth, Penguin Books, p. 183 for his description of 'dividing practices'.

59 Slee, R. (1994) *Changing theories and practices of discipline.* London, Falmer Press.

60 Fulcher (1989a), p. 191.

61 See Ibid., Fulcher (1988 and 1989a).

62 Macdonald, I. (1981) Assessment: A social dimension. In L. Barton and S. Tomlinson (Eds) *Special education: Policy, practices and social issues.* London, Harper and Row, pp. 102–103.

63 Ibid., Fulcher (1988), p. 37.

64 Ibid., p. 3.

65 Op. cit. Thomas and Loxley (2007), pp. 3–4.

66 Skidmore, D. (2004) *Inclusion: The dynamic of school development.* Buckingham, Open University Press, pp. 6–7.

67 Van Morrison, *No Religion,* (Days like this) 1997.

68 Gilroy, P. (2000) *Against race: Imagining political culture beyond the color line.* Cambridge, Mass., Harvard University Press.

69 Op. cit. Thomas and Loxley (2007), p. 7.

70 Ibid., p. 8.

71 Ibid., p. 85.

72 See Bruner, J. S. (1990) *Acts of meaning.* Cambridge, Mass., Harvard University Press; Clough, P. (2002) *Narratives and fictions in educational research,* Buckingham, Open University Press; Denzin, N. K. and Lincoln, Y. S. (1998) Handbook of qualitative research. Strategies of qualitative inquiry, Thousand Oaks, Calif., Sage Publications.

73 Gillborn, D. (2008) *Racism and education: Coincidence or conspiracy?* Abingdon, Routledge. p. 26.

74 Ibid., pp. 13 and 14.

75 Allan, J. (2005) Inclusion as an ethical project. In S. Tremain (Ed.) *Foucault and the government of disability.* Ann Arbor, The University of Michigan Press), pp. 281–297.

76 Ball (2007)

77 Ibid., p. 3.
78 An exception to this was the work of Stephen J. Ball whose work she draws on to elaborate notions of discursive practices.
79 Op. cit., Fulcher (1989), p. 4. (Author's own emphasis.)
80 Daniels, H. (2006) The dangers of corruption in special needs education. *British Journal of Special Education*, 33(1), 4–10.
81 Rosenthal, R. and Jacobson, L. (1968) *Pygmalion in the classroom; teacher expectation and pupils' intellectual development*. New York, Holt.
82 Good, T. L. and Brophy, J. E. (1973) *Looking in classrooms*. New York, Harper and Row.
83 Slavin, R. E. (2009) *2 million children: Success for all* (2nd Edition). Thousand Oaks, Calif., Corwin Press.
84 Harlen, W. and Malcolm, H. (1999) *Setting and streaming: A research review*. Edinburgh, Scottish Council for Research in Education.
85 Ireson, J. and Hallam, S. (1999) Raising standards: Is ability grouping the answer? *Oxford Review of Education*, 25(3), 343–358.
86 Sizer, T. R. and Sizer, N. F. (1999) The students are watching: Schools and the moral contract. Boston, Beacon Press.
87 Oliver, M. (2009) *Understanding disability: From theory to practice* (2nd Edition). Basingstoke, Palgrave Macmillan; Snyder, S. L. and Mitchell, D. T. (2006) *Cultural locations of disability*. Chicago, University of Chicago Press; Armstrong, F. and Barton, L. (1999) *Disability, human rights and education: Cross-cultural perspectives*. Buckingham, Open University Press.
88 Barton, L. (1988) *The politics of special educational needs*. London, Falmer Press.

6 From segregation to integration to inclusion and back (a policy reprise)

1 Foucault, M. and Faubion, J. D. (2001) *Power: The essential works Volume 3*. London, Allen Lane, p. 383.
2 Slee, R. (1993) The politics of integration: New sites for old practices? *Disability, Handicap and Society*, 8(4), 351–360.
3 Bernstein, B. B. (1996) *Pedagogy, symbolic control and identity: Theory, research, critique*. London, Taylor & Francis, p. 7.
4 A close reading of Bernstein (1996), pp. 6–12 is highly recommended to understand his conception of democratic education and the rights (Enhancement, Inclusion and Participation) and conditions (Confidence, Communitas and Civic discourse) which apply and the levels (Individual, Social and Political) that these operate at.
5 Wolfensberger, W. (1972) *The principle of normalization in human services*. Toronto, National Institute on Mental Retardation; Wolfensberger, W. (1983) National Institute on Mental Retardation and Georgia Advocacy Office Inc. *Normalization-based guidance, education and supports for families of handicapped people*. Downsview, Ontario; Atlanta, Ga., National Institute on Mental Retardation, Georgia Advocacy Office, Inc; Wolfensberger, W. (1992) *A brief introduction to social role valorization as a high-order concept for structuring human services* (2nd Edition). Syracuse, NY, Training Institute for Human Service Planning, Leadership and Change Agentry. For a critique of Social Role Valorization see chapter 6 of Oliver, M. (2009) *Understanding disability: From theory to practice*, (2nd edition) Basingstoke, Palgrave Macmillan.
6 Touraine, A. (2000) *Can we live together? Equality and difference*. Cambridge, Polity Press.
7 Ibid., p. 195.

8 Peter McLaren as quoted in hooks, b. (1994) *Teaching to transgress.* New York, Routledge.

9 See Nussbaum, M. C. (2004) *Hiding from humanity: Disgust, shame, and the law.* Princeton, Princeton University Press and Nussbaum, M. C. (2006) *Frontiers of justice: Disability, nationality, species membership.* Cambridge, Mass., Belknap Press of Harvard University Press.

10 Giroux, H. A. (2009) *Youth in a suspect society: Democracy or disposability?* New York, Palgrave Macmillan.

11 Norwich, B. (2008) *Dilemmas of difference, inclusion and disability: International perspectives and future directions.* London, Routledge, p. 19.

12 Minow, M. (1990) *Making all the difference: Inclusion, exclusion, and American law.* Ithaca, New York, Cornell University Press.

13 Dahl, R. A. (1982) *Dilemmas of pluralist democracy: Autonomy vs. control.* New Haven, Yale University Press.

14 Berlin, I. (1990) *The crooked timber of humanity: Chapters in the history of ideas.* London, John Murray.

15 Goodhart, D. (2004) Too diverse? *Prospect*, 30–37.

16 Stocker, M. (1990) *Plural and conflicting values.* Oxford, Clarendon Press.

17 Terzi, L. (2008) Beyond the dilemma of difference: The capability approach to disability and special educational needs. In L. Florian and M. McClaughlin (Eds) *Disability classification in education.* Thousand Oaks, Corwin Press, pp. 244–262.

18 Ibid., p. 249.

19 Sen, A. (2002) *Rationality and freedom.* Cambridge, Mass., Belknap Press of Harvard University Press, p. 86.

20 Sen, A. (2009) *The idea of justice.* Cambridge, Mass., Belknap Press of Harvard University Press, p. 258.

21 Kuklys, W. (2005) *Amartya Sen's capability approach: Theoretical insights and empirical applications.* New York, Springer.

22 Op. cit. (Sen, 2009), p. 258.

23 Ibid., pp. 258–259.

24 Dorling, D. (2010) *Injustice: Why social inequality persists.* Bristol, Policy Press.

25 Crawford, C. (2004) Fulfilling the social contract in public education. Paper presented at the National Summit on Inclusive Education, Canadian Association for Community Living and Canadian Teachers' Federation, Ottawa.

26 Corbett, J. and Slee, R. (2000) An international conversation on inclusive education. In F. Armstrong, D. Armstrong and L. Barton (Eds) *Inclusive education: Policy, contexts, and comparative perspectives.* London, David Fulton, p. 134.

27 Ibid., p. 134.

28 Ibid., pp. 134 and 135.

29 Booth, T. (1996) Stories of inclusion: Natural and unnatural selection., in: B. E. and J. Milner (Eds) *Exclusion from school: Inter-professional issues for policy and practice.* London, Routledge; Booth, T. and Ainscow, M. (2004) *Index for inclusion: Developing learning, participation and play in early years and childcare.* Bristol, Centre for Studies on Inclusive Education.

30 Parsons, C. (1996) *Exclusion from school: The public cost* (Revised Edition). London, Commission for Racial Equality; Parsons, C. (2009) *Strategic alternatives to exclusion from school.* Stoke-on-Trent, Trentham Books.

31 Tomlinson, S. (1981) *Educational sub-normality: A study in decision-making.* London, Routledge and Kegan Paul.

32 Gillborn, D. (2008) *Racism and education: Coincidence or conspiracy?* Abingdon, Routledge, p. 62.

33 Ibid., p. 63.

34 Ibid., p. 63.

35 Touraine, A. (2000) *Can we live together? Equality and difference*. Cambridge, Polity Press, p. 265.

36 Rieser, R. (2008) Implementing inclusive education: Commonwealth guide to implementing Article 24 of the UN Convention on the Rights of People with Disabilities. London, Commonwealth Secretariat.

37 Op. cit. Norwich (2008).

38 Artiles, A. and Dyson, A. (2005) Inclusive education in the globalization age: The promise of a cultural-historical analysis. In D. Mitchell (Ed.) *Contextualizing inclusive education*. London, Routledge, pp. 37–62.

39 United Nations (2010) *Enable – Rights and Dignity of People with Disabilities*. Geneva, United Nations (March) www.un.org/disabilities/ (retrieved at 12.52 on 7 April 2010.

40 Reynolds, H. (1999) *Why weren't we told? A personal search for the truth about our history*. Ringwood, Viking; Rowley, C. D. (1970) *The destruction of Aboriginal society*. Canberra, Australian National University Press; Rowley, C. D. (1971) *The remote Aborigines*. Canberra, Australian National University Press; Rowley, C. D. (1971) *Outcasts in white Australia*. Canberra, Australian National University Press.

41 Op. cit. Minow (1990); Jones, M. and Basser Marks, L. A. (1998) *Disability, divers-ability, and legal change*. The Hague, M. Nijhoff Publishers; Uditsky, B. (1993) From integration to inclusion: The Canadian experience. In: R. Slee (Ed.) *Is there a desk with my name on it?* London, Falmer Press.

42 Cook, S. and Slee, R. (1999) Struggling with the fabric of disablement: Picking up the threads of the law and education. In M. Jones and L. Basser Marks (Eds) *Disability, divers-ability and legal change*. The Hague, Martinus Nijhoff.

43 Slee, R. (1996) Clauses of conditionality. In L. Barton (Ed.) *Disability and society: Emerging issues and insights*. London, Longman.

44 Op. cit. Cook and Slee, 1996.

45 Dickson, E. (2005) Disability discrimination in education: Purvis v New South Wales (Department of Education and Training), amendment of the education provisions of the Disability Discrimination Act 1992 (Commonwealth) and the formulation of Disability Standards for Education. *University of Queensland Law Journal*, 24(1): www.austlii.edu.au/au/journals/UQLJ/2005/11.html (retrieved 15 October 2008 at 12.50); Rattigan, K. (2004) Case Note: Purvis v New South Wales (Department of Education and Training). A Case for Amending the Disability Discrimination Act 1992 (Commonwealth), Melbourne University Law Review, 48. www.austlii.edu.au/au/journals/MULR/2004/17.html (retrieved 15 October at 13.42); Human Rights and Equal Opportunities Commission (1999) Mr. Purvis v New South Wales Department of Education and Training. www.hreoc.gov.au/disability_rights/decisions/comdec/1999/DD000140. htm (retrieved 15 October, 2008 at 12.45); op. cit. Cook and Slee, 1996.

46 Human Rights and Equal Opportunities Commission (1999) Mr. Purvis v New South Wales Department of Education and Training. www.hreoc.gov.au/disability_rights/decisions/comdec/1999/DD000140.htm (retrieved 15 October, 2008 at 12.45).

47 Op. cit. (Touraine), p. 265.

48 Attorney General's Department, Australian Government (2006) Disability Standards for Education 2005. www.ag.gov.au/www/agd/agd.nsf/P./Human rightsandanti-discrimination_DisabilityStandardsforEducation (retrieved on 15 October, 2008 at 13.28).

49 Ibid.

50 Minow, M. (1990) *Making all the difference: Inclusion, exclusion, and American law*. Ithaca, Cornell University Press; Campbell, J. and Oliver, M. (1996)

Disability politics: Understanding our past, changing our future. London, Routledge; Norwich, B. (2008) *Dilemmas of difference, inclusion and disability: International perspectives and future directions.* London, Routledge; Jones, M. and Basser Marks, L. A. (1998) *Disability, divers-ability, and legal change.* The Hague, Nijhoff Publishers.

51 UNESCO (1990) World Declaration on Education For All. Geneva, United Nations. www.unesco.org/education/efa/ed_for_all/background/jomtien_declaration.shtml (retrieved at 11.23 0n April 8th, 2010).

52 UNESCO (1994) Final report. World conference on special needs education: Access and quality. Report for UNESCO (Paris).

53 Ibid., pp. viii–ix.

54 See, for example, Deno, E. (1970) Special education as developmental capital. *Exceptional Children*, 37(3), 229–237.

55 Onaga, E. E. and Martoccio, T. L. (2008) Dynamic and uncertain pathways between early childhood, inclusive policy and practice. *International Journal of Child Care and Education Policy*, 2(1), 67–75; Jordan, A. (2007) *Introduction to inclusive education.* Mississauga, Ont., J. Wiley and Sons Canada, p. 46.

56 Troyna, B. (1993) *Racism and education: Research perspectives.* Buckingham, Open University Press; Mirza, H. S. (2009) *Race, gender and educational desire: Why black women succeed and fail.* London, Routledge.

57 Daniels, H. and Garner, P. (Eds.) (1999) *Inclusive education: Supporting inclusion in education systems.* London, Kogan P., p. 4.

58 Op. cit. Artiles and Dyson (2005), p. 39.

59 Ibid., p. 40.

60 Op. cit. (Norwich), p. 20.

61 See McGough, R. (1990) *Blazing fruit.* Harmondsworth, Penguin Books.

62 Galbraith, J. K. (2004) *The economics of innocent fraud: Truth for our time.* Boston, Houghton Mifflin, p. xi.

63 Ibid., p. ix.

64 Slee, R. (2006) Limits to and possibilities for reform. *International Journal of Inclusive Education*, 10(2), 109–119.

7 Building authority, dividing populations and getting away with it (exposing a system of rationality)

1 Campbell, C. (2002) Conceptualisations and definitions of inclusive schooling. In C. Campbell (Ed.) *Developing inclusive schooling: Perspectives, policies and practices.* London, Institute of Education, University of London, p.11.

2 Compiling a list of these researchers would inevitably result in omissions and cause offence that deflects from the argument. The stalwart activist Keith Ballard captures a neat representation of this argument. In Ballard, K. (1999) International voices: An introduction, in K. Ballard (Ed.) *Inclusive education: International voices on disability and justice.* London, Falmer Press, p. 1. Tony Booth registered the point early in his work and one can find it in more elaborate form and strident pitch in his most recent presentations. Booth, T. (1998) The poverty of special education. In C. Clark, A. Dyson and A. Millward (Eds.) *Theorising special education.* London, Routledge.

3 Allan, J. and Slee, R. (2008) *Doing inclusive education research.* Rotterdam, Sense Publishers.

4 Kearney, A. (2008) Barriers to school inclusion: An investigation into the exclusion of disabled students from and within New Zealand schools. Unpublished PhD, Massey University; see p. 212.

5 Kesey, K. (1964) *One flew over the cuckoo's nest.* New York, Viking Press.

6 Allan, J. (2008) *Rethinking inclusive education: The philosophers of difference in practice*. Dordrecht, Springer, p. 60.

7 Allan, J. (1999) *Actively seeking inclusion: Pupils with special needs in mainstream schools*. London, Falmer Press.

8 Willis, P. E. (1977) *Learning to labour: How working class kids get working class jobs*. Farnborough, Eng., Saxon House.

9 Furlong, V. J. (1991) Disaffected pupils reconsidered: The sociological perspective. *British Journal of Sociology of Education*, 12(3), 293–307.

10 Mills, C. W. (1959) *The sociological imagination*. New York, Oxford University Press; Oliver, M. (1990) *The politics of disablement*. London, Macmillan Education.

11 Here I am thinking of the work that Marie Shoeman is doing to produce an alternative funding model for more inclusive schools in the Republic of South Africa, the work that Glenda Strong, Julie Green and their colleagues are doing in closing the hospital special school at the Royal Children's Hospital in Melbourne (Australia) and opening the Education Institute to keep children connected and build a research agenda for maintaining learning for children with chronic and long-term illnesses, or the work undertaken by Trudy Smith in her school in remote Mt Isa in Queensland (Australia) to spread the learning of sign language first throughout the school and then through the community to establish translation as a function of a growing bilingualism.

12 Fulcher, G. (1989) *Disabling policies?: A comparative approach to education policy and disability*. London, Falmer.

13 Rose, N. S. (1990) *Governing the soul: The shaping of the private self*. London, Routledge; Rose, N. (2007) *The politics of life itself: Biomedicine, power and subjectivity in the twenty-first century*. New Jersey, Princeton University Press.

14 Keynes, J. M. (1936) *The general theory of employment, interest and money*. London, Macmillan, pp. 33–34.

15 Op. cit. (Bauman).

16 Henry, J. (1971) *Pathways to madness* (1st Edition). New York, Random House; Henry, J. (1971) *Essays on education*, Harmondsworth, Penguin.

17 Billington, T. (2000) *Separating, losing, and excluding children: Narratives of difference*. London, Routledge Falmer, p. 94 (my emphasis).

18 Rose, S. (2005) *The 21st century brain. Explaining, mending and manipulating the mind*. London, Vintage; Laurence, J. and McCallum, D. (2009) Inside the child's head. Histories of childhood behavioural disorders. Rotterdam, Sense Publishers; Tait, G. (2010) Philosophy, behaviour disorders and the school. Rotterdam, Sense Publishers.

19 Rose, N. (2007) *The politics of life itself. Biomedicine, power and subjectivity in the twenty-first century*. New Jersey, Princeton University Press.

20 Nussbaum, M. C. (2004) *Hiding from humanity: Disgust, shame, and the law*. Princeton, Princeton University Press, p. 305.

21 For an example of changing patterns of referrals of children with behaviour disorders it is useful to refer to Graham, L. J. and Sweller, N. (2010) The inclusion lottery: Who's in and who's out? Tracking inclusion and exclusion in New South Wales government schools. *International Journal of Inclusive Education* and Graham, L. J., Sweller, N. and Van Bergen, P. (forthcoming) Detaining the usual suspects: Charting the use of segregated settings in New South Wales government schools in Australia.

22 Foucault, M. (1973) *The birth of the clinic: An archaeology of medical perception*. London, Tavistock Publications.

23 Ibid. (Rose, 2007), p. 9.

24 Ibid., p. 10.
25 Ibid., pp. 10–11.
26 Foucault, M. (1965) *Madness and civilization: A history of insanity in the age of reason.* New York, Pantheon Books; Foucault, M. (1977) *Discipline and punish: The birth of the prison* (1st American Edition). New York, Pantheon Books.
27 Gilman, S. L. (1982) *Seeing the insane.* New York, J. Wiley, Brunner/Mazel Publishers; Gilman, S. L. (1988) *Disease and representation: Images of illness from madness to aids.* Ithaca, N.Y., Cornell University Press.
28 Rose, N. S. (1990) *Governing the soul: The shaping of the private self.* London, Routledge.
29 Op. cit. (Gilman, 1982).
30 Foucault, M. and Faubion, J. D. (2001) *Power. The essential works Volume 3.* London, Allen Lane, *The birth of social medicine*, pp. 134–156. See also: Dean, M. (1999) *Governmentality: Power and rule in modern society.* London, SAGE.
31 The analyses, contrary to the recent representation of Paul Cooper, are multi-disciplinary, reflexive and interrogative rather than conclusive. His description of a psychosocial perspective is radically incomplete and astonishingly unreflexive of the position he restates. See Cooper, P. (2008) Like alligators bobbing for poodles? A critical discussion of education, ADHD and the biopsychosocial perspective. *Journal of Philosophy in Education,* 42(3–4), 457–474.
32 Rose, S. (2005) *The 21st century brain: Explaining, mending and manipulating the mind.* London, Vintage.
33 American Psychiatric Association (2000) *Diagnostic and statistical manual of mental disorders: DSM-IV-TR* (4th Edition). Washington, DC, American Psychiatric Association.
34 Fleck, L. (1979) *Genesis and development of a scientific fact.* Chicago, University of Chicago Press.
35 Op. cit. (Rose 2007).
36 Fleck, L. (1979) *Genesis and development of a scientific fact.* Chicago, University of Chicago Press, as referenced by Nikolas Rose (2007), p. 12.
37 Kuhn, T. S. (1962) *The structure of scientific revolutions.* Chicago, University of Chicago Press.
38 Op. cit. Rose, p. 14.
39 *The Economist,* 'And man made life', 22 May, 2010, p. 11.
40 *The Economist.* 'Genesis redux', 22 May, 2010, p. 88.
41 Op. cit. (Rose, 2007), p. 16.
42 Rose, Steven. (2005) *The 21st century brain: Explaining, mending and manipulating the mind.* London, Vintage.
43 Foucault, M. (1974) The Birth of State Medicine, the second of two lectures delivered at the University of Rio de Janeiro and first published in 1977. In Foucault, M. and Faubion, J. D. (2001) *Power.* London, Allen Lane, pp. 140–141.
44 Rabinow, P. (1996) *Essays on the anthropology of reason.* Princeton, NJ, Princeton University Press.
45 Rose, N. and Novas, C. (2006) Biological citizenship. In A. Ong and S. Collier (Eds) *Blackwell companion to global anthropology.* Oxford, Blackwell.
46 Op. cit. (Rose, 2007), p. 27.
47 Ibid., p. 27.
48 See Cohen, S. (1985) *Visions of social control: Crime, punishment, and classification.* Cambridge, Polity Press and Rose, N. S. (1990) *Governing the soul: The shaping of the private self.* London, Routledge.

49 Sachs, J. (2005) *The end of poverty: How we can make it happen in our lifetime*. London, Penguin.

50 Op. cit. (Rose, 2007), pp. 29–30.

51 Op. cit. (Nikolas Rose, 2007), pp. 31–32.

52 Greenberg, G. (2010) *Manufacturing depression: The secret history of a modern disease*. London, Bloomsbury Publishing.

53 Ibid., p. 11.

54 Cooper, P. (2008) Like alligators bobbing for poodles? A critical discussion of education, ADHD and the biopsychosocial perspective. *Journal of Philosophy in Education*, 42(3–4), 457–474, p. 457.

55 Ibid., p. 462.

56 Laurence, J. and McCallum, D. (2009) *Inside the child's head. Histories of childhood behavioural disorders*. Rotterdam, Sense Publishers; Graham, L. (Ed.) (2010) *(De)constructing ADHD: Critical guidance for teachers and teacher educators*. New York, Peter Lang; Danforth, S. (2009) *The incomplete child: An intellectual history of learning disabilities*. (New York, Peter Lang; Tait, G. (2010) *Philosophy, behaviour disorders and the school*. Rotterdam, Sense Publishers.

57 Reynolds, D. and Nicholson, R. I. (2006) Follow-up of an Exercised-based Treatment for children with reading difficulties, *Dyslexia*. www.dore.com.tw/about/images/FollowUpStudyReynoldsNicolson2006.pdf (retrieved Monday 14 June, 2010 at 13.40); Christensen, C. M., Horn, M. B. and Johnson, C. W. (2008) *Disrupting class: How disruptive innovation will change the way the world learns*. New York, McGraw-Hill Professional; Gardner, H. (1999) *Intelligence reframed: Multiple intelligences for the 21st century*. New York, Basic Books.

58 Rose, S. (2005) *The 21st century brain. Explaining, mending and manipulating the mind*. London, Vintage, p. 4.

59 Ibid., pp. 253–263.

60 See also op. cit. (Laurence and McCallum), p. 79.

61 American Psychiatric Association. (2000) *Diagnostic and statistical manual of mental disorders: DSM-IV-TR* (4th Edition). Washington, DC, American Psychiatric Association.

62 Kutchins, H. and Kirk, S. A. (1997) *Making US crazy. DSM: The psychiatric bible and the creation of mental disorders*. New York, Free Press, p. 14.

63 Ibid., p. 16.

64 Ibid., p. 17.

65 Op. cit. (Greenberg), pp. 38 and 39.

66 For discussions of women and madness see Appignanesi, L. (2009) *Mad, bad and sad: A history of women and the mind doctors from 1800 to the present*. London, Virago.

67 Ibid., p. 16.

68 Op. cit. (Greenberg), p. 15.

69 Ibid., pp. 14–15.

70 The phrase is borrowed by Greenberg (and others) from W. H. Auden's elegy 'In Memory of Sigmund Freud'. Op. cit. (Greenberg), p. 9.

71 Barkley, R. A. (1990) *Attention-deficit hyperactivity disorder: A handbook for diagnosis and treatment*. New York, Guilford Press.

72 Op. cit. (Steven Rose), pp. 258–259.

73 Slee, R. (1998) High reliability organisations and liability students – the politics of recognition. In R. Slee, G. Weiner and S. Tomlinson (Eds) *School effectiveness for whom?* London, Falmer Press, pp. 101–114.

74 CHADD 2008–2009 Annual Report (retrieved online 14 June, 2010 at 15.24) www.chadd.org/AM/Template.cfm?Section=Reports1andTemplate=/CM/ContentDisplay.cfmandContentID=13228.

75 Ecclestone, K. and Hayes, D. (2009) *The dangerous rise of therapeutic education*. London, Routledge.

76 Furedi, F. (2004) *Therapy culture: Cultivating vulnerability in an uncertain age*. London, Routledge.

77 Arnold, C. (2008) *Bedlam: London and its mad world*. London, Simon & Schuster.

78 Goleman, D. (1996) *Emotional intelligence: Why it can matter more than IQ*. London, Bloomsbury.

79 Op. cit. (Furedi), p. 413.

80 Furlong, V. J. (1991) Disaffected pupils reconsidered: The sociological perspective. *British Journal of Sociology of Education*, 12(3), 293–307.

81 Connell, R. (1987) *Gender and power: Society, the person and sexual politics*. Sydney, Allen and Unwin.

82 Ibid., pp. 193–194.

83 Polk, K. (1984) The new marginal youth. *Crime and Delinquency*, 30, 462–480.

84 McLeod, J. and Yates, L. (2006) *Making modern lives: Subjectivity, schooling, and social change*. Albany, State University of New York Press.

85 Ball, S. J., Maguire, M. and Macrae, S. (2000) *Choice, pathways and transitions post 16: New youth, new economies in the global city*. London, Falmer Press.

86 Tomlinson, S. (1981) *Educational subnormality: A study in decision-making*. London, Routledge and Kegan Paul.

87 Parrish, T. (2002) Racial disparities in the identification, funding and provision of special education. In D. Losen and G. Orfield (Eds) *Racial inequality in special education*. Cambridge, MA, Harvard Education Press.

88 Grant-Thomas, A. and Orfield, G. (2009) *Twenty-first century color lines: Multiracial change in contemporary America*. Philadelphia, Pa., Temple University Press.

89 Oswald, D. P., Coutinho, M. J. and Best, A. M. (2005) Community and school predictors of overrepresentation of minority children in special education. In D. J. Losen and G. Orfield (Eds) *Racial inequality in special education*. Cambridge, MA, Harvard Education Press, pp. 1–13.

90 Ferri, B. A. and Connor, D. J. (2006) *Reading resistance: Discourses of exclusion in desegregation and inclusion debates*. New York, Peter Lang.

91 Gillborn, D. (2008) *Racism and education: Coincidence or conspiracy?* Abingdon, Routledge.

92 Gillborn, D. and Mirza, H. S. (2000) *Educational inequality: Mapping race, class and gender: A synthesis of research evidence*. London, Office for Standards in Education.

93 Tomlinson, S. (2008) *Race and education: Policy and politics in Britain*. Maidenhead, McGraw-Hill Open University Press.

94 Ford, J., Mongon, D. and Whelan, M. (1982) *Special education and social control: Invisible disasters*. London, Routledge and Kegan Paul; Barton, L. and Tomlinson, S. (Eds) (1984) *Special education and social interests*. London, Croom Helm.

95 Tait, G. (2010) *Philosophy, behaviour disorders and the school*. Rotterdam, Sense Publishers; Laurence, J. and McCallum, D. (2009) *Inside the child's head. Histories of childhood behavioural disorders*. Rotterdam, Sense Publishers; Rose, S. (2005) *The 21st century brain. Explaining, mending and manipulating the mind*. London, Vintage; Graham, L.J. and Sweller, N. (2010) The inclusion lottery: who's in and who's out? Tracking inclusion and exclusion in New South Wales government schools. *International Journal of Inclusive Education*.

96 Bennett, S. and Wynne, K. (2006) *Special education transformation: The*

report of the co-chairs with the recommendations of the working table on special education. Ottawa, Queen's Printer of Ontario.

97 Riddell, S. (2008) The classification of pupils at the educational margins in Scotland: Shifting categories and frameworks. In L. Florian and M. J. McLaughlin (Eds) *Disability classification in education: Issues and perspectives.* Thousand Oaks, Corwin Press, pp. 109–128.

98 Graham, L. J., Sweller, N. and Van Bergen, P. (forthcoming) Detaining the usual suspects: Charting the use of segregated settings in New South Wales government schools in Australia. *Contemporary Issues in Early Childhood.*

99 McRae, D. (1996) *The integration/inclusion feasibility study.* Report for New South Wales Department of School Education, Sydney.

100 Op. cit. (Graham, Sweller and Van Bergen), p. 2.

101 Ibid., p. 2.

102 Wald, J. and Losen, D. J. (2003) Defining and re-directing a school-to-prison pipeline. *New Directions for Youth Development,* 99(Fall), 9–15.

103 Ibid., p. 12.

104 Semmens, R. (1990) Delinquency prevention: Individual control or social development. *Youth Studies,* 9(3), 23–29; Polk, K. and Schafer, W. E. (1972) *Schools and delinquency.* Englewood Cliffs, NJ, Prentice-Hall; Polk, K. (1984) The new marginal youth. *Crime and Delinquency,* 30: 462–480; Pearl, A. (1972) *The atrocity of education.* St. Louis, New Critics Press; Knight, T. (1975) Locked-in or locked-out: The powerlessness of the student role. School determinants of delinquent behaviour. In L. F. Claydon (Ed.) *The urban school.* Melbourne, Pitman; Coventry, G. (1988) Perspectives on truancy reconsidered: From victim blaming to educational crisis. In R. Slee (Ed.) *Discipline and schools: A curriculum perspective.* South Melbourne, Macmillan.

105 Bodna, B. (1987) People with intellectual disability and the criminal justice system. In D. Challinger (Ed.) *Intellectually disabled offenders.* Canberra, Australian Institute of Criminology.

106 Levin, B. (2005) *Governing education.* Toronto, University of Toronto Press.

107 Fulcher, G. (1989) *Disabling policies? A comparative approach to education policy and disability.* London, Falmer.

108 Her Majesty's Inspectorate (1978) Behaviour units: A survey of special units for pupils with behavioural problems. Report for Department for Education and Science, London.

109 Mongon, D. (1988) Behaviour units, 'maladjustment' and student control. In R. Slee (Ed.) *Discipline and schools: A curriculum perspective.* South Melbourne, Macmillan.

110 See op. cit. Slee, 1995, pp. 79–83; also Parsons, C. (1996) *Exclusion from school: The public cost.* London, Commission for Racial Equality.

111 Department for Children, Schools and Families (2007) Schools and pupils in England, January 2007 (final). In Department for Children, Schools and Families, London, DCFS.

112 Department for Children, Schools and Families (2009) Schools, Pupils, and their Characteristics. January 2009 (Provisional). London, DCSF.

113 Lamb, B. (2009) *SEN and parental confidence. Lamb inquiry review of SEN and disability information.* Report for Department of Children, Schools and Families (London), p. 13.

114 Ibid., p. 13.

115 Beckett, F. (2007) *The great city academy fraud.* London, Continuum, p. 12.

116 Ibid., pp. 13–15.

117 European Agency for development in Special Needs Education (2009) *Development of a set of indicators – for inclusive education in Europe.* Report for EADSNE, Odense, Denmark, p. 9.

118 Wilkinson, R. G. and Pickett, K. (2009) *The spirit level: Why more equal societies almost always do better*. London, Allen Lane, p. 103.
119 Ibid., p. 105.
120 Teese, R. and Polesel, J. (2003) *Undemocratic schooling: Equity and quality in mass secondary education in Australia*. Carlton, Melbourne University Publishing, p. 2.
121 Willms, D. (2003) Raising the learning bar. Paper presented at the Canadian Society for the study of Education. Halifax, May; Willms, D. (2003) Literacy proficiency of youth: Evidence of converging socioeconomic gradients. *International journal of Educational Research*, 39: 247–252.
122 Hargreaves, A. and Shirley, D. (2009) *The fourth way: The inspiring future for educational change*. Thousand Oaks, Calif., Corwin Press, pp. 51–55.
123 Blanden, J., Gregg, P. and Stephen, M. (2005) Educational inequality and intergenerational mobility. In S. Machin and A. Vignoles (Eds) *What's the good of education? The economics of education in the UK*. Princeton, Princeton University Press, 99–114.
124 Op. cit. Levin, p. 120.
125 Ibid., p. 119.
126 Dorling, D. (2010) *Injustice: Why social inequality persists*. Bristol, Policy Press.
127 Fulcher, G. (1987) Bureaucracy takes round seven: Round eight to commonsense? *The Age*, Melbourne, 14 April.
128 Ball, S. (2008) *The education debate*. Bristol, Policy Press, p. 193.
129 Ibid., p. 193.
130 Ball, S. (2007) *Education plc: Understanding private sector participation in public sector education*. London, Routledge, p. 184.
131 Op. cit. (Hargreaves and Shirley).

8 Considering other possibilities – the irregular school

1 Dorling, D. (2010) *Injustice: Why social inequality persists*. Bristol, Policy Press, p. 1.
2 See Vincent, C. and Ball, S. J. (2006) *Childcare, choice and class practices: Middle-class parents and their children*. London, Routledge; Ball, S. J. (2003) *Class strategies and the education market: The middle classes and social advantage*. London, Routledge/Falmer.
3 Ballard, K. (1999) *Inclusive education: International voices on disability and justice*. London, Falmer, p. 176.
4 Slee, R. (2005) Education and the politics of recognition: Inclusive education – an Australian snapshot. In D. Mitchell (Ed.) *Contextualizing inclusive education*. Abingdon, Routledge.
5 Apple, M. W., Au, W. and Gandin, L. A. (2009) Mapping critical education. In M. W. Apple, W. Au and L. A. Gandin (Eds) *The Routledge international handbook of critical education*. New York, Routledge, p. 16.
6 Said, E. W. (2000) Travelling theory reconsidered. In E. W. Said (Ed.) *Reflections on exile and other literary and cultural essays*. London, Granta Publications, pp. 436–452.
7 Ibid., p. 437.
8 Brantlinger, E. (2004) The big glossies: How textbooks structure (special) education., in: D. Biklen (Ed.) *Common solutions: Inclusion and diversity at the centre*. New York, Syracuse University Press.
9 Booth, T. and Ainscow, M. (2004) *Index for inclusion: Developing learning, participation and play in early years and childcare*. Bristol, Centre for Studies on Inclusive Education.

10 Bernstein, B. B. (1996) *Pedagogy, symbolic control and identity: Theory, research, critique*. London, Taylor & Francis.

11 Lewis, J. (1989) Removing the grit: The development of special education in Victoria 1887–1947. Unpublished PhD thesis, Melbourne, LaTrobe University.

12 Nussbaum, M. C. (2004) *Hiding from humanity. Disgust, shame, and the law*. Princeton, Princeton University Press, p. 305.

13 Diawara, M. quoted in Connell, R. (2007) *Southern theory: The global dynamics of knowledge in social science*. Cambridge, Polity, p. 89.

14 Nussbaum, M. C. (2006) *Frontiers of justice: Disability, nationality, species membership*. Cambridge, Mass., Harvard University Press, p. 210.

15 Armstrong, F. (2003) *Spaced out: Policy, difference and the challenge of inclusive education*. Dordrecht, Kluwer Academic.

16 Mike Oliver quoted from an interview with the authors: Allan, J. and Slee, R. (2008) *Doing inclusive education research*. Rotterdam, Sense Publishers, p. 58.

17 Kauffman, J. M. and Hallahan, D. P. (2005) *The illusion of full inclusion: A comprehensive critique of a current special education bandwagon* (2nd Edition). Austin, Tex., Pro-Ed.

18 Eagleton, T. (1994) Ideology and its vicissitudes in western Marxism. In S. Zizek (Ed.) *Mapping ideology*. London, Verso, p. 193.

19 Op. cit. (Allan and Slee).

20 Oliver, M. (1992) Changing the social relations of research production? *Disability Handicap and Society*, 7(2), 101–114.

21 Op. cit (Nussbaum, 2006), p. 209.

22 Knight, T. (1975) Locked-in or locked-out: The powerlessness of the student role. School determinants of delinquent behaviour. In L. F. Claydon (Ed.) *The urban school*. Melbourne, Pitman.

23 Hargreaves, A. and Shirley, D. (2009) *The fourth way: The inspiring future for educational change*. Thousand Oaks, Calif., Corwin Press, p. x.

24 Nussbaum, M. C. (2010) *Not for profit. Why democracy needs the humanities*. Princeton, NJ, Princeton University Press, p. 6.

25 Ibid., p. 6.

26 Dewey, J. (1916) *Democracy and education: An introduction to the philosophy of education*. London, Free Press.

27 Op. cit. (Nussbaum, 2010), p. 10.

28 Pearl, A. and Knight, T. (1998) *The democratic classroom. Theory to inform practice*. Cresskill, NJ, Hampton Press.

29 Luke, A. (2003) After the marketplace: Evidence, social science and educational research. *The Australian Educational Researcher*. 30(2), 87–107.

30 Education Queensland (2001) The New Basics Project, Brisbane, Queensland Government. http://education.qld.gov.au/corporate/newbasics/ retrieved 17 July 2010 at 16.19.

31 Lingard, B., Mills, M. and Hayes, D. (2006) Enabling and aligning assessment for learning: Some research and policy lessons from Queensland. *International Studies in Sociology of Education*, 16(2), 83–103.

32 Op. cit. (Pearl and Knight), p. 3.

33 Touraine, A. (2000) *Can we live together? Equality and difference*. Cambridge, Polity Press.

34 Sennett, R. (2004) *Respect: The formation of character in an age of inequality*. London, Penguin, p. 21.

35 Watson, D. (2003) *Death sentence: The decay of public language*. Milson's Point, Random House Australia.

36 Op. cit. (Sennett, 2004), p. 20.

37 Kenway, J. (1990) Education and the right's discursive politics. In S. J. Ball (Ed.) *Foucault and education*. London, Routledge.

38 www.sarai.net/publications/readers/07-frontiers/176–186_longoni.pdf retrieved at 13.18 on Monday 12 July, 2010.
39 I am grateful to Kevin McDonald who generously shared his presentation with me to use. See also Longoni, A., Bruzzone, G. A., Aguerreberry, R. and Lebenglik, F. (2008) *El Siluetazo*. Buenos Aires, Adriana Hidalgo Editora.
40 Chapman, G., Cleese, J., Gilliam, T., Idle, E., Jones, T. and Palin, M. (1979) *The Life of Brian*. Film script. http://montypython.50webs.com/scripts/Life_of_Brian/23.htm retrieved at 13.25 on 12 July, 2010.
41 Rose, M. (1995) *Possible lives: The promise of public education in America*. Boston, Houghton Mifflin; Bernstein, B. B. (1996) *Pedagogy, symbolic control and identity: Theory, research, critique*. London, Taylor & Francis; Touraine, A. (2000) *Can we live together? Equality and difference*. Cambridge, Polity Press; Apple, M. W. and Beane, J. A. (2007) *Democratic schools: Lessons in powerful education* (2nd Edition). Portsmouth, NH, Heinemann; Pearl, A. and Knight, T. (1998) *The democratic classroom: Theory to inform practice*. Cresskill, NJ, Hampton Press.
42 Alur, M. and Bach, M. (2010) *The journey for inclusive education in the Indian sub-continent*. London, Routledge.
43 Op. cit. Dorling, p. 307.

Index